The Inside Story

Robert Schuller

The Inside Story

Robert Schuller

Michael & Donna Nason

WORD BOOKS
PUBLISHER
WACO, TEXAS

A DIVISION OF
WORD, INCORPORATED

ROBERT SCHULLER: THE INSIDE STORY

Printed in the United States

Library of Congress Cataloging in Publication Data

Nason, Michael
Robert Schuller: The inside story

1. Schuller, Robert Harold. 2. Reformed Church—United States—Clergy—Biography. I. Nason, Donna. II. Title.
BX9543.S36N37 1982 285.7'32'0924 [B] 82–50512
ISBN 0–8499–0300–9

Contents

Foreword

"Look," my wife said, grabbing at my sleeve with one hand and pointing with the other, "it's Dr. Schuller." Glancing up, I caught my first glimpse of the man who would forever alter the course of my life. He was tall, much taller than I had imagined, with a full head of silver hair. He stood awkwardly off to the side of the room, talking to the woman who stood next to him, his spectacled eyes searching for a familiar face.

"We'd better go introduce ourselves to him," Donna said, interrupting my thoughts. "After all, we are the ones who invited him." It was 1972, the end of a long campaign for me. I had been on a year's leave of absence from my job as assistant to the president of a large California-based fireworks firm, on loan to the Committee to Reelect President Nixon. I had spent months running the Orange County office, reveling as I always did in the glamour and the excitement of politics. Politics had been in my blood since childhood and had really dominated my life since my teenage years. Now, at age thirty-one, I was just about ready to make my real entrance into public service. I was already a veteran of fourteen campaigns, stretching all the way back to Eisenhower when I was ten. I knew all the right people, had been carefully groomed, and was planning to enter into the next race for California State Assembly as a candidate. Right now, on Halloween Eve, I was flushed with success and ready to tackle the world.

We were giving a large dinner party to thank the hundreds of volunteers in our area. It had been my wife's idea to invite Dr. Schuller. "We need an invocation, don't you think?" she had said. Actually, I hadn't thought about it at all. I was a Christian, born again some two years earlier along with my wife as we struggled for meaning and hope in dealing with the tragic accident suffered by our then two-year-old daughter Tara. She was left profoundly brain damaged and quadriplegic; it had been a terrible blow to us. Our lives would have been unbearable were it not for the peace and strength of the Holy Spirit and our special relationship with a risen Lord who knew our great needs and answered our prayers, even giving us a new baby whose arrival we were anticipating at that time.

But this was different. This was politics. My thoughts were on little else in the closing weeks of that momentous campaign. At Donna's insistence, I had phoned Dr. Schuller's office to ask him to come to the party and offer a few words of prayer. Had I known more about the man, I doubt that I would have been so flippant in the call nor so confident in its outcome. Sure, I knew he pastored a large church up in Garden Grove; it was the one with the big tower with the cross on top that lit up at night. I'd seen it from the freeway many times. And I knew he was on TV, too. Donna watched him sometimes, and I'd seen bits and pieces of the program as I wandered in and out of the family room on Sunday mornings. But for all I knew, it was just one of those small productions that was only seen in the greater Los Angeles area. Anyway, I felt I was important too. I spoke with the staff at the White House nearly every day. Even though he didn't normally accept invitations of that sort, Dr. Schuller agreed to come. And here we were about to meet—the politician and the preacher.

"Hi, I'm Mike Nason, the chairman for the dinner," I said, shaking the outstretched hand. "This is my wife, Donna." "Bob Schuller," came the reply in a rich voice, with just a hint of an accent. "I'd like you to meet my wife Arvella." She was nearly as tall as he and spoke with quiet dignity. A few moments of small talk, and I was off. There were so many last minute details to attend to. It was Donna who stood and talked with the Schullers, sharing our mutual faith in our Lord, exchanging stories about our children. As I darted to and from the dinner table, Bob questioned me about my background and duties in the current campaign. I thought he was extremely polite and a very good conversationalist to take such an interest in a stranger, asking and then listening intently. I could sense his warmth and sensitivity.

"You know," he began in a confidential manner, "I'm about

ready to wage a campaign of my own. Possibility thinking has taught me to set goals. Right now 'The Hour of Power' is on six television stations in six markets around the country. I have as my goal that I would like to be on forty TV stations with my program.'' Then he looked me straight in the eye. ''How'd you like to run my campaign for me?''

I had three immediate and admittedly disjointed thoughts. 1) This is the nicest man I've ever met. Imagine going to such lengths to be friendly. 2) He couldn't afford me even if he were serious, which he isn't. 3) Working for a preacher is bound to be very boring, and I'm sure there wouldn't be enough to keep me busy or interested. I thanked him very sincerely, if a bit incredulously, telling him I was quite happy where I was.

Bob dug into his pocket with his big hand and pulled out a tan business card with a sketch of Christ on the flap. ''If you ever change your mind, please give me a call at this number,'' he replied, undaunted. ''Even if you don't, call anyway. I'd like to speak with you more.''

Donna and I drove home elated, I about the success of the party, she about the job offer from Dr. Schuller. Shortly after the elections, she finally convinced me to give Dr. Schuller a call. By this time, I was quite embarrassed, thinking he had probably forgotten all about me by then. But he hadn't. I was invited over to the church, which he called the campus, for a private meeting. Once I had parked and walked through the beautifully landscaped gardens and into the fourteen-story Tower of Hope, even I became a bit intimidated. What business did I, a cocky kid, have in taking up the time of a man like Robert Schuller? I'd done some checking and knew that he was no ordinary man, but one called by God for some very special purposes which probably weren't apparent even to him yet.

But he received me so cordially that I was put immediately at ease. We struck an affinity for each other right away, talking and sharing private dreams and goals like old friends. It was to be but the first of many such meetings. We worked together for nearly a year trying to help Christian pastors imprisoned behind the Iron Curtain as well as working for religious freedom for Christians in Afghanistan. I spent hours working as a volunteer. For me, it was a labor of love. Love for the God I served and an increasing love and respect for the man and the ministry of Robert Schuller. When at last he offered me a job as his administrative assistant, I jumped at the chance.

In the ensuing ten years, I have traveled all over the world with Robert Schuller. I have produced his television program, "The Hour of Power" for nine of those years, handled his public relations and speaking engagements, bought the television time for the program across the country, and acted as president of his in-house advertising agency. When I first came to work for him, in the brashness of youth, I promised him that I would make his name a household word in ten years. I am older and wiser now, and doubt that I would make such a bold claim today, but it turned out to be prophetic. In God's timing and with His help and the dynamism of Robert Schuller, the promise was kept.

I have lived, loved, argued, cried, and laughed with Robert and Arvella Schuller and their family through these last ten years. I have watched their phenomenal rise to fame, experienced with them the agony and the ecstasy of the construction of the Crystal Cathedral. Dr. Schuller himself has said I probably know him better than any person on earth save his wife. I have found our friendship and work together to be the most exciting and satisfying I have thus far experienced. I have certainly never been bored nor in lack of stimulating and creative activity. I never went into politics nor have I ever been sorry for my decision against it, for God had other plans for me.

So come with me as I reveal to you Robert Schuller as I have come to know him. My wife Donna, being the journalist in the family, has put pen to paper to record the life of one of the most fascinating men of our century. Robert Schuller—is he for real? Come—let us show you. . . .

1

The TV Evangelist from California

It was one of those dreary January days. Outside my office the wind swirled and rain beat against my window. It was a fitting tribute. Former Vice-President Hubert Humphrey was dead. Quite a few of us on staff at "The Hour of Power" were gathered around the TV set, watching the preparations for the funeral. The three television networks were all there. The snowy Minnesota landscape was full of activity—cars coming and going, people scurrying about. All the pomp and dignity of a state funeral.

We were all wondering about Bob. He had been a close friend of Hubert for many years and cared very deeply for both him and his wife Muriel. Even before Humphrey's death had been announced to the press, his family had contacted me at home in an effort to reach Dr. Schuller, who was on an airplane at the time. Before the country heard of the death, Muriel and Hubert's daughter Nancy Solomonson, at her mother's request, had already asked Bob to speak at Hubert's funeral. Bob, and all of us, had felt it was a great honor and a wonderful testimony to the friendship they had shared.

All of us in the room that day knew the great responsibility Bob felt to be speaking to such a prestigious group, not to mention all the press coverage the funeral would receive. He had worked especially hard on his message, wanting one that would minister to Muriel and the family as well as to the president, vice-president, other office holders, the grieving country, and even the world.

Our phones in Mascom, our in-house advertising agency for "The Hour of Power," had been ringing off the hook from the press ever since the news broke; and we had been careful to answer all questions carefully and courteously, supplying all information requested, as was our policy. When the networks had called requesting information on Robert Schuller, it had been given with pride in the man and in his work. After all, he was a figure of national prominence, well known all over the world. A diplomat, a churchman, a philanthropist, a TV personality well respected in all sectors of the country.

And then it came—the slap in the face which caught us all so off guard and hurt as well as angered each of us. Chris Kelly of CBS News was talking, saying a bit about the people who were to speak at the funeral. Knowing his news department had been well supplied with biographical information on Dr. Schuller, we were anxious to hear what he would say. His voice took on a condescending tone as he began. "Robert Schuller, a TV evangelist" (he virtually spat out the title as if it were a bad word) "from California, has been added to today's service. No one seems to know anything about him, and I can say there have been eyebrows raised here about his being included. We're not sure who asked him to be here," he continued.

My face flushed and anger made my cheeks hot and my eyes sting. "Why?" My mind formed the words over and over again. Why such an unwarranted attack on the personal integrity of such a man? I never received an answer.

I thought back to the first breakthrough we had had with station WDCA in Washington, D.C., in 1975. Bob had seen the potential in it even then. "Any fool can count the seeds in an apple, but only God can count the apples in one seed." It was a simple little phrase, some people called it corny, but Bob believed in it. Intuitively, he knew there was a lot of potential waiting in Washington to receive the seed of the gospel of Christ. He had been so excited when I told him we finally had gotten the coveted position in Washington. "Just imagine," he had mused, "the opportunity we have here to influence our country for good through her lawmakers. It's a tough job administrating our country—these people need to know Jesus, they need a positive faith."

The first letter we received from Hubert Humphrey had meant a great deal to Bob. It was handwritten, expressing his and Muriel's feelings in a beautiful, simple way. They watched "The Hour of Power" both in their home in Waverly, Minnesota, and in Washington, D.C., and spoke of the comfort and inspiration it brought them. Hubert stated at that time that he would really like to meet Bob if he were ever in the D.C. area.

About six months later., Bob and I were flying to the capital for a speaking engagement. His eyes lit up as he realized how he would be able to meet personally with Senator Humphrey. We were given an appointment with him in his office, and I know Bob was quite excited as well as a bit nervous in that first meeting. He sensed the importance of it, knowing it was only the beginning.

As it happened, the Senate was in session that day, and pressing business was being conducted. The senator was unable to leave long enough to meet Bob in his office, but chose instead to see him in the Senate reception area. It was a large room, very ornate, with carving on the walls and even the ceiling. Encircling the room, and definitely the most dominant characteristic, was a series of enormous, beautifully draped, French-style windows with large wooden window sills.

A Senate page was sent to tell Senator Humphrey of our arrival, and he came out shortly afterward. He was a small man, obviously full of energy and enthusiasm. His whole face broke into a big grin when he caught sight of Bob; and he hurried over to greet him with a vigorous handshake and a warm embrace. He spoke cordially to me, and then excused himself and Bob for the talk they had both desired for so many months.

They went over to the side of the room, and Hubert sat up on the windowsill of one of the large windows. Bob pulled up a chair, and there they sat, knee to knee for some twenty minutes or so. There are those times when greatness—fame, wealth, power—mean nothing. This was one of these times. It was man to man, person to person, heart to heart. A real friendship was being forged, and it was humbling for me to witness it.

They spoke of many things. Hubert, who had experienced the power and position of vice-president under Lyndon Johnson, who had known the bitterness and rejection of defeat when he lost his bid for the presidency against Richard Nixon, and who had then gone on to be elected once more United States senator from Minnesota, had fought many of his own private as well as public battles. "Bob," he said, "I can't tell you how much your *Possibility Thinkers Creed* has meant to me. It has helped me so often and brought me through so many trials.'' And he repeated it, ''When faced with a mountain, I will not quit. I will keep on striving until I climb over, find a pass through, tunnel underneath, or simply stay and turn the mountain into a gold mine, with God's help.''

They concluded their visit deep in prayer together, hands clasped, heads bowed. Tears streamed down the senator's wrinkled cheeks and fell onto his dark blue suit. Then a quick handshake, and he was gone.

They didn't meet again personally during the next few years, but continued their friendship through correspondence, each learning more about the other. When Hubert's cancer began to seriously spread, attacking him with all its vengeance, Bob sent telegrams to the hospital and prayed.

It's odd, but no one seemed to take much notice in Washington when Hubert quietly slipped home to Waverly to die. In November 1978, Bob was on his way to speak to a group in Minneapolis when Fred Gates, Humphrey's long-time aide, called. ''Could you come by Waverly and see the senator?'' he asked. ''It would please him so.''

Fred Gates picked up Bob at the airport and began the forty-five minute drive to the Humphrey home. With forced cheerfulness, Bob asked, ''What can I do for Senator Humphrey today?'' Fred's reply was earnest, ''Please, see if you can't get him to return to Washington. He needs it, he deserves it. The doctors say he won't live past Christmas.''

Bob felt this was a heavy trip Fred had laid on him, and immediately became silent and withdrawn. Wondering. Worrying. Praying. It was bitterly cold as he walked toward the house, the wind lashing at his face as if to taunt him. He had seen pictures of Hubert in the news, but even they hadn't prepared him for the cruel toll the cancer had taken of his body and soul. So gaunt and so thin, gone was the sparkle, the energy. He was down, depressed in body and spirit, when Bob arrived.

As Bob has often said, ''I'm glad I can pray with my eyes open,'' for this was surely a time for prayer. To draw him out, Bob began asking Hubert about the favorite stories and one-liners from the senator's many speeches. Hubert, in turn, asked Bob about his. Then

Hubert had Muriel go get his book of remembrances, and Bob and Hubert looked through it together. Gradually, his spirits began to improve somewhat, and at the end of forty-five minutes Hubert felt well enough to painstakingly draw on his coat and hat and walk Bob out into the cold to his car.

Just as he was leaving, Bob felt the moment was right. "Hubert," he said, patting his back affectionately, "you should go back to Washington. You owe it to yourself." The senator brightened. "You're right; I'm going to do it," he determined.

The rest is history. President Jimmy Carter himself diverted Air Force One through Waverly on his way back from a swing through the West Coast and personally escorted the failing senator back to Washington. There were dinners and parties, honors and accolades for a dying man who enjoyed his greatest popularity in his last days.

During these brief weeks in the capital, Senator Humphrey called Bob to thank him for his suggestion and to ask his permission to use in his and Muriel's last Christmas card together, the phrase Bob had made famous—"God loves you and so do we."

"Isn't it strange," Bob had said, "the way events turn out? Here you are. You served as vice-president, you lost your try for the presidency against Nixon, then were elected senator again, and are back in Washington now enjoying the just deserts of a long life of public service. Your popularity has never been higher. You are held in esteem by all the American people, but the man who defeated you so overwhelmingly is now in virtual exile in San Clemente. You know, Hubert, there's only one person in the country today who could extend a hand of forgiveness to Richard Nixon."

"You're right, Bob," the old gentleman was quick to reply, "and I know you mean me. I think I'll give him a call." He was as good as his word, calling Nixon to wish him a happy sixty-fifth birthday. Later, Nixon called Hubert to wish him a Merry Christmas.

There were many who didn't think Richard Nixon belonged at Humphrey's funeral, and a newsman made such a comment to one of Humphrey's aides. "If you knew the senator," he replied, "you would understand."

What attracted Hubert Humphrey and Robert Schuller to each other? Their positive Christian faith. Neither knew the word impossible. Hubert had devoted his life to human rights, to helping the poor of our country achieve their potential, just as Dr. Schuller has spent years helping the poor in spirit to see the God-given potential for goodness each one has. Jesus cuts across all barriers.

Dr. Schuller's remarks at Senator Humphrey's funeral were just one more occasion when he was thrust into the limelight. His words were powerful, full of compassion, and silenced, at least for a time, most of his critics. Even Chris Kelly had nothing negative to say. Ted Kennedy turned to Jacob Javits, who sat next to him at the funeral. "Who is that man? I'd like to meet him. He gives me hope." But that's another story. Right now, let's go back to the beginning.

2

Down on the Farm—God Calls

The corn stood in·tall, straight rows, nearly ready for harvesting. Soon the fields would be stripped and prepared once more. The little vegetable garden had yielded its crops of yellow and green beans, cabbage, onions, carrots, potatoes, lettuce, tomatoes. The family had feasted on them all summer, and Jennie had carefully cut the cabbage into fine strips and salted it and placed it in crocks down in the cellar so it would ferment and become a staple of the coming winter—sauerkraut, a family favorite. The crocks stood, even then, next to the crocks of fried bacon which had also been salted and put under lard last February when Tony had done the butchering. With painstaking work, Jennie had canned the leftover vegetables which were also stored up for the long winter ahead.

It was Indian summer on the endless Iowa plains, that brief respite between summer's relentless heat and the arctic winter blasts. The sky, sparkling in the warm sunshine, was so big and so blue that it seemed to spread out like a huge canopy over the fertile black soil. Here and there wispy clouds chased each other across the prairie, playing hide and seek with the wind. The big white clapboard farmhouse stood out in bas-relief against a background of gently undulating hills and sky, as far as the eye could see.

Inside, a large Dutch American family gathered around the old wooden table for supper. There would be fried potatoes, eggs, pickles, tomatoes, cabbage, and lettuce. But first, the blessing. Anthony, tall and thin, his arms well veined, his hands coarse and calloused, bent his white-haired head to pray. Jennie, her light brown hair streaked with gray, smoothed a wayward tendril back into the bun at the base of her neck, heaved a heavy sigh, and folded her work-worn hands across her swollen belly, smiling and patting it ever so slightly as she did so. "It won't be long now," she whispered to herself as they began to pray.

Lined up on either side of the table were the children: Jasmine, so grown-up now at fourteen, and already doing a woman's share of the work; and thirteen-year-old Henry, quiet and soft-spoken. Then there was nine-year-old Margaret and eight-year-old Violet. For eight years now there had been no more children. Jennie was really past the childbearing years, and her pregnancy had come as a great surprise to her, though not an unwelcome one. Tony had seemed especially pleased when she had told him, but acted as if he had almost expected it, smiling broadly and beaming at her with his quiet, gentle eyes.

Anthony Schuller knew a secret. A secret he would keep for the next twenty-three years. One day last fall he had knelt among the furrows of his newly tilled field, gazing up as the last rays of the setting sun spread their golden fingers across the sky and shone softly over the nearby box elder trees. He had been lost in thought, and as he continued to mull his idea over in his mind, his thoughts became a prayer. The good Lord had given him one son and three daughters. They were fine young people, children of the soil, lovers of the rich dark earth, happy in their home and anxious to continue the life their parents had taught them. "But oh, Lord," he breathed, "could you give me just one more son? Please? One who won't be content on the farm, one with dreams, with visions. Oh Lord, please send my Jennie and me a son who will grow up to be a minister."

It was September 16, 1926, when the first contractions began, and Jennie could at last see the end of an uncomfortable change-of-life pregnancy. As the hours dragged on, she took to her bed, and outside her room the house buzzed with activity. Tony at length called for the doctor, who arrived shortly thereafter. Soon the awe-struck children could hear the lusty cries that signaled the arrival of their baby brother. "Robert Harold Schuller," Tony announced proudly. "I knew it would be a boy." His soft eyes shone with an almost unearthly joy as he looked up toward the ceiling and uttered a hearty, "Thank You, Lord." Then he turned his attention again to the young people before him. "We'll call him Harold," he beamed.

But even then he didn't share his secret. If this new Schuller were to become a minister someday, it would be because God Himself called him to be one, not because it was expected of him, not just to please his father.

By the time he had learned to toddle around, Harold loved to follow his father as he did his chores around the farm. He adored the quiet, gentle man with the strong arms and the big heart, and would watch in fascination as he carried the pails across the yard and into the cool, damp barn to milk the cows. Down in the cellar, Tony kept rows and rows of cigar boxes full of nuts and bolts, bits of string, wires, all sorts of things to fascinate a very small boy. There in his own special place, he would repair farm and home equipment, and even take time to make broken toys like new again for his young son.

How Harold loved it when spring came to the prairie. It seemed the whole world was clean and new. There was a freshness, a beauty about everything, from the tender green shoots poking their heads up in the fields to the buttercups that were blooming everywhere. Wild roses trailed red and pink along the fences, where wild plum trees tantalized with promises of future delights. He soon learned to look forward with increasing excitement to the arrival of the baby chicks, and would wait, dancing with anticipation, for the eggs to hatch their precious cargoes of yellow fluff. With squeals of glee, he would take the soft, newly hatched creatures and rub their downy baby feathers against his cheek. Sometimes, in his exuberance and out of his great love for the tiny birds, he would squeeze them too tightly; he didn't want to let them go. Tony would smile, his hazel eyes crinkling at the corners, understanding; and in his simple, homespun way, pour out wisdom that Harold would remember. "Don't hold so tight," he'd admonish. Harold stood there, still clutching the tiny chick to his breast, looking up at his dad with wide brown eyes. "But I love it so." Tony stroked the soft brown hair, "If you love it so much, you have to let it go." The gaunt farmer rarely spoke, but when he did, he always had something meaningful to say.

Jennie Beltman Schuller had spent all her life there in the cornfields of Iowa. She and Anthony had married when they were both well into their twenties and had settled down quite naturally to the farming life they had always known. But there was within her a yearning that was never quite fulfilled. One she didn't really understand. She had inherited the drive of her grandfather, a Dutch baron. He had left Holland in 1887 and come to America with the dream of establishing a Dutch colony in Texas, but fell victim to two tragedies which were to leave him a broken man. He was deceived in business dealings with some oil companies and lost all he had worked for in a disastrous flood that hit Galveston. He finally settled down in Orange City, Iowa, leaving a legacy of leadership, vision, and strength for his granddaughter Jennie.

Even when he was a small child, Jennie could see these traits in her younger son and hoped and prayed he would be able to follow where his dreams led him. She was Harold's greatest encouragement and critic during his growing up years, always insisting that he strive for excellence in whatever he was doing, always challenging him to achieve his potential. After all, she had big plans for him; he was going to be a doctor.

She had a real love of music, and gave her young son piano lessons. She could be a real slave driver, pushing and prodding through the hours of practice that are misery for small children. Once, when he was to play in a recital, she made Harold go over the conclusion again and again. It had to be perfect. "You can make a mistake in the beginning or even in the middle; the people will forget it—so long as you make the ending glorious."

Jennie had a younger brother of whom she was extremely proud. Henry Beltman was a missionary to China, and often they would speak of him as they sat around the supper table. When the youngest Schuller child heard that his uncle from China was to visit them, he could hardly control his excitement. To young Harold, Henry seemed an enigma, so far away and mysterious, telling other people about the Jesus that Harold had grown to love. The farm was a little island, isolated from the outside world by its very nature, as well as by its geography. The anticipation of a visitor all the way from China conjured up oriental fantasies that flamed in young imaginations.

When the big day actually arrived, Harold spent all morning running barefoot across the splintered porch and down the path to the end of the walk, craning his head around the gate, hoping to catch the first glimpse of his fabled uncle and asking no one in particular, "How much longer? When is he coming?"

And then, unmistakably, there it was. A dot way down at the end of their road that grew larger as it approached, taking on shape, color, dimension. The battered Ford inched its way through the gravel, dwarfed by the cornstalks that loomed on either side, and finally pulled up in front of the house, sending billows of dust scurrying in its wake. "Henry!" Jennie cried as she ran out of the house, hurriedly drying her hands with a dishtowel. The tall young stranger gathered her up in his arms. "Where's that new son of yours?" he queried, his eyes darting about the yard.

Harold, for all his enthusiasm, was suddenly shy of this dashing young missionary; and was standing at the gate, peering up at him with wide-eyed curiosity. "You must be Robert," Uncle Henry boomed as he bounded over to the five-year-old. Placing a big hand on each of the boy's shoulders, he laughed his approval and ruffled the boy's hair affectionately. "I think you're going to be a preacher some day."

The words were prophetic, and though they may havc been lightly spoken, they were not lightly received by the child. "A minister," he thought to himself. "That's what I want to be when I grow up." It was a sobering thought to a five-year-old boy, one that reached out and touched his very soul with excitement, and at that moment God put a seal on the boy's life. He had been called and he knew it. God had called him, and even though he wasn't sure what it meant in its entirety, Robert Harold Schuller, in five-year-old sincerity, accepted that call.

Later that evening, the whole family had gathered around the table. The air was heavy with spices—cinnamon and nutmeg. Harold pressed the prongs of his fork against his plate, scraping up every flaky crumb of pastry and each slice of fresh, sweet apple. Mom's apple pie was his very favorite. Every now and then he paused to peer up into the faces of his parents, his attention fixed on his dad's quiet, gentle eyes and his mother's, fiery with determination. "What will they think?" he wondered silently. He was waiting for just the right break in the conversation to make the most important announcement of his young life. "Dad," he said, looking straight into the kind eyes of the old farmer, "I've decided. I'm going to be a minister when I grow up." When the old man heard the words he had been longing to hear since the birth of his second son, his heart skipped a beat, and his face registered delight, but he spoke not a word of his secret. He couldn't. Not yet.

There was a genuine change in Harold from that time forward. He had grown up loving Jesus. His mother and father had taught him of the loving Shepherd from his infancy. They observed a strict Sunday sabbath in their home—church and quiet time, prayer and Bible study. His parents lived their faith. He always knew it was real to them, and so it became real to him from a very early age. It was easy to believe in a loving Father in heaven when his own father was so loving and kind. It was easy to believe in a God who could mend broken hearts and make lives new again as he watched his own father lovingly and painstakingly make old toys new again. After all, couldn't his daddy fix everything?

But to his faith, a new dimension was being added—a genuine desire to preach and a true compassion for people who were hurting. Each night as he said his prayers, added onto the long list of God blesses, was the request, "Lord, please make me a preacher when I grow up."

Tony had prayed for a son who wouldn't be suited to farming, one who would be a dreamer of dreams, a visionary with the courage to work for his visions. But there were times when these traits could be troublesome around a big farm with lots of work to be done. Time and time again, Harold would have the cows back late for their evening milking. He just simply lost track of the time. Hardly a day went by when he wasn't dreaming of his vocation.

He spent hours standing on the cool green grass of the low hills, "tending" the cows. They had thirty Ayreshires, and their massive red and white frames were scattered hodge-podge across the meadow, some gnawing lazily on the sweet grass, others lying contentedly beneath the willows, chewing their cuds. But he didn't see them. Their images blurred and finally changed shape entirely until, to the boy's heart, they became people.

He saw seas of people who were hurting and needed to know the healing power of Jesus. And there, overlooking the lazy Floyd River, as it meandered toward the Missouri, he spent hours practicing his preaching, gesturing wildly and raising and lowering his voice dramatically. He was developing the preaching style that would eventually win him world acclaim, the theatrics that would either draw people to him or turn them off entirely. He was destined from the beginning to speak in the out-of-doors or in vast halls. His style demanded it, being most unsuited to the restrictions of a small enclosure.

These were bad years, Depression years. Harold was surrounded with so much love, he didn't really notice the lack of material comforts too much. And besides, most everyone else in the little triangle of Iowa towns, Alton, Newkirk, and Orange City, was in pretty much the same shape. Many's the night, in the blistering cold of an Iowa winter, when Harold would wake up to the sound of the wind racing around the house and feel snow blowing in through the poorly sealed windows of his bedroom. He would snuggle down even deeper under the covers and try to stay warm; only to awaken to drifts of snow built up in the corners and along the baseboards. There was no running water in his home, no indoor plumbing, no electricity, and no heat. A single stove stationed in the living room burned coal to warm the house, and Jennie heated her wash water over the kitchen stove, which the children were expected to keep supplied with corn cobs for fuel. A hand pump in the kitchen must be drained each cold night to keep it from freezing.

Difficult as the winters were, sometimes the summers were even worse. They lived in the Dust Bowl, and in the thirties it was often bleak and frightening. The drought swept in from the Dakotas. It was a dry wind, dusty and fierce, and destruction followed in its wake. Its whistling called to the rich black soil like a pied piper and gathered it up in great gusts from the neatly plowed fields. Like a child playing keep-away, the wind tossed the soil here and threw it there until it swirled in and out of the gullies and canyons. The Schuller family, like most of the Dutch Reformed farming community, prayed for rain. But the heavens were dry.

One year, it got so bad that the family walked around the farm doing their chores with towels tied over their faces to keep from suffocating in the driving dust. It was a sad harvest that year. Usually Anthony Schuller harvested one hundred wagon loads of corn. Harvest was a time of grueling labor, but a time which brought with it a keen sense of accomplishment, a feeling of security in the provision for the family. But this year there was a total crop failure, the likes of which had never been seen in this country before, or since; and when Tony finished harvesting his corn, just one old wagon stood in the yard in the midst of the swirling dust. It was half full.

That night, Harold witnessed something he would never forget. There was an air of gloom that pervaded everything, but as the family gathered at the table for their evening meal, they joined hands and Anthony looked up and thanked God. "I thank you, God," spoke this simple farmer of great faith, "that I have lost nothing. I have regained the seed I planted in the springtime." He had used half a wagon load of corn for seed, and he had harvested half a wagon load back. He was grateful to God, considering that he had lost nothing, while other farmers were griefstricken, blaming God and asking through gritted teeth and clenched fists why they had lost their entire harvest—ninety loads or a hundred loads of corn. They counted their losses by what they had hoped to accomplish.

Harold would remember all his life what his father said. "You can never count up the 'might have beens' or you will be defeated." Many farmers gave up that year, selling their farms, practically giving them away, and moving away from all they held dear. But not Anthony and Jennie Schuller. That wise Dutch farmer, with no more than a sixth-grade education, went right back and planted that half a wagon load of seed the next year. Years later, Robert Schuller would take this homespun wisdom and change the words to "Never look at what you have lost; look at what you have left."

Despite his hours upon hours of exuberant preaching to the cows, Harold remained basically a quiet, shy person during his growing-up years. Unwittingly, he was forging his basic personality. In public and with family and close friends he became dramatic, persuasive, even a ham; but in private, on a one-to-one level or when with a very few people, he would be quiet, personable, but rather restrained.

He loved his mother's wonderful cooking, especially the sweets, so that even as he was growing up to his full height of six-feet-two inches, he was always overweight and poor at sports. He had to endure the humiliation of not being chosen to play on athletic teams at Floyd Independence School, the one-room country schoolhouse where first through eighth grades were taught.

However, his years of preaching practice paid off in high school when he became captain of the tiny school's debating team. He also excelled in drama and voice, but didn't like math. Jennie labored diligently, making sure that her youngest son, who was now the only one at home, completed his schoolwork assignments, often finding him in bed asleep when he should have been studying. Harold's parents were strict and demanding, but like the God they served, they always tempered their justice with mercy and never asked Harold for less or more than the best he could be.

Harold had always set his sights on college. A minister in the Reformed Church of America had to have a college and seminary education. Harold's performance in school was consistently inconsistent. The amount of studying he was willing to put in on any given subject was in direct proportion to whether or not he felt it would further him toward his goal of the ministry. By the age of six, he already realized that a good minister was a good communicator, and asked to be allowed to memorize a poem and recite it at the school's Christmas pageant as a beginning in public speaking.

English, history, speech, drama, debate—these were his favorites all the way through school. For goal-oriented Harold, they were concrete steps toward the ministry. He worked hard at them, and his grades were good. Other subjects, though, like math and science, were courses to be plodded through, giving them as little time and attention as possible. He ruefully admits now that the knowledge obtained from them would have made many a good sermon illustration, but at the time he couldn't make the connection and felt that for him they were a waste of time.

There were fourteen students in Harold's graduating class, the largest in the history of Newkirk High School up to that time. Gregarious, people-oriented, goal-centered Harold Schuller ranked somewhere in the lower half. He was only sixteen years old that momentous June day in 1943 as he stepped forward to receive his diploma. And he was in such a hurry to reach his goal that he left immediately for summer school at Hope College in Holland, Michigan. The next seven years of intense preparation would be difficult mentally and financially, but no one expected the bizarre turn of events that would show both the utter impossibility and the complete possibility of all that he hoped to accomplish.

3

Preparation—God Molds

It was the first time this youngest son of Anthony and Jennie Schuller had really been away from home. It took him hours to travel by bus into Michigan. And he went alone. Farm folks like his parents just simply didn't travel. Perhaps this would have been a good time for Tony to tell Harold of his prayer. But no, if his son had not succeeded in college or seminary, then God wouldn't really have called him. Besides, if he knew how much it meant to his father and for some reason was unable to complete his plans, his guilt would be much worse; so the wizened old farmer, his hair snowy white by now, kept his silence in wisdom.

For Harold, Holland, Michigan, was a wondrous place, so much larger and more cosmopolitan than Alton, Iowa. Located in the Southwestern portion of the state, Hope College was built along the shore of Lake Michigan. He had never seen such a large body of water. The college was steeped in tradition—ivy grew up the side of the old Dutch buildings, and beautiful oaks and elms, already more than a century old, graced the grounds. It would have been easy for a sixteen-year-old, away from home for the first time, to sow a few wild oats in the big city, but Harold didn't have time for that. The call was too strong.

He settled down to studying for his preministerial degree, focusing on psychology and history for a Bachelor of Arts. This was especially hard since he has never been fond of studying and, even today, would rather talk than listen. Once again he joined the debating team, winning a prize for his oratory. And because he loved to sing, he joined a quartet. He also took the opportunity to begin using his first name, Robert, and soon was known as Bob to everyone.

Money was scarce. His parents were still recovering from the Depression and couldn't help with his education, so he took a job as a janitor, cleaning toilets in an elite women's club. Later he became a busboy and eventually a waiter at an exclusive summer resort. The Castle at Castle Park was a haven for people like Mrs. Sligh of Sligh Furniture and the Reynolds family of Reynolds Aluminum. Having been raised on a farm, he had never been inside a fine restaurant before. For the first time, he realized there was an ordinary way to do something and a way to do the same thing superbly. Simple little things like setting a table became grand productions at the Castle. First there was a snowy white tablecloth, starched and ironed smooth and crisp, then beautiful fine china and crystal and even sterling silver. And to finish it all off, a napkin folded to perfection. The results of this careful attention to detail were stupendous. The years he worked as a waiter were times of learning a lesson in excellence—a striving for perfection and a realization that often the perfection comes in the details. These concepts have profoundly affected his ministry in so many ways, and as he will often say with a smile and chuckle, "God is in the details."

Two bad habits Bob got into during his college days had to do with both the lack of money and the need to eat. In those days, during and just after the second World War, Hershey bars were quite popular and felt to be very nutritious, giving quick energy. They were cheap, a nickel apiece, and Bob got into the habit of eating these tempting candies as meals in themselves when money was scarce. The other, much worse than the first, was smoking cigarettes. Many may wonder how a fine young Christian man in study for the ministry could possibly pick up such a bad habit, but actually there's a good reason for it.

As a child, Bob attended church regularly at a little country chapel of the Dutch Reformed Church. In that conservative Dutch culture, smoking was very proper. It's a matter of different customs among Christians in different parts of the world. Now mind you, the women didn't wear make-up, not even lipstick, nor did they do much to their hair. These were considered quite worldly sins. But a good preacher always smoked. The elders and deacons smoked and most of the men in Bob's family smoked. The women did not smoke; at that time, it was considered a sin for a woman to smoke in rural Dutch Iowa. So it was really quite natural for the young man away from home to start smoking as a way of expressing his adult status and preparing for the ministry.

Being poor, often with no money for food, he soon learned that smoking killed his appetite, which at the time was quite expedient, so he began to smoke regularly. Before he knew it, he was hooked, and smoked two packs a day. When he was broke he would smoke each cigarette down so far that he would take a toothpick and put it through the stub to get that last hot drag. He was that Dutch. It was a terrible addiction that lasted about twelve years and which brought him much sorrow. He tried so many times to quit, tearing up the package with great intentions only to come back later to the wastebasket and fish out the longest piece of broken cigarette he could find and smoke it. It was a humiliating experience for a positive thinker to find it impossible to control his own desires.

Finally, one January first he made a New Year's resolution, promising again to quit smoking. "Jesus," he prayed in desperation, "with your help, I'm going to quit smoking and never start again. Liberate me, Lord." And He did.

One summer, Bob arranged to take his quartet on a singing tour across western America. They left Holland, Michigan, in an old 1939 Pontiac, owned by friend and quartet member Ken Leestma. It was brutally hot as the Arcadian Four, including a fifth member who came along to play the organ, motored across Minnesota and Iowa and worked their way toward their destination, Southern California. Bob and Bill Miedema, who were both heavy smokers, were relegated to the back seat.

The quartet sang old-time gospel music and performed in churches along the way. Prior to their departure from college, Hope College President Irwin Lubbers had called them in and given his blessing for the venture, telling them to give greetings from their college to the churches they visited. Because of his gift of gab, bass singer Bob Schuller was given the job of speaking for the group. The rest of the quartet would sit together in the back row of the sanctuary, blushing and giggling as Bob enlarged upon the official capacity of the quartet. With each stop, President Lubbers' farewell speech became more elaborate, the significance of the quartet amplified. It was during one of these exceptionally adjective-riddled speeches that one of the boys gave Bob his nickname. For the next several years, he was known as Bull Schuller to his close circle of friends.

When they finally reached Southern California, it looked like paradise to Bob. He was fascinated by all that sunshine, and the palm trees, and the orchards dripping with juicy oranges. The Pacific Ocean, all shimmering blue, thundered against the rocks in secret coves, and all around rose the mountains, silent sentinels grazing the sky.

The quartet hadn't planned on making any money on the tour; in fact, they had to raise their own expenses. But they hadn't counted on car trouble. They ended up having to buy four new tires, a new transmission, a new radiator, and finally had to have the entire engine rebuilt. They tapped all their savings and eventually had to borrow money from the Artesia Reformed Church in California before they could begin the trip home. When they at last limped into Lincoln, Nebraska, they pulled into a sleazy downtown hotel and learned that they had only enough money for four of them to sleep in a room together. They drew straws to see which one would sleep in the back seat of the car. Bob got the car. Needless to say, they returned to Holland, Michigan, with a wealth of memories never to be forgotten.

The next summer stands out in stark contrast to the carefree fun-filled singing tour. It held so much promise, and Bob was really looking forward to spending a summer with his aging parents on the farm. He had been home for only a few days and had just gotten unpacked and settled when disaster struck. It was late afternoon, and the sky was shaping up for a good rain storm. Giant, fierce-looking black thunderclouds were churning overhead as if God Himself were stirring them with a stick, and soon the hot wind began to blow with a fury, banging the wooden gate against the fence and sending the small animals scurrying for cover. From out in the pasture a cow bawled distractedly. Bob's riding horse stood erect in the field, his ears cocked, his mane and tail blowing in the wind. He held his head high and sniffed the air. Danger. He could smell it.

Tony grew roses, tenderly caring for the delicate flowers and prizing their fragrant blossoms. As he glanced anxiously up toward the sky, he called to his son, "Looks like it's going to hail tonight;

let's find all the buckets and boxes we can and cover the roses so they won't be destroyed." As they began, lightning pierced the sky and was immediately answered by a deafening clap of thunder. It was growing darker by the minute, closing in, and the old farmer shouted in to his wife who was just putting a batch of bread into the oven. "Hurry, Jennie. Looks like hail's coming fast. Come, help us cover the roses."

The three worked quickly, and then watched in increasing dismay as the dark clouds formed a huge lump in the sky. It looked like someone was blowing it up like a balloon. Then it elongated and dropped, hanging suspended in the furious sky, swaying, slithering like a snake ready to strike. A tornado, racing from the Northwest, livid with rage, and heading straight toward them. Mother, father, and son made a mad dash for the storm cellar, but Jennie knew it wasn't safe even there. "We've got to get out of here!" she shouted. "We've got to go *now!*"

They streaked across the yard, in their terror almost knocking over the buckets that were over the rosebushes. In an instant they were in the car, slipping and sliding down the driveway in a wild race for their lives. At ninety miles an hour, they drove through the rain that by now was falling in big angry drops. When at last they reached the top of the hill, out of the path of the funnel, they switched off the car and sat paralyzed as they watched the tornado sweep across a wide swath of sky, hoping and praying that it hadn't touched down on their farm. Just as unexpectedly as it had appeared, the funnel collapsed back into the sky and disappeared. It was suddenly calm.

The trio slowly made their way back home, looking closely at the other farms along the way. There were a few broken tree branches, but no major damage anywhere, and their spirits began to rise. They each took a deep breath as they began their ascent up the final hill before their farm. Nostrils flared, hair on end, they inched their way up. They could always see the tip of their barn halfway up the hill, and their eyes were peeled to the spot. Hoping. But it wasn't there.

"It's gone! Jennie, the barn is gone!" Tony cried to the wind. As they crested the hill and looked down, their worst fears were confirmed. Not only the barn, but all nine buildings were gone. Everything. All that remained were the clean white cement lines of foundations. There was no rubble. Over two hundred trees were gone, yanked up by their roots, not even leaving their stumps behind. The winds had picked them up like so many thistles and deposited them a half mile away. Electric wires crisscrossed the road. A dead pig lay motionless in the driveway, her three babies still trying desperately to nurse. Bob gasped; there in the grass lay his horse, a fourteen-foot-long two-by-four driven clean through his middle.

Tony's bony hands gripped the steering wheel, strangling it with his anguish until his veins under the gray hair of his hands turned purple and swelled as if they would pop. At last he let go and pounded the wheel with his fists, shouting all the while, "Jennie, it's all gone! Thirty-three years worth of living and working and it's all gone in ten minutes. Where is it? Where's the rubble?" And he stepped out of the car and walked slowly down the road, leaning heavily on his cane. A sixty-six-year-old man, his back stooped from a lifetime of hard work, stepping over the sparking wires, walking around the empty yard where minutes earlier his home had stood. He reached down and picked up part of a wall plaque that had hung in their kitchen. Originally it had said "Keep looking to Jesus." He returned to the car and handed the broken plaster piece to Jennie. "Keep looking," it said. And through the tears, they prayed. They prayed to a God they loved and trusted. Yes, they loved and trusted Him even in the midst of tragedy; and the God who rides on the wings of the storm comforted them in their loss. It was quiet. And from the quiet came peace. From the peace came guidance.

They drove west to the home of their married daughter, Violet Mouw, knowing she would care for them that night. And as they drove, Tony already had a plan. This simple man didn't know the meaning of defeat, to give up just wasn't in his vocabulary. "Mother," he began, "remember that big old four-story house in Orange City they've been dismantling? The back end of it is still standing like the Leaning Tower of Pisa. They've been trying to sell it for fifty dollars. I think we can take it and build us a new home."

The next day they drove into Orange City and bought the house. But they had to remove it, shingle by shingle. Bob and his dad climbed up to the top of that four-story roof and started removing shingles. "Be careful; don't break them." They saved every nail and every shingle. Then they got down to the sheeting and removed every nail with crowbars and straightened each one out individually. They went down to the studs and removed every piece of oak flooring. Tony became enthusiastic as they worked. "Boy, they don't build houses like this today. You can't get two-by-fours like this anymore."

Finally, after three weeks of back-breaking work, the father and son had removed piles of shingles; piles of shingle nails; six penny nails and twelve penny nails. They had piles of two-by-fours, two-by-eights and two-by-sixes; they had sheetings, one-by-sixes and one-by-tens; and they had good oak flooring. The basement of the house was made of cinder blocks. They dropped a wrecking bar in through a hole in the wall, attached a long chain to it, tied the chain to Bob's brother-in-law's tractor, and pulled down the wall. Then they went in with hammers and chipped the old cement off the cinder blocks, carefully saving each one. They loaded a wagon with their precious supplies and hitched it to the tractor and pulled it the ten miles to the farm and started right away to build a new home, complete with out buildings. Nine farms were destroyed in that tornado, but Anthony Schuller was the only farmer to completely rebuild a demolished farm. It is still standing, and Bob's older brother Henry lives there to this day.

Many years later, a stooped-over, white-haired grandmother would tell this story to her grandchildren; and she would always close her story with an admonition for them to remember: "No problem is so big that God won't give you the strength to see you through." And a distinguished silver-haired gentleman would stand in an all-glass church and lecture on prayer with these words. "When I talk about meditation, I'm not talking about some fad that has just been imported from another country and is being sold for a certain number of dollars. I'm telling about the kind of meditation and prayer that is offered free from Jesus Christ. It's been around two thousand years. It works when the roof falls in, and it works when the walls cave in, and it works when the floor gives away under you. I know what I'm talking about. I've lived it and I know it works."

Living through the tornado and spending the summer helping his parents pick up the pieces of their lives was an experience that would speak strongly to young Robert of the power of faith in a disaster. It would serve to emphasize the reality of the faith of his parents, and of his own faith, still young compared to theirs. His love and devotion to a loving and powerful God would be strengthened beyond anything he had ever known as he sweated and struggled and prayed his way through that summer.

Some might wonder that he didn't give up his quest for the ministry right then, disillusioned and discouraged by tragedy and defeated by adversity, and resign himself to spending his time helping his parents rebuild the farm instead of returning to college in September. But actually, he was spurred on to even greater visions by the event, because more than any other single occurrence of his life, he could see the miracle-working power of God. He could feel His tender loving care. He could really understand Jesus' words in the Sermon on the Mount as He said, "Blessed are those who mourn, for they shall be comforted." And by his parents' stubborn refusal to bow down to defeat and by their continued faith and trust in God, he was inspired to press on toward his goal of the ministry, confident of the support God would give him in his task. He knew firsthand of the power to transform lives and situations for good that is implicit in the gospel of Jesus Christ, and he was more excited than ever to proclaim this Good News to the world.

Robert Harold Schuller received his Bachelor of Arts degree from Hope College in 1947, and went on to enter Western Theological Seminary, also in Holland, Michigan. The Reformed Church in America is an old, historic denomination, the oldest continuously operating denomination in the United States. It was brought over by the Dutch in 1628, as they came to colonize the new land, settling in New Amsterdam, which would later become New York. Over the years, this conservative church, with a history stretching all the way back to the Reformation and the teachings of John Calvin, changed its name from the Dutch Reformed as it was known in Holland, to the Reformed Church in America. But essentially, it was the same in theology and church government as it was when originally imported to this country. Western Theological Seminary was much like the church it served—extremely orthodox, very conservative, ultra Dutch, and small.

It was an exhilarating day for Bob as he walked its venerated halls for the very first time, knowing that he was on the last leg of the journey that would take him to the goal that had consumed his interests and his time for the past sixteen years. At last Bob was in his element. No more was he required to spend his time on courses that were not essential to his goal. Studying for the ministry was sheer joy, and his grades reflected his attitude. He earned A's in everything from Hebrew to Preaching. He read the Bible in its original languages and was fascinated by its eternal truths once more. Truths that were always old and always new at the same time, and thought even then of ways to speak these truths in words that would be easy for his future congregations to understand.

One day, in his middle year of seminary, Bob was in a coffee shop with some upperclassmen. They were nearly ready to graduate and were discussing various churches across the country which they felt would really be prestigious assignments. The competition was fierce, with each graduate pitted against the other for the most important position. The campus was seething with jealousy as first one and then another received their calls, with much criticism directed against those who were called to larger, more affluent congregations. Bob was repulsed by their venomous attacks, and later that night did some hard thinking about his own career.

It was common knowledge that from seminary to retirement, ministers sought to better their church assignment, trying to work their way up from assistant pastor to senior pastor, from a small, insignificant church to a larger, more prestigious one. As Bob mulled this over in his mind, he was shocked to discover that ambition and drive for personal achievement had taken root in his own life. Later, he was to say that these emotions literally scared the hell out of him. He perceived that he was pregnant with ambition, full of the desire to make a name for himself, to do something great with the one life he had to live. Intuitively, he realized this driving force could be either a halo or a horn, a star to guide or a stone to weigh him down. The choice was his. Recognizing he had a serious problem, he prayed for guidance. He didn't want to covet and scheme to land a job in some great church, feeling this was an extremely negative way to begin his ministry.

About that time, his professor of homiletics assigned him a term paper which was to be written on George Truett. He knew nothing about him, but as he began to study his life, God spoke to him in a very real way. Mr. Truett had come to a tiny congregation in Dallas, Texas, as a young man. Rather than transferring from one church to another, Truett decided to spend his entire life right there. He and his wife labored together for forty years, leaving behind one of the greatest churches in America, First Baptist of Dallas, the largest Baptist church in the country.

Bob saw in Truett's life the answer to the driving energy and ambition that he wanted to channel for good in his own. He determined then that he would never covet any man's job, nor aspire to the upper echelons of denominational politics. He would not scrap with the other graduates over the biggest, best churches. Instead, he would ask for a small church, one in a growing area where there were large numbers of people without a living faith. That way, his only competition would be his own last year's record. "Give me a chance, Lord," he prayed. "I'm a young man; please lead me to some place where I can spend forty years and build a church from scratch."

As part of their seminary training, the students were required to spend at least one summer on assignment. Bob was assigned to an Indian mission in Macy, Nebraska. That summer was a meaningful one for him, and he became knowledgeable about the Omaha Indians with whom he worked, building a deep love for these native Americans. In those days, you rarely saw anyone on an Indian reservation but Indians, and perhaps a white person there as an official missionary or government worker. Blacks, Orientals, or Mexican Americans just weren't seen on an Indian reservation at that time.

So it was quite a shock for Bob to see a young black man kneeling in front of the little church. He was a huge man, and it impressed Bob to see him kneeling there on the sidewalk, his hands folded, looking up at the spire and praying. He went out to welcome him and to show him Christ's love, and was disturbed by the faraway look in his eyes. It seemed as if he must have had some sort of deep problem, so troubled were the murky waters of those brown eyes. It seemed that the best way to reach him was just lots of Christian love, accepting and nonjudgmental.

They spoke at some length, and he told Bob that he had just come to town. "Do you have a place to stay?" the ministerial student asked. He didn't, so Bob suggested that he sleep on a couch downstairs in the basement of the church, explaining that there would be a youth meeting that evening and that he was welcome to attend. He introduced him to the young people and was pleased when he stayed to enjoy the music and the singing. At the end of the meeting, the teenagers went home, Bob went to bed in the adjoining parsonage, and the black man went down into the basement.

Early the next morning, the fledgling pastor was awakened by frantic banging on the door. He opened it, and there stood his visitor, brown eyes glaring at him wildly from whites that seemed to be on fire with rage. His lower lip was stuck out defiantly, and his entire stance was that of a lion ready to pounce. "Follow me," he barked. Bob didn't know what to expect, but could see the man was in no mood for an argument, and followed him into the church and down into the basement. He went into the kitchen, opened the drawer where the huge butcher knives were kept, and pulled out some records, one of which was a child's recording of Little Black Sambo. He left the drawer with the gleaming butcher knives conspicuously open. Then he turned to Bob with the records and asked in a voice as cold as ice, "Where did you get these?"

"Well, I'm not sure," Bob answered. He tried to inflect his voice with courage, but it was hard. His own hopes for survival were shrinking by the minute.

Then the man pulled himself up to his full height, glaring with an obsessed intensity, his eyes sparking, as he explained with exaggerated calmness: "I will tell you who I am. I am an angel sent from heaven to study this church and you." At this, his eyes began burning even more intensely. "I find sin here. These records are sinful." He was shouting now. "I will destroy you and I will destroy this church." And he began moving closer to the butcher knives.

In helpless terror, Bob shot a prayer off to the God he had always trusted to protect him. "Help . . ." And then, in divine wisdom, he turned calmly to the enraged man. "You know what? You are right. I know, because I'm an angel too. I was sent here too. Do you know what I must do? Tonight at the stroke of midnight, when the clock chimes bong, bong, bong . . . ," and he counted to twelve, bonging louder with each one. "At the stroke of midnight, I will take a huge sledge hammer and smash these records." Bob held him with his eyes. The man glanced down to the butcher knives, beckoning to him from the drawer, hesitated a moment and looked back at Bob. "Good, good," he said. "Well, I must be about my Father's business " And he turned away and walked out

The immediate threat gone, Bob realized that he was wringing wet with perspiration yet felt oddly cold. He went to the nearest telephone and called the authorities, who came at once and picked up the man. Later they told Bob that the big man was an escapee from a mental hospital for violent psychotics, located in the suburbs of Lincoln, Nebraska. They had been looking for him for some time.

Does God care? Yes. Does He answer prayer? Yes. Can He enter a man's mind by the power of His Holy Spirit and speak words with a conviction the man himself didn't know he had? Yes. And it was in this manner that God continued to reveal Himself to Bob Schuller, shaping, molding the man He had called.

But He was not only shaping and molding Bob, for He knew in His wisdom that what would be needed in the ministry for which He had called Bob was not a solo performance, but a duet. It would require two voices carefully blended in harmony, each singing a different part. How long ago had He picked out Arvella DeHaan for the co-lead in the play? In the recesses of eternity?

She was a quiet country girl, growing up in one of the same trio of towns, Newkirk, Iowa. She was raised on a farm in an equally loving and strict Dutch Reformed family. She also loved Jesus as her Savior from an early age and sought to serve Him. She dreamed of serving Him on the concert stage as an organist and spent her growing up years working steadily toward this goal. She was a dreamer, a setter of big goals; and she was a hard worker.

Arvella was four years younger than Bob; and even though they attended the same high school of seventy-four students, she didn't know him personally. She entered as a freshman the year he was leaving as a senior. Her older brother Johnny was a friend of the dynamic, fun-loving Bob Schuller, and she had watched admiringly as the two put on talent shows for the school. It was hard not to notice Bob, as he loved to be the life of the show, the clown who tried to steal all the scenes.

But then he graduated, and it was her turn to become involved in the music department. She sang in a mixed quartet that was so good they went all the way through the state contests, winning every one but the very last big all-state competition. They probably could have won that one too, had they not spent the previous evening riding the roller coaster in Iowa City, screaming themselves hoarse.

But Arvella's consuming love was the organ. She dreamed of attending college and becoming a concert organist, but her plans were dashed by the outbreak of World War II as were so many other young people's. Her two older brothers left, one for the Pacific, the other for Germany; and she was left as the oldest DeHaan child to help hold the home front together. Her father needed help with his work in the fields, her mother needed help with the four younger children, and so she put her dreams aside and went to work. I would say that strength of character still characterizes Arvella today. She seems quite happy to remain relatively in the background while her famous husband gets most of the glory. But she labors tirelessly in his behalf, deriving her greatest satisfaction in the knowledge that she has done her part to the best of her abilities, which are considerable.

With so much work to be done, Arvella had little time to practice her organ, but would steal a few moments whenever she could to go down to the little Dutch Reformed Church in Newkirk, Iowa, to play. The moment she sat down on the organ bench and touched her fingers to the keys, she was transported beyond time and space to the great day when she would sit upon the concert stage, a beautiful long gown swirling gracefully around her ankles as her feet, in shoes that matched her gown, flew over the pedals and her fingers raced across the keyboard. And thus lost in her daydream, she would spend hours playing the organ in the tiny empty church. The music would soar, filling the air with its powerful beauty, and then cascade to a soft note of bittersweet contrast.

One day as she practiced, she didn't hear the door open, nor did she notice that a young man had entered and was standing quietly in the background, afraid to speak, afraid to move, lest the spell be broken. So taken was he, by the enchanting sounds of the music and the tall, thin girl who created it, that he stood there for some time, his senses overwhelmed by the beauty of the moment—the sound of the music, the look of the girl, the dark coolness of the old church, the fragrance from flowers outside the open window.

Finally he approached her. Still unaware of his presence, her lips were pursed in rapt attention, her eyes riveted to the notes on the page before her. "Hello, there," his words cut through the music like a knife, the spell was broken. Her long fingers left the keys and flew to her throat in self-conscious alarm. He had intruded unknowingly into her dream. Did he know? She wondered. Her brown eyes were wide with surprise as she took in the tall young man with a glance. "You startled me."

"I'm sorry," he was quick to reply. "I guess you didn't hear me come in. You were pretty involved. That must be why you play so beautifully. Let me introduce myself. I'm Robert Schuller, the visiting minister here this week. You must be Arvella."

"So that explains why he's here," she thought to herself, remembering him vaguely from high school. But she answered him shyly, lowering her eyes so that they were hidden under her dark lashes. "Yes, I'm Arvella. I suppose you want to discuss the hymns for this Sunday?" Bob had quite a struggle keeping his mind on the hymns. How could he possibly be interested in something so mundane when his heart was already racing away, totally captivated by the country girl with the deep, sensitive eyes?

For weeks he could think of little else. *Love at first sight* is such a trite phrase used to describe almost anything but real love, but surely between these two there had been such stirrings in two hearts prepared by God to respond to each other in such a way. After their first date, Bob wrote to his best friend back at Hope that he'd met the girl he was going to marry.

It was late May. Bob had just completed his first year of seminary and was home for the summer. The long, hot days were heavy with the excitement of two hearts learning to care for each other. When he returned to Michigan in the fall, they began a long distance courtship with letters full of promises and plans. Bob hocked nearly everything he owned to buy Arvella a diamond ring, and on a weekend visit, they became engaged.

It was an engagement of hopes and dreams shared mostly in letters, for distance kept them apart most of the time. Seminary summers were kept busy with service assignments, and the school year was grueling and regimented, so the young lovers had very few dates and were able to spend very little time together. Classes ran from Tuesday through Saturday, and Sundays were spent preaching in different area churches. Mondays were for traveling from the church or for study.

One Tuesday, seminary president John Mulder announced that he would be away from town the coming weekend, from Friday to Tuesday. Lonesome Bob decided to seize the opportunity in order to pay a visit to Arvella. He even succeeded in convincing Warren Hietbrink to ditch school with him so they could drive to Iowa together. It seemed like a great plan, but President Mulder strode into school unannounced on Saturday and discovered the deceit of two of his most promising students. He had all weekend to build up steam, and by the time Bob returned on Tuesday morning, Mulder was livid with rage.

He called them into his office and proceeded to scald them with his anger and disappointment. He announced their misconduct to the entire student body and held them up as bad examples. Bob went in afterwards and begged Mulder to forgive them and bury the hatchet. He refused. A week or so later, it was Bob's turn to lead the school in chapel services. As he bowed his head to pray, he shot a furtive glance at President Mulder's impassive face. "Dear Lord," he began, "when we bury the hatchet, may we not keep the handle above the ground."

It was a great disappointment to Bob that three years of advanced studies in seminary only qualified a person for what was called a Professorial Certificate. He felt that after all that work, at least a graduate deserved some letters after his name indicating an advanced degree. He learned in his freshman year that to qualify for a B.D. degree, it was necessary to prepare a full-fledged thesis of doctoral proportions. He presented his topic before the board of the seminary in his first year there, and they approved it.

In the sixteenth century, John Calvin wrote a classic four-volume work entitled *The Institutes of the Christian Religion,* which became one of the foundations of reformed Christian theology. The lawyer turned reformer included no indexes, topical or textual, nor had any been prepared up to that time. Bob Schuller spent his three years of seminary preparing a topical scripture index to the entire four volumes.

It was a monumental task that required tremendous discipline. Bob read and reread the books until he became intimately acquainted with John Calvin. His own mind was young and able to absorb knowledge like a sponge. Looking back, Bob credits his three year in-depth study of the writings of John Calvin with giving him the ability to see gaps in the great reformer's theology which he has filled in with his own theology of self-esteem. Thirty-two years after Robert Schuller completed his project on Calvin's multivolume work, Western Theological Seminary presented him with a leather-bound copy of his index. It remains one of his most prized earthly possessions.

The last few months in seminary were like watching a movie being played in double speed. There were all the exams and last-minute preparations for graduation. Waiting for the call to that first church was especially nerve-racking for everyone. And then there was the wedding. All the little details that must be planned and agreed upon by the bride and the groom and both families; getting that many people to agree on one plan is always a chore. But at last the plans were made, the wheels set into motion.

When Bob graduated from seminary that spring, he won two coveted prizes of which he is extremely proud. He won first prize for sermon delivery and second prize for sermon content. To win both awards was highly unusual. But it was an enormous satisfaction to him and still is. "It does you no good," he says, "to be a fantastic communicator if your messages have no substance. Likewise, you can have all the substance in the world and go nowhere if you are not able to communicate it."

Robert Schuller graduated from Western Theological Seminary in the first week of June, 1950. He and Arvella DeHaan were married a week later on June fifteenth. The next Sunday, Bob was ordained into the ministry of the Reformed Church in America and took on the responsibility of his first pastorate.

Bob had been called to pastor the Ivanhoe Reformed Church in Ivanhoe, Illinois, a suburb of Riverdale on the far south side of Chicago. The church had been larger at one time, but controversy and a split had caused the membership to dwindle down to only thirty-eight members. It wasn't exactly a prestigious assignment, but then Bob hadn't asked for prestige. He had asked for the opportunity to build a church from the ground up, a chance to spin the magic of his dreams; faith, hope, love, courage, and lots of hard work.

The president of Western Theological Seminary had felt that Robert Schuller showed great promise, and he was anxious that he not waste himself on some of the arguments that were sweeping the denomination at the time. Violent disagreements over details of the second coming of Christ were prevalent, and he felt it would be a shame if the fledgling pastor became embroiled in them and wasn't able to achieve his potential. He contacted a friend, Raymond Beckering, who pastored Hope Church in Chicago, and asked him and his wife Harriet to take Bob and his bride under their wings.

Dr. Beckering made it a point to contact Bob, and the two were drawn to each other right away. Their similar Dutch-American backgrounds and their positive faiths gave them an immediate affinity. Bob asked Ray to be the officiating pastor at his ordination, which was held right at the little church in Ivanhoe.

As he stood there in his long black robe that day, surrounded by other pastors of the church, and took his vows into the ministry, his heart swelled with thanksgiving to God for having led him into such a wonderful vocation and for giving him the ability to answer that call. The goal at last had been reached. He was twenty-three years old and had labored nineteen of those years just preparing himself for the great task which now lay ahead of him. Far from having reached the top, he was again at the bottom, ready to begin the next challenge.

His new wife Arvella was there to witness this great milestone in both of their lives. Jennie and Anthony, who had never been outside of the small farming community where they had lived all their lives, would be sharing the grand event in spirit only. How could they brave a trip all the way to the suburbs of Chicago? It might as well have been the moon. But unknown to Bob, a dear old man with a great big heart and the gentlest eyes in the midwest, spent fourteen hours bouncing around in an old bus, his workworn hands folded over his hat. Every now and then he would reach up a long finger and brush a tear from his cheek, smile a secret smile, and clutch anew at the brim of his hat.

When he reached Chicago, Tony took his very first taxi ride. It took longer than he had expected, and he could hear the strains of the organ through the closed doors of the little church in Ivanhoe when he arrived. The service had started without him. He hesitated a moment, looking up into the cloudless sky and far beyond. "Thank you."

Then he carefully navigated the steps with his cane, an arthritic old man with a twenty-three-year-old secret that was burning a hole right through his heart. He stood near the back of the church, watching the ordination of his son through his tears. He had asked, and God had answered. How precious was his God! When Tony shared with his son the secret he had kept for more than twenty-three years, Robert Schuller felt the call of destiny on his life as never before.

Bob plunged into his first church with a vigor and enthusiasm that was just bound to be contagious. Before long, the community was buzzing about the dynamic new pastor at the Reformed Church. He wasted no time worrying about the problems that had caused the split in church membership, but preferred to forge ahead into new directions, driven forward by the force of his own excitement in the work.

He began a canvassing of the neighborhood on foot, ringing doorbells and meeting the people, sharing the enthusiasm. In the course of four years, the little congregation grew from thirty-eight to four hundred. The Sunday school was so crowded, that as an outreach Bob instituted a branch Sunday school some blocks away which swelled to seventy-five children. He led the growing church in a massive building program, doubling the size of the sanctuary, adding a steeple and a cross, and constructing a brick parsonage across the street.

There was no money for advertising, but even then Bob exhibited a natural talent for it, often coming up with ingenius ways to attract the attention of the local press and thereby getting free publicity. When the trim was to be painted at the new parsonage, he arranged for two crews of twenty men each to trade shifts one Saturday. One group arrived at eight in the morning and stayed until noon; the second shift came at noon and stayed until dark. At the changing of the groups, a full forty men were there, complete with numerous ladders and buckets and paintbrushes, all perched precariously at various angles and heights about the house. At this point, Bob had the newspaper photographer there to take pictures.

When the steeple was completed and it was time for the cross to be lifted into place, Bob decided to do it himself. A full crew of reporters were on hand to watch the young pastor—their clicking press cameras recording the event as he rode up in the crane, proudly waving the cross dramatically to the congregation below and gently placing it atop the slender steeple.

Halfway across the continent, Bob's mentor Ray Beckering was now serving a church in Los Angeles. He had risen in denominational ranks and was a member of the extension committee of the Classis of California. Orange County, to the south of Los Angeles, was on the brink of an incredible population explosion, and the committee felt that now was the time to begin a mission church there. Ray remembered Bob Schuller, feeling that his energy and dynamism could flourish in Southern California among the orange groves. No one else on the board had any other ideas, so Ray was elected by default to give Bob a call to the area.

Bob was negative to the whole idea. California was a long way away from his and Arvella's families, and he already knew that they wouldn't travel there for visits. If the mission failed, they'd be stuck out there in the wilds of the West Coast alone. But he couldn't ignore the drive that burned within him. At least, he reasoned, he could go take a look.

The trip revived memories of his college musical tour, and he was again awe-struck by the natural beauty, the churning energy, and the vitality of California. The aerospace industry was booming there, hundreds of new people poured into the county daily, entire new communities were springing up in the middle of the orange groves. It was a fertile mission field just waiting to be cultivated. But the task seemed so great, the distance so overwhelming that Bob started back to Chicago still undecided.

He was traveling by train, and the endless miles of track formed a bridge of prayer for him as the train hurtled toward the horizon. It braked to a stop high up in the mountains of Arizona. It was nearly midnight, but Bob was wide awake. As he lay in the upper bunk of that railroad car, staring out the window, snow-covered pines shimmered in the light of the full moon. The moment was suspended in time and space, the eternal and the temporal fused forever as a single deer bounded from behind a tree, its tiny hooves joyously dancing into the stardust, spraying the night with a trail of fresh snow.

"The greatest churches have yet to be organized." As swift as the deer Bob received God's words into his heart and made them his own.

4

In Search of a Dream—God Leads

THERE WAS SNOW on the ground that February day as Bob and Arvella Schuller loaded their old Chevrolet with their few meager belongings and lovingly tucked three-year-old Sheila and baby Bobby into the back seat. Their breath hung in puffs of steam as they carried their things from the little parsonage. This was it. There would be no turning back now. They were committed to the mission church they hoped to found in California. Whether it brought them success or failure, happiness or despair, it was in God's hands.

From his experience at Ivanhoe, Bob was emphatic on two points about the new work in California. He was going to begin his new church with an organ, and without mimeographed Sunday bulletins. The Ivanhoe congregation had given the Schullers a farewell gift of four hundred dollars to use as they saw fit, and Bob was determined to use it in the purchase of a two-manual organ. As they drove across the country, they stopped at a music store in Sioux City, Iowa, that was run by an old friend, Howard Duven. He agreed to sell Bob the coveted organ, accepting the four hundred dollars as a down payment. The balance would be paid out in thirty-six monthly installments of thirty-eight dollars each. The denomination had already promised them a salary of four thousand dollars a year, so Bob calculated that he could just make the payments with his tithe. Arrangements were made to have the organ delivered to California.

It was a grueling drive, but at least the roads were dry. That was more than they had expected in crossing the country in February. On the second day, they stopped for lunch at a little coffee shop in

Albuquerque, New Mexico. As they munched their hamburgers, Bob was lost in thought. Just before their departure, a denominational representative had phoned him to say that there were simply no halls to rent for the new church. "It's impossible to find a meeting place," he had commiserated. "Impossible."

Bob mulled the negative word over in his mind and finally blurted out, "It can't be impossible."

Arvella turned from the children and looked at him in confusion. "What?"

"There's bound to be some place where we can hold services for the church," Bob determined. "I know it can't be impossible."

Without another word, he grabbed a white paper napkin from the table, pulled a pen from his pocket, and began to write:

1. Rent a school building
2. Rent a mortuary chapel
3. Rent a Masonic Hall
4. Rent an Elk's Hall
5. Rent a Seventh Day Adventist's Church
6. Rent a Jewish Synagogue
7. Rent an empty warehouse
8. Rent an acre of ground and pitch a tent
9. Rent a drive-in theatre.

At various times, Bob has pulled different events from his past and given them credit for the birth of his Possibility Thinking, but I believe he usually admits that it was born in that coffee shop in Albuquerque, New Mexico. The tack he used there is still one of the basic tenets of his own personal philosophy. "When you are faced with an impossible task, write down the numbers one through ten, pray for guidance, and write down ten different ways that the impossible might be accomplished."

The crumpled napkin was thrust into Bob's pocket where it remained as the young pastor and his family traveled across the desert into California. Later he was to say that the value of that napkin couldn't be measured in dollars; it was invaluable. "You don't need money," he has said on many occasions. "What you need are ideas. If you have the right ideas, you'll get what you need."

It was late in the afternoon of February 27, 1955, when Bob and Arvella and two cranky children pulled into the driveway of the little eighty-five-hundred-dollar parsonage provided for them by the denomination. They had driven through the mountains and through the desert and through the mountains again. Now they were surrounded by orange groves. They climbed stiffly from the car, stretched their arms and legs, and began carrying suitcases into the house. They were immediately struck with the precariousness of their situation. The Reformed Church had given them a check for five hundred dollars. That and the mortgaged organ which would soon be arriving were their only assets.

They had driven all the way across the country for a dream. There was no organized church, not even one as poorly organized as Ivanhoe had been. There was no building. There were no members. There was no office. There was nothing at all. Nothing but twenty-eight-year-old Robert, twenty-four-year-old Arvella, three-year-old Sheila, six-month-old Bobby, five hundred dollars, and a dream. That's all.

The first thing Bob did was to look up other members of his denomination in the area. To his dismay, he found that there were only two families. Realistically, he had to admit that the odds were against even as few as seventy-five families in the Reformed tradition moving into the Garden Grove area within the next ten years. From the outset, Bob did not want to take members from other churches. Since there were none of his own, there was really no choice. He would have to find a way to attract some of the more than 50 percent of the public who, for one reason or another, chose not to participate in organized religion.

Before he could attract the unchurched, he would have to have a place for them to meet, and that was his next course of action. Within a few days after their arrival, Bob had exhausted the first eight possibilities he had written on the list in Albuquerque. His ninth and final choice was the drive-in theatre. He and Arvella had attended services held in a drive-in once in Spirit Lake, Iowa, so he knew it was possible even though unconventional. On the sixth day, more or less in desperation, Bob went to the manager of the Orange Drive-In Theatre and asked to rent it on Sunday mornings. It so caught the man off guard that he couldn't come up with an answer that day, but a week later he called to say Bob could have it if he wanted it. "What'll it cost?" Bob queried. "Well," the manager thought for a moment. "It costs me ten dollars to have the sound man come out here and switch the sound control on and off. So I guess I'll charge you the same. Ten dollars." It was a deal.

Little did Norman Miner know what a deal he had made. Curiosity got the best of him, and he began to listen secretly over a speaker in his office at the drive-in to Bob's messages each Sunday. Over a period of time, the power of the living God came to dwell within him, and he was converted to a life of faith.

Bob took the five hundred dollars from the denomination and opened up a bank account in the name of the Garden Grove Community Church. Even in its name, he was aiming for the unchurched, knowing the title Reformed Church wouldn't be at all attractive to them.

Now that the meeting place had been arranged, it was time to begin spending some of that money. First, publicity. Bob always says that you should make a statement and make it bold. Let the people you want to reach know you're in business. So for twenty-five dollars, he had a four-by-eight-foot sign painted and posted on a triangular frame and set up under a palm tree in front of the drive-in. "In three weeks we will be starting what will become Orange County's newest and most inspiring Protestant Church. On Sunday, March 27, 1955, at 11:00 A.M., first services will be held in the Orange Drive-in Theatre."

Next came the all important newspaper ads. Bob took out a big ad in the *Independent Press Telegram*, taking advantage of every positive aspect of the drive-in. Calling it Southern California's beautiful drive-in church, they added "Worship in the shadows of rising mountains, surrounded by colorful orange groves and tall eucalyptus trees. Worship as you are . . . in the family car." They spent seventy-five dollars for a microphone that Bob could jack into an outlet of the sound system on the roof of the snack bar at the theatre. That way, he could stand up there and preach to the people who would be listening through the drive-in speakers placed in their cars. One hundred and ten dollars was spent for rough lumber which Bob used to build his first altar and a fifteen-foot cross, and an additional twenty-five dollars was used to purchase a used trailer on which to pull the organ.

Hoping to impress the unchurched, Bob wrote Norman Vincent Peale and told him of his plans. Dr. Peale was extremely generous, writing back an encouraging letter and giving his permission to quote him extensively. Bob admits to grabbing on to Norman's coattails, quoting him in his newspaper ad as well as in the fifty dollars worth of brochures he had printed.

By this time, they were nearly through the five hundred dollars; however, Bob was insistent from the very beginning to create a "success" image. As he has been known to say since, "You can spoil the whole money tree if you give the impression that you are having financial problems." That's not an unscriptural or an un-Christian comment; it's just simply a realistic assessment of human nature. And he wasn't saying it because he hoped to make a fortune for himself either. But when you are trying to build a church from scratch and you've already run out of scratch, you are going to have to get some money from somewhere just to break even each Sunday.

The bold statement had been made, but unfortunately not everyone agreed with it. In fact, no one actually thought what they were doing was a good idea, except maybe Dr. Beckering. He felt that Bob's booming theatrical preaching style would go over better in a large open-air arena like the drive-in than in a small enclosed one. Everyone else's reactions ranged from sympathy to downright anger. One pastor friend came over eight days before the opening service and proceeded to lambaste Bob and Arvella for holding worship services in a "passion pit." Bob countered by reminding him of St. Paul's sermon on Mars Hill in Athens. But the minister was not to be put off. His criticisms devastated Bob, who swears that impossibility thinking is contagious. His self-confidence was shattered, but he had already spent all the money, the advertisements had run. He had no choice but to continue. Bob tossed and turned for most of that Saturday night, finally falling into a restless slumber about three in the morning.

When he rose bleary-eyed that Sunday, only one week before the first service was scheduled for the drive-in, Bob was still reeling from the tongue lashing he had suffered the previous night. He sat despondently at the little breakfast table, looking from Arvella to Bobby, to Sheila, and back again, trying to compose himself. Finally, he forced a smile, "I know," he proposed, "why don't we hurry and get dressed and drive up to services at Hollywood Presbyterian this morning? We can hear Dr. Lindquist speak. God knows we need a lift."

Raymond Lindquist, pastor of Hollywood Presbyterian Church, the largest Presbyterian Church in the world, was another of the men Bob really admired. During his days in seminary, he had read a big spread about Dr. Lindquist and his church that had appeared in *Life* magazine. He had visited Western during Bob's matriculation there, and Bob had overheard him advise some students not to accept a call to a church unless they were planning to spend their whole lives there. Bob had felt it was another sign from God that he was to remain in one church for his entire ministry. Hoping for some further inspiration, preferably something that could buoy him up for the next difficult week, Bob drove his young family the hour's drive into Hollywood, barely getting the children placed in the nursery in time to make the start of the second service.

He and Arvella inched into a pew toward the back of the sanctuary and opened their bulletins. The title of the morning's message leaped off the page. "God's Formula for Your Self-Confidence." Bob involuntarily shuddered and sighed—thinking to himself that maybe some of Dr. Lindquist's self-confidence would rub off on him; he sure needed some. Ray Lindquist's resounding voice soon broke the quiet as he began his message with a scripture from Philippians. The words of that passage echoed in Bob's head that day, and he grabbed onto the promise they held for him and never let it go. "Being confident in this one thing, that God who has begun a good work in you, will complete it" (Phil. 1:6).

"God got you started in life," the minister boomed. "It's He who has helped you to get where you are today. You can trust Him to continue. God will not quit on you. There may be times when you quit on God, but God will never quit on you." And, at that moment, unknown to Dr. Lindquist, Bob Schuller and his young wife received God's words and were strengthened, their hope and confidence in their God and themselves renewed. With God's help, they would build His church. They would.

The next day Bob went to a church in Los Angeles and asked to borrow their choir for the first service. It had about thirty members, and as an afterthought, he asked, "Do you think they could each come in a separate car?" That way, the fifteen-hundred-car drive-in would have at least thirty cars. Bob was hoping that maybe another ten might show up for the first service, and really be the beginning of his congregation.

That Saturday he worked hard on his first message in California, choosing as his text "If you have faith as a grain of mustard seed, you can say to this mountain move, and nothing will be impossible to you." It was quite a struggle to get the shiny new mahogany organ up onto the little trailer and bolt it down, but Bob and Arvella, their faces dripping with sweat, managed to do it together. The back seat of the car was loaded with the offering plate; Bob's pulpit Bible; the microphone; and, just in case, raincoats and umbrellas. Bob checked the air in the trailer tires, and knew he had done all he could. He turned his eyes heavenward, "It's up to You."

The big day finally arrived, March 27, 1955. Bob's mouth was as dry as cotton. "What if nobody comes? What if they don't like the drive-in? What if they don't like me?" But just as soon as these negative thoughts entered his mind, he would counteract them with positive ones. "Of course people will come. Yes, they will love worshiping outdoors, and they are not coming to know and like me, they are coming to know and love the God I serve. If God be for me, who can be against me?"

It was a beautiful spring day in Garden Grove, the sun was shining warmly and a soft breeze stirred the air as Bob mounted the stairs to the top of the snack-bar roof. The birds were singing and the air was alive with the sweet smell of orange blossoms. Arvella, the little girl who dreamed of playing the organ on stage, sat proudly at the console of the little electric organ, her fingers nimbly skimming the keys. This was their day, hers and Bob's. God had given them the dream, and they had taken the chance and made the commitment. She glanced proudly over at her young husband, his brown hair moving softly in the breeze, standing so straight and tall in his flowing black robe; and she swallowed a lump in her throat as he raised his arms to the congregation of fifty cars below and exclaimed enthusiastically in his dramatic voice, "This is the day which the Lord has made; let us rejoice and be glad in it."

In speaking of that historic day in an interview with the *Los Angeles Times* many years later, Arvella was to say, "There was no stained-glass window, no gold cross, no props. Just a microphone and Bob standing alone on a sticky tarpaper roof. He had to dip into his own imagination and become an entertainer, an inspirer. Call it theatrical presence and you won't be far wrong."

Later that afternoon, while the children were napping, Bob and Arvella counted up their first offering. They had received a grand total of $83.75. They were excited, not over the amount of money, but just in the challenge of the commitment they had made. They could each feel that they were in the right place at the right time, that God's plan for their lives was just beginning to unfold. The years of preparation were complete, and something very special was just getting under way. They knew it.

On Monday morning, Bob sat down at his little portable typewriter, which was set up at the dining table, and typed out another press release. "Southern California's first drive-in church got off the ground yesterday with an attendance of over half a hundred cars. The people who came were told that they were fortunate to be a part of an exciting program that God was planning in Orange County."

Bob and Arvella Schuller believed it. And their enthusiasm was contagious. Their little congregation began to grow, and Bob first came to know them by their cars. There was the brand-new Lincoln, some Chevrolets and Fords, and a battered old green Buick that always parked in the back row. "Gee," Bob would make a mental note, "Bob Smith must be out on maneuvers this week; I don't see his car." Or, "Rosie must be sick today; the old green Buick isn't here." He made a point of greeting each one personally, beaming from behind his glasses and smiling broadly at everybody. In fact, Bob Smith, who now works full time for the ministry, recalls that his jovial personality and rotund appearance in his bulky clerical robes made Bob Schuller take on a quality not unlike Santa Claus. Twinkly and vivacious, with a kind word for all. He also remembers that then, as now, Bob was always looking for volunteers. At one time the young serviceman (Bob Smith) had sixteen different jobs to fulfill in the little church; everything from soundman to Sunday-school teacher.

Since they didn't have a church office or building, all of the church business was handled from their tiny home. Arvella had to keep her bustling household of small children clean and ready for company at any time. When there were counseling sessions, she had to keep the children quiet and out of the way and had to have them scrubbed and in bed in time to help lead Bible study and choir practice.

Those first seven years were the toughest for Bob and Arvella personally. Their little house had brown asphalt floors, and it was years before they could afford floor coverings. There was no money for curtains, so they made do with newspapers and sheets at their windows. They had taken a cut in pay to come to California, and they felt it sorely. Jennie Schuller did her best to help. Occasionally, on birthdays and special occasions, she would send anywhere from two to five dollars along with a letter. It was a real luxury for the young family to receive such a generous gift.

One day, after paying their tithe and the family bills, Bob was chagrined to realize that there was no money left whatsoever. Not one cent. They ran out of milk and were not able to buy any for their young children. Bob was frantic. He searched through the house to see what he might have of value. All he could find were some postage stamps. He took them to the post office, but they refused to exchange them for money. He took them to the grocery store, but there also he was refused. They would not take the stamps in trade for milk.

He dragged himself home, a defeated man, dejected and despondent. He stopped at the mailbox and drew out a letter from his mom. As he opened it, a five-dollar bill fell out. It was like money from heaven. "I know there's no special occasion, honey," the letter read, "but I've been thinking about you and praying for you and thought you could use this."

Over the months, the church was growing; God was blessing their efforts and crowning them with success, and as they saw their dream begin to take root and expand within their congregation, it was a rich source of joy for the young pastor and his wife. It was not without their own hard work, though, through long hours and sometimes very undesirable conditions.

Most of the country thinks of proverbial spring when they think of Southern California; and in most cases they are correct in that assumption, but not always. There were those days when Bob stood up on the top of that snack-bar roof in heat that would have blistered the heartiest of midwest farmers. The hotter it got, the stickier the tarpaper became, until he could hardly pull his feet from it as he strode across the roof, dramatically making the various points of his sermon, sweat dripping from his hair onto his face and splashing onto his robe. And underneath that black robe, his entire body seemed to be melting. Then there were the Santa Ana winds which swept across Orange County from the deserts, bringing not only the unbearable heat, but gusts strong enough to nearly knock a large minister off the roof during his message, swirling his robes and twisting them about his legs.

But worst by far were the rainstorms. Winter is the rainy season in California, and while it rarely rains any other time of the year, December, January, and February are sometimes extremely wet months. Poor Bob would stand up there in the rain for two hours straight at times, a beach umbrella perched over him in an attempt to keep dry while big drops pelted it and were blown underneath it into his face. Sometimes he could barely see the cars below and wondered if preaching to the cows on his father's farm might have been an easier profession.

One day, as he was waving his arms and delivering a particularly intense message, a big gust of wind swooped under and turned his umbrella inside out. The heavy rain attacked him viciously from overhead and all sides; even inside his robes, he was shivering from the cold. But the congregation never knew. He never missed a word or skipped a beat, but kept right on gesturing and speaking as if nothing had happened, as if standing on a soaking wet tarpaper roof in the pouring rain were the most normal thing in the world.

Sometimes it wouldn't be raining when the Rev. Schuller began his sermon. The children would all be seated over at the outdoor picnic tables. All of a sudden it would start to rain. And the drive-in would become one big free-for-all. Children would be screaming and running around; parents would run to corral their little ones and take them to the shelter of their cars. In the midst of the mayhem, Bob just kept right on preaching. If he was going to preach, he was going to do it right, regardless; and he did, time after time. He's always required a lot from his employees, but never more than he has required from himself. It must be perfection, in the overall and in the details; nothing else is acceptable.

As that first year rolled into the second, and the little congregation grew, they realized that now they would be able to build a permanent home for the Garden Grove Community Church. Bob was ecstatic.

No more tarpaper roof, no more rain in the winter, blinding sun in the summer. He could preach in a normal church like everybody else.

The denomination loaned them four thousand dollars to buy two acres of land at the corner of Chapman and Seacrest, promising Bob that one of the local ranchers who put up buildings on the side would draw up plans for the new church at no charge. Bob was aghast. Since his early college days he had had a growing love of fine architecture. As he had been able, he had studied this field which so fascinated him. There was no way he was going to build his very first little chapel without the aid of the best architect he could find. The committee flatly refused to loan him money for such a frivolous expenditure, but Robert Schuller is not one to have his plans thwarted so easily.

On his own, he contacted a young architect in Long Beach. "You don't know me," he began, "but my name is Robert Schuller. I'm twenty-nine years old, and I'm building a new church. I don't have any money, but it's very important to me that the building be designed by a good architect. If you'll draw the plans, I promise that you'll be paid completely within my lifetime." Even though Richard Shelly knew the young pastor made only three hundred dollars a month, he trusted him and took a chance. His complete bill was four thousand dollars; but the little congregation, spurred on by the enthusiasm of their minister, contributed enough extra to pay for it. They collected an additional ten thousand dollars cash, took out a bank loan for the remainder, and built the lovely little chapel for seventy thousand dollars.

Week by week the construction revealed more of the details to the anxiously awaiting pastor and his flock. Finally it was nearly complete, a storybook chapel, with three sides of brilliantly colored stained glass in a modern design and a big cross right in the middle of the sanctuary.

But one evening during a consistory meeting in the Schuller home, a serious problem was brought up under new business. "What about Rosie Gray?" There were gasps about the room as the significance of the situation struck home. Rosie was an elderly woman, the wife of an old rancher. Some years earlier she had suffered a debilitating stroke, leaving her paralyzed and unable to speak. But she could understand. Her husband had cared for her lovingly all these years, and when the drive-in church had held its very first service, Rosie and Warren Gray had been there. They had been touched by the faith of the young minister and his wife, and both had accepted Christ as their Savior there in their car in the drive-in. Bob had even baptized the two of them, and Rosie, though unable to speak and tell what knowing Jesus meant to her, had expressed herself eloquently by the tears which trickled down her wrinkled cheeks that day. The old rancher had become an active member of the new church and a staunch supporter. His relationship with Jesus had changed his life, and Rosie was happier than she had been since before her stroke. But she couldn't walk; she could barely sit up. Her husband carried her from her bed to the car and propped her up with pillows to bring her to church, where she left inspired to face another week without speech or movement.

They just couldn't let Rosie and Warren Gray down. They debated and argued into the night. Finally, after much prayer, they knew what must be done. Like it or not, the drive-in worship services must be continued. Rosie wasn't expected to live much longer, so it probably wouldn't be but for a few months.

On dedication day, September 23, 1956, Bob stood outside the entrance of the chapel at 9:30, ringing the bell in the courtyard and greeting everyone with an infectious smile as became his routine each Sunday. After the thrill of standing in his very own pulpit on the carpeted floor of his very own beautiful chapel during the 9:30 A.M. service, volunteers hauled the little organ onto the trailer and threw on what other articles were needed for worship. And pastor, choir, and organist made a mad dash for the Orange Drive-In Theatre, where Bob once again donned his robe and climbed onto the rooftop of the snackbar for an 11:00 A.M. repeat of his earlier service. It was a hectic schedule, but it was worth it for Rosie.

As the months wore on, though, Bob noticed a most unusual phenomenon. The congregations at both locations were growing and thriving. At first, he had expected to be delivering a message to one car, but each week the number grew. It became apparent that some people preferred worshiping in their cars. Perhaps they too, like Rosie, had some handicap that kept them from entering a church. Or maybe the handicap was not a physical one, but a spiritual one; people who just couldn't get up their courage to actually walk inside a real church could work up to it gradually by starting out in the drive-in. Some folks didn't own the clothing they felt was required to attend regular services, but they could worship God unashamed from the privacy of their car. Couples with sick children, and those with babies they didn't want to leave in a nursery came. Teenagers who overslept and didn't have time to prepare for services properly came, too. There were all sorts of reasons, but Bob got the message loud and clear. There was a need for the drive-in services, and Rosie Gray wasn't in his congregation just by accident, but by design—God's design.

All during these first two exciting, backbreaking years, Bob had made it a point to wage a massive foot-campaign on the nearby areas of Orange County. Hour after tiring hour he would tramp on foot up and down the quiet, tree-shaded streets of Garden Grove, Orange, Santa Ana. He wanted his church to grow and prosper, but in keeping with his original promise, he never wanted to take members from another's flock. He wanted to attract the unchurched, so he went looking for them. His goal was to compile a large mailing list which he considers the first line of publicity, the way to build a church.

But Bob had always been a bit shy with strangers, especially on a one-to-one level. The thought of going up to people's homes and asking them questions frankly threatened him with great fears of rejection. At first he walked timidly up to the door, hoping that the owners would be away from home. More than once, he would walk up to the front porch only to find that his courage had left him entirely, and he would turn and leave without ever touching his finger to the bell. He felt so certain that going door to door was the way to build his church, that he prayed, asking God for guidance. How could he do it?

He did it through his imagination. He would imagine that the people inside the house were warm, wonderful folks who were dying to meet a new minister. He told himself that behind those doors was someone who was destined to become one of his best friends and staunchest supporters. And it worked.

He went up to each home, ringing the doorbell. When it was answered, he always began with the same question, "Are you active and involved in a church?" If the answer was "yes," as it sometimes was, he would express his pleasure, thank them very much, and go on to the next house. But if the answer was no, as was often the case, he had a whole battery of questions for the interview. First, he would ask them why they chose not to attend church. "You're intelligent, so you must have good reasons why you don't go."

At first he was amazed by the answers. Having been raised in a strict Christian home and having attended church with pleasure all of his life, he just hadn't thought about the reasons expressed. Some people were just too busy with their own lives, landscaping their yards on Sunday or mowing the grass. Some liked to sleep late, others preferred to take their family out to breakfast or brunch. Others said Sunday was the only free day they had and they certainly weren't going to waste it by going to church. It saddened Bob, because he knew that if a church was providing what it should, people would think it well worth their effort to get up early or miss breakfast in a restaurant to attend and receive the uplift and inspiration to get them through the next week.

Everywhere he went, he saw people who were hurting, leading empty lives, lives without the love of a God who was waiting in the wings to be called in to set them free. There must be some way to reach these lonely people—there must be. So he began to ask them what sort of programs they would like to see offered in a church, if they did attend one. "I'm single—do you have anything for single people? Some place where I can go and share my problems with others and receive real help and understanding?" It crushed Bob everytime he had to say "No, not yet, but someday." "I'm an elderly, retired person, and I'd sure like companionship with others my own age. Do you have a program for senior citizens?" "Not yet, but someday," would come the wistful reply.

"I have teenage children. Do you have a special program just for them?" Sadly, "Not yet, but someday we will have." "Do you have special programs for women?" "How about something for college-age young people?" "We're just newlyweds, looking for other couples our age with our interests—do you have a program for us?" "Not yet," the young minister forced a smile and replied with determination, "but someday."

Day after day, week after week, Bob spent all his spare time ringing doorbells. In the course of two years he rang over three thousand doorbells. He walked until he thought his sore feet and aching legs couldn't go another step, and then he'd walk some more. He asked people about the Bible, his favorite book since childhood; and to his surprise he found that most people didn't even know the difference between the Old and New Testaments and couldn't care less. They weren't familiar with the names of the books in either one and had no idea how to look anything up in one. The words John 3:16 meant nothing to them; they just couldn't identify. That's when he realized that giving Bible studies on Sunday morning during a worship service would turn off most of the unchurched people entirely. They wouldn't be able to follow one, even if they were interested, which they weren't.

They hated dark, drab churches, and they hated the superior, holier-than-thou attitudes they found in those churches even more. Many thought church music was boring, even depressing, and hopelessly out of step with modern America. Others complained that they had been to churches where nobody spoke to them or acted the least bit friendly; they hated that. They thought many churches were full of hypocrites who played goody-goody on Sundays and then went out and did whatever they wanted to the rest of the week.

Then he asked the people what sort of a church they would want to attend. They wanted light, beauty, tranquility, beautiful music, friendly people, programs that suited their needs, sermons that weren't *boring*—better yet, sermons that weren't even sermons! They wanted a place where they could feel comfortable, where they wouldn't feel someone was pointing the finger at them all the time. They wanted to be inspired, not put down.

"If there were such a place, would you go to it regularly?"

"Yeah, I guess so. Why, do you know of one?"

"No, not yet, but someday."

Bob was finally forced to admit that his little church was not offering a single thing that the unchurched masses wanted. They were not at all interested in his Sunday-morning expository sermons from the Bible, or Wednesday-evening prayer meetings. They didn't care about Bible lectures. The people who wanted those things were already in church. He decided at that point that he would never again use his pulpit as a teaching platform. It was quite a revolutionary concept then. I think it still is. He came to realize that church should not just be a place where the Bible is preached and prayer meetings are held. It shouldn't just be a building where youth societies meet and women get together to sell cakes to pay the bills. It should be all of those things, but it should be more. Much more.

His two model churches, First Baptist of Dallas and Hollywood Presbyterian, were staffed to serve. Jesus had wanted His people to serve, even saying that the greatest would be the servant of all. Bob felt he had a legitimate mandate to serve, to provide for his community the programs it needed.

He figured it would take a membership of six thousand to support all the programs the people wanted, and in fact needed, and to pay the staff of nine full-time ministers it would take to administer such a church. So, he set his goal. He began to see his church as a missionary outreach into Orange County, a large place that was growing all the time with a constant influx of people from all over the country. If a missionary were called to China, like his Uncle Henry had been, he would first go and see the needs of the people. If it were medical care, he would arrange to have doctors come in regularly and eventually maybe try to build a hospital. If there was no schooling for their children, then the mission would see about setting up a school and bringing in teachers. The whole idea was to meet the people's needs in Christian love so that they could actually see and feel that love in a tangible way and know it was real. Then they would be curious to know about the God who inspired such love and would come to the mission's services on Sunday to learn more about Him. This was the dream of Robert Schuller. Orange County, California, had hurting people too—people who wouldn't dream of setting foot inside a church and yet who desperately needed God to fill up the emptiness of their lives. There were people who suffered from deep problems within themselves and in their interpersonal relationships. Bob's mission church, the Garden Grove Community Church, would step in as it was able and begin filling the people's needs. It would lead them to Christ by the services it would offer to the community.

At this time, Norman Vincent Peale's books were on the best-seller list. As Bob visited homes throughout the area, the books he saw more than any others on the coffee tables of the unchurched were those of Dr. Peale. His ideas on positive thinking were sweeping the country; he was putting Christianity in terms no one else had thought of at that time in quite that way, and the public was eating it up. Bob

Schuller had always had a positive faith, one that was ingrained in him from his childhood and expanded by his own experiences. His nature was a positive one, he was attracted by positive people and ideas, and Dr. Peale and his writings both fascinated and challenged him. They reached deep inside Bob, to ideas and thoughts buried in his heart and mind that he had never taken a close look at before. He felt an immediate kinship with the older man he so admired; and as he continued reading, praying, and studying, his own viewpoints were enhanced and expanded. He was exhilarated, excited as God's Holy Spirit spoke to him in new ways and taught him concepts that had previously been only random thoughts.

Bob Schuller credits Dr. Peale with fine tuning his own positive faith and laying the foundation for his own Possibility Thinking that was to come. Peale's writings showed Bob that positive thinking was an effective tool to use to reach out to the unchurched with the gospel, and Peale's success showed him that he could pursue that course with credibility. Of course, he knew that Dr. Peale was criticized by the mainline church and that he, too, would be criticized if he went too heavily into the positive side of Christian theology. But he had to; he was called to do it; he knew that. No matter what, he had to pursue the course that he knew God was setting for him. It was right, and he had to do it. And so he plunged ahead and began to incorporate more and more positive theology into his messages and into his dealings with his congregation and the vast number of unchurched people he hoped to reach.

Bob had never heard Dr. Norman Vincent Peale preach, but he sure would have liked to. He knew of him and his enormous church in Manhattan through denominational sources—they were both members of the Reformed Church in America. Slowly the idea began to form; he would ask Dr. Peale to come to Orange County and preach at his church. It would be an excellent way to attract the unchurched, help build the church and get good media coverage at the same time. He had a natural flair for the dramatic and a keen knowledge of what would appeal to the secular world. And it would be filling a need; surely, as the people heard Dr. Peale speak, their hearts would be touched and inspired, their lives renewed through God's Holy Spirit.

He had the little chapel, but knew it would be way too small to accommodate the numbers of people who would want to hear Dr.

Peale. The drive-in theatre would be perfect. But would someone of Norman Peale's prestige be interested in flying across the country just to speak in a drive-in theatre? In typical Robert Schuller fashion, he decided not to tell him. He would write the letter, he would tell the truth—he just wouldn't tell *all* the truth.

And so the letter was sent. It described in glowing terms the beauty of the open-air church, the mountains, the orange blossoms; it said each member of the congregation had a comfortable chair by an open window; it spoke of excellent freeway access and parking for fifteen hundred cars. Why, he was inviting Dr. Peale to come to the largest, most beautiful church in California. That's Bob Schuller. He purposely paints a picture that is every word true but that doesn't necessarily give the whole impression. He doesn't see this as being deceitful; it's just that he's so great with the adjectives, and in the positive way he views things, he's really describing them as he feels they are. Did he think Dr. Peale would accept his invitation? Yes, he did. Every time Bob writes a letter to anybody asking them to come, he is thinking positively that they will. He is disappointed when he gets a "no." Usually his unique combination of prayer, faith, possibility thinking and sheer brass does the trick. Sure enough, a letter of acceptance was received: Dr. Peale would love to come and address his congregation.

Bob was elated. Now that he had his foot in the door, he was certain of the outcome. He shot back another letter. "So excited you're coming and just to set the record straight . . ." and in a casual, positive manner he told the famed theologian that he had accepted an invitation to speak in a drive-in. Dr. Peale was most gracious and honored the young pastor's positive-thinking approach, coming to preach on June 30, 1957.

For weeks, the little church had been in a stir, preparing for its distinguished guest. When the big day finally arrived, it was one of those June scorchers. By ten o'clock it was ninety degrees, with the sun blazing like wildfire out of control. Already cars were lined up on the Santa Ana Freeway, trying to reach the drive-in; it was one of the worst traffic jams the area had known, with cars backed up for miles, tempers flaring as the sun beat down on the roofs.

There were so many people who wanted to hear Dr. Peale that there wasn't room for them all in the drive-in; two thousand cars jammed into the spaces, five hundred more than the capacity of the theatre. Over eight thousand persons sat baking in the sun that day, some of them packed to overcrowding in their cars; and they hung on the famous minister's every word.

He was a small man, very small when compared with Bob Schuller's six feet three inches, and very vivacious. He so exuded enthusiasm and vitality that he appeared to twinkle, and in that respect he was very like the youthful minister he had come to help. When it came time for Bob to introduce Norman to the crowd, he stepped dramatically up to the microphone, grinning from ear to ear. "Now I'm going to introduce you to the greatest positive thinker who ever lived. More people have read his words than any other's." Dr. Peale beamed approvingly. "His name is Jesus Christ and here to speak about him is Norman Vincent Peale." With flushed face, Peale stepped to the pulpit, peering out at the cars through his wire-rimmed glasses. "Pray for me," he said in his gravel voice. He went on to electrify the crowd.

In spite of his size, Dr. Peale's strong voice could have probably been heard all over the theatre even without the public-address system. He told the throng that they could never find happiness and peace amid the tensions of a modern world without first finding Jesus Christ. Then he asked them if they thought Jesus would condemn them for their sins if He were with them that day. He paused dramatically and then roared out his answer, "No. He would say . . . 'There is something greater in you than has been demonstrated.' " He closed with a challenge to the crowd to change their thinking and believe that any human being can be anything he wants to be through the power of Jesus Christ.

It was the fulfillment of a dream for Bob to meet and hear his mentor preach, and he was watching closely to see if he could pick up any pointers to help him in his own delivery. It wasn't that he wanted to copy Dr. Peale, but just that he admired him so and wanted to model his ministry after such a successful one. Bob wanted to be the very best minister he could be, he wanted to be as effective as possible, and it was only natural that he wanted to study the methods used by one of the most powerful communicators of that decade.

Bob loved his treatment of sin, taking a negative subject and turning it into a positive one. This would become a trademark of Schuller as well in the years to follow; instead of chiding people for their sins he would challenge them to reach for better things, the perfection and beauty of character demonstrated by Jesus. It was a matter of semantics, finding new ways to articulate old truths that would be appealing to the unchurched. St. Paul had said that we are to be all things to all men in the carrying of the gospel; and in Orange County, California, Robert Schuller was seeking to exemplify that command.

Dr. Norman Vincent Peale's visit to Garden Grove Community Church gave Bob's ministry another spurt in growth. Dr. Peale had been extremely kind to Bob, spending time with him and giving him pointers on church growth.

Several years later, when the Garden Grove Community Church was well on its way to the fulfillment of its dreams, Norman Peale returned once more to preach at the dedication of the glass-sided sanctuary and again at the groundbreaking ceremonies for the Tower of Hope. Bob gives Dr. Peale much of the credit for his own success, feeling he owes him a debt he will never be able to repay.

Within two years of the dedication of the stained-glass chapel on Chapman Avenue, it was literally bursting at the seams. In a three-year period, Garden Grove Community Church had grown from a membership of two, Robert and Arvella Schuller, to five hundred persons. Many think of it as a wealthy church in a wealthy neighborhood, but actually just the opposite is true. Central Orange County is a mixture of ethnic groups and financial incomes. Sure, there are some affluent areas nearby; but on the whole, these suburbs, which are made up of many different cities, are middle income areas, even below middle in many parts. In those days especially, the area was extremely conservative, both financially and politically. There were still many farmers in the area, though they were selling out one by one to the big land developers. It was a study in contrasts. The beautiful scenery and fantastic weather, coupled with cheap land and big aerospace contracts, attracted new people from all over the country. They came to California in droves. Yet, there was still that conservative atmosphere that pervaded everything: Let's not change the status quo.

But Bob Schuller, though conservative in many ways, has never been fond of the status quo. He's a mover, a dreamer, a visionary. He loves the challenge, the excitement of change. He has an uncanny knack for predicting the future, knowing instinctively the trends, being able to read the signs of change and to see how these are going to affect his ministry. He is a man of action, not discussion. This is not to say that he makes a habit of rushing in where angels fear to tread, although he has been known to do that, too; but simply that he is usually so far ahead of everyone else that it is often frustrating for him to wait while everyone else catches up with him. Some people never do.

In 1958, he was a restless man. He could read the signs. Orange County was transforming before his very eyes from a basically agricultural community to a sprawling series of suburbs. Land prices were escalating as the demand increased. His own little two-acre church was inadequate for the needs of the people—the ones who already belonged and the ones he knew instinctively would come. The chapel only seated two hundred and fifty people, and he wanted the membership to grow. He knew that if a church is over three quarters full, it will begin to die. The people must feel comfortable—they must know that if they don't come, the church will be empty, and they must know that when they do come there will be a good seat in which to sit.

He was getting tired of the trek he had been making to and from the drive-in every Sunday for the past two years. There must be a better way. He began looking for a place to expand, not realizing that he was opening Pandora's box. And the frightening specters that poured forth were to haunt him for years, nearly crushing his dream and in the process, the fiber of enthusiasm that is Robert Schuller.

5

Unification Brings Division—God Tests, God Delivers

To the casual observer, the Garden Grove Community Church seemed to be growing and prospering under the direction of Robert Schuller, appearing to be a happy community of Christians serving God in unity of purpose. But there was an undercurrent of discontent, a burgeoning spirit of restlessness among almost everyone, from the pastor on down. It seemed to start with the addition of Bob's assistant.

In retrospect, it's interesting how many of the key people disagree on the circumstances involving the hiring of the church's first assistant minister. It is definite that he was hired while Bob was away on vacation, but whether this was with or without his consent is uncertain. Consistory members are adamant that they never went behind Bob's back, but Bob himself says they did. According to him, the young graduate seminarian came door-to-door selling Fuller Brushes, calling at the house of one of his elders who ended up offering him a job.

Others, though, maintain that it was the positive thrust of Bob's whole personality that allowed the problem to get started. They say Bob was aware of the graduate's negative attitudes, which may have stemmed from the seminary he attended, but was sure he could change him. He was an extremely legalistic young man, critical and narrow-minded, what Bob would today call an impossibility thinker. One of Bob's chief advisors, Ray Beckering, says that he tried to talk Bob out of hiring this particular man, but that he was tantalized by the possibility of turning this negative thinker into a positive one.

Looking back, Bob says that he was a nice enough guy, but you should never try to hitch up a pacer and trotter together. They just can't take the wagon to the same place at the same time.

From the very beginning, Bob had not been your average preacher. He had been fairly traditional, but with gusto, with theatrics. As his own personal theology began to develop further, he began mixing possibility thinking, self-love, and psychology with his Bible preaching. His months of doorbell ringing and his study of Dr. Peale had each had an important effect on his strategy, style, and substance, and subtle changes were occurring. Although his basic beliefs had not altered, nor have they altered to this day, his ways of expressing them had. He was an evangelical with a flair.

This was in contrast with his assistant pastor who was of the definite, traditional, hard-nosed school. He lived and breathed fundamentalism in its most straight and narrow sense. Later, Schuller's staff members would jokingly call this kind of Christian a foaming fundamentalist. But at that time he was anything but a joke. He spoke the traditional language of the fundamentalist and Bob didn't—a language some call "Christianese," because nobody can understand it but Christians. And, of course, that's why Bob Schuller doesn't use it. He is not trying to reach Christians, he is trying to speak to the unchurched and he talks to them in their language.

At any rate, a conflict began to emerge over the difference in the two ministers and in their vastly different outlooks on ministry. There were murmurings about Bob's lack of Bible teaching from the pulpit on Sunday mornings, comments of "I'm not getting fed." Little factions arose, creating friction, and the natural ringleader of these was the assistant pastor. All of Bob's possibility thinking couldn't bring about the desired change in his assistant, and the young man began to undermine the senior pastor with the congregation. Secret meetings were held, accusations made. Instead of working as a team toward the end that Christ be served and God glorified, the assistant minister developed a following among the people for himself, emphasizing the differences between their leaders.

It was at about this same time that Bob began to realize the need for a change of location in order to unify the walk-in and drive-in churches. It was obvious to him that the two acres occupied by the little chapel would not be appropriate for the dream that was ever expanding in his and Arvella's minds. And he knew that time was of the essence. With the increasing encroachment of industry and home-building on the farmlands and the subsequent escalating costs of property and construction, something would have to be done soon, before it was too late. But he was afraid to share his dreams with the congregation—afraid of their rejection, afraid of failure. Perhaps he would have never gotten up his courage had he not read a positive sentence on a church calendar one day: "I would rather attempt to do something great and fail, than attempt to do nothing and succeed."

He had to try. He took the plunge and began to tell others about his plans. It proved to be the proverbial straw that broke the camel's back. Two groups of people arose, in complete opposition to each other, and there appeared to be no neutral ground. It was a difference in attitudes, in vision, in scope as much as in theology or doctrine. A certain percentage of the congregation was solidly behind Bob, but there were those whose only interest was in maintaining the little stained-glass chapel. They didn't want a big church, didn't even want the drive-in. They couldn't bear to change things, were afraid to break up the camaraderie that had developed at the chapel. They weren't keen on further building at all, but if it became necessary they were sure it could be done on their little two acres at Chapman and Seacrest. Many of these proved to be the ones who were already skeptical of Reverend Schuller, and some even questioned his Christian commitment. They rallied around the assistant pastor and together worked toward defeating Bob's plans.

He could see his dream breaking apart before his very eyes and often felt helpless to stop it. His assistant was a called minister. He had no ability to fire him. He could be let go only by action of the consistory, and even that had to be on the gravest of grounds. The fact that he disagreed with his senior pastor on nearly everything was not an acceptable reason, and no one knew that better than Bob.

He knew that there were secret meetings being held regularly, that members of the congregation and his assistant were formulating plans to see to it that his own dreams would never be realized. But he wasn't sure exactly who was for him and who was against him. The stress was insufferable. In board meetings he would lash out at people, "Were you part of that secret meeting? Well, were you?" This only served to fan the flames, giving the younger assistant more ammunition. Now to his other list of grievances, he could add that the pastor was developing mental problems.

Bob, who has developed some perspective over the years, and can even semi-joke about it, has admitted that the entire episode was enough to make a paranoid out of anyone. "And just because you're paranoid doesn't mean people aren't saying things about you behind your back." Insecurities buried since childhood reared their ugly heads, the greatest one being the fear of failure. And failure was and is the one thing that frightened Robert Schuller more than any other. His nerves were raw, his hair turned prematurely gray practically overnight. He was haunted by terrifying specters; what if he flipped out and killed his wife and children? My God, he was going crazy. *Life* magazine came out with an issue articulating "Why Ministers Are Cracking Up," and he knew he would be the next one to go berserk.

He began to have regular night terrors, that horrifying instant when he was suddenly wide awake, lying there in a bed soaked with sweat, trembling all over, his eyes wide in an almost hysterical fright. He spent those hours in darkness, doubting. "Oh God, take me please. Just a fatal heart attack would solve all my problems. Give me a way out gracefully. Please." His body shook with sobs. Had he been a different sort of person he might have committed suicide, but his very nature cried out against the obscenity of such an act.

The power struggle went on for nearly two years, sapping the vitality and enthusiasm out of Bob until there was practically nothing left. One night he was startled out of a restless sleep, adrenalin pumping through his body as if his very life were threatened. "Jesus, I claim to know You. I tell others that You're alive. But I don't really know You. I've never really touched You. What do You want from me? Maybe You're not even there. Maybe I've just been brainwashed, indoctrinated. Have I hypnotized myself to believe in a God who doesn't exist?" He gulped, dabbing frantically at his eyes as he lay in the darkness. "Jesus, if You are really alive, if You can hear me, heal me. Heal me before it's too late. Reach into my brain and take out this terrible compulsion, this insanity. Deliver me from myself, from my obsessions, my anxieties. Please."

And he lay there overcome. In a moment, under the bones of his skull, he felt it. Another dimension, another presence from beyond time and space. A finger pressing, probing into the gray matter. He could feel the flesh separate to give it room as it delved deeper. Slowly he could feel that icy finger begin to ascend back toward the crown of his head; it was dragging something behind it. It passed between his bones, lifting the psychic poison through his skull. Gone. The darkness was gone.

It is often said that God always breaks his servants before he can really use them; and in 1958, Robert Schuller was a broken man. In addition to the ills at church, he was experiencing the first real physical difficulty of his life. He had developed a bulbous nose—large, round, and red. The appearance was quite disturbing to him. As one long-time member of the church recently recalled, "It's hard to look dignified when you resemble W. C. Fields."

But it wasn't the appearance that bothered him the most. The under layer of skin kept on growing, and day by day it was becoming noticeably worse. Bob would be officiating at a wedding or a funeral or perhaps preaching his Sunday-morning message when he would feel his nose begin to run. When he reached up to wipe it, he would invariably discover to his embarrassment that he had blood trickling down his face.

Surgery was the only remedy, and Bob almost considered leaving the public eye before he consented to place himself under the surgeon's knife. When at last it was performed, the surgery was nearly overdone, leaving noticeable scars which further attacked the self-esteem of the now gray-haired, broken-hearted young man. Years later he was to say that there is no great person alive who has not been hurt deeply, that sometimes we must be broken to become more beautiful. Possibly his most famous saying on this subject is "Turn your scars into stars."

Something deep within Bob's spirit wouldn't give up, wouldn't accept defeat. He clung to the words of his grandfather, a Dutch immigrant farmer. He remembered seeing him walk to the top of a hill, drive a stake into the ground, and tie a red handkerchief to it. Then he would walk stubbornly back down the hill and pierce the grassy Iowa prairie with the sharp tip of his plow. He'd whip his oxen and, with his eye fixed on that waving red flag, he'd forge ahead. His furrows were always straight and even. "Harold," he would say, "no matter what happens, keep your eye on the flag. Don't look back or you will plow a crooked furrow." And then he would always quote the same Bible verse with fierce determination: "No man having put his hand to the plow and looking back is fit for the Kingdom of God."

One night, after he had spent hours in prayer, Bob grabbed a pencil and a piece of paper and wrote down the words that God gave him, his own battle cry as a Christian soldier. They would become his testimony of God's faithfulness. St. Paul once wrote, "Out of your weakness shall come strength." Robert Schuller took this concept, paraphrased it in modern English, and called it the Possibility Thinker's Creed.

> When faced with a mountain,
> I WILL NOT QUIT.
>
> I will keep on striving until I climb over, find a pass through, tunnel underneath, or simply stay and turn the mountain into a gold mine, with God's help.

The press has had a heyday with that one; and theologians, both liberal and conservative, have picked it apart. It's been said to be too me-centered and not enough God-centered, that Robert Schuller depends too much on himself and not enough on the miracle-working power of God. Some have seen the creed as being materialistic, taking the gold mine aspect to mean earthly riches rather than the analogy it was intended to convey. Actually, it is based on faith, the faith that perseveres because it is placed in the God who promises to persevere with us, causing all things to work together for our good when we are called according to His purpose. And Bob Schuller has always known that he was called to God's purpose and has never deviated from his headlong and sometimes headstrong course of its pursuit.

So he continued to preach, to smile, to encourage, and to press forward toward the acquisition of new property. The vision was so strong, the call so great, that he could not be deterred from it.

Sooner or later the immovable object must do battle with the irresistible force; a confrontation was inevitable. It came in the form of a congregational meeting. Nearly the entire congregation turned out to decide the burning issue of expansion. Lines were drawn, boundaries set, encampments fortified.

"I cannot, I will not," Bob began, "continue to pastor two separate congregations in two different locations. It is unthinkable. I was called to build one church, not two. I offer you three choices. *Number one,* we drop the drive-in ministry. The sick and the old and the handicapped will just have to stay home and listen to the radio. *Number two,* we could separate the two churches entirely. Each would have its own pastor, its own board. I would resign from both, leaving each free to choose its own direction. *Number three,* we can merge the two churches. We can sell this property, secure a larger piece, and build a new creative development; what I call a walk-in, drive-in church."

Anytime you are a dreamer, you create new areas of conflict.

Bob, with all his natural eloquence, put his dream before the group. He drew them word pictures of the great church he envisioned, reaching out into Orange County with all its programs to help the unchurched. He gave them his honest opinion of what would happen were the two churches to split. The little chapel would never be able to expand beyond its two acres, remaining a mediocre, medium-sized church unable to service the needs of the growing community. "It would be like trying to shoot a herd of elephants with a twenty-two caliber, single-shot rifle."

"But Reverend Schuller, where are you going to get the money to buy that kind of property? How can we afford to build buildings like you're talking about?"

"I'm not worrying about money." Bob met them with a steady gaze. "Our job is to create great ideas, to dream with God, and to trust Him to provide us with what we need to make His dream come true. The question is not, 'How much will it cost?' The really important question is, 'Will this be a great thing for God? Is it what he wants?' If so, then He will find the solution to the financial problem if we just give Him time."

The session was stormy, with heated debate issuing from both sides. Feelings were strong in each direction, the future thrust of the church at stake. Robert's Rules of Order had been thrown right out the window. Finally, in an attempt to get the meeting back on the right track, Dr. Wilfred Landrus, a professor of education at nearby Chapman College, scribbled a motion on the back of an envelope.

"I move that this congregation, under God, go on record as

favoring integration; and that we authorize the consistory to conduct further study toward acquiring property for this purpose."

Bob sucked in a deep breath of air and slowly let it out, his hands at his chin in a characteristic attitude of prayer. This was it. He looked over at Arvella, whose eyes were wide with apprehension but who, nevertheless, smiled encouragingly. The motion was seconded. A vote was taken. It was not what you would call a clear-cut vote of confidence, but the motion was carried. The margin was narrow, fifty-four to forty-eight, but substantial enough to let the opposition know that there was little point in reviving the issue.

After all the others had gone, Bob and Arvella were still sitting there, thinking—feeling the importance of the decision. Knowing it signaled the beginning of yet another chapter. As they rose to go, Bob noticed the crumpled envelope on which the decisive motion had been scrawled. He picked it up and slipped it into his pocket.

The next morning, when he opened the front door to get the paper, Bob found a small stack of envelopes and books there on his front porch. Among them was the treasurer's report along with his letter of resignation; the clerk's resignation accompanied the minutes of the previous night's meeting. There were also letters of resignation from the vice-president and even Bob's personal secretary. Bob shook his head as he walked into the house. "And I thought they were on my side."

It appeared to be a hollow victory. Feelings had run so high on both sides that a reconciliation was impossible. The rift was complete.

One by one, families began to leave. In all, about forty persons left the church, and with each one Bob felt a little of himself slip away, too. "Oh God," he prayed, "I won the battle, but I've lost the war. Please take over; I can't do it. It's too hard."

Out of the silence came the Lord's answer, "I will build *My* church."

Up until then Bob had thought that he and Jesus were partners in building *their* church. But at that thought, he sprang to his feet and in dramatic Schuller style thrust his arm in the direction of his empty chair. "Okay, Jesus Christ. Then *You* do it," he challenged. "You be the head of this church. You take command. You solve the problems and handle the problem people."

"Schuller," he heard His Lord speak, "We can get by without

these people: the secretary, the clerk, the treasurer, even the vice-president. But not unless I am in control of your life. You step down, Schuller, and I'll step up, and we'll make it go."

"Okay, Lord. You take over. I'm so tired. Do you mind if I go on vacation?"

God had wrested the reins of leadership away from Robert Schuller. From that moment on, the center chair in the board meetings of the Garden Grove Community Church has been left unoccupied. It's saved for the Guest of honor, the Chairman of the board—Jesus Christ.

During Bob's four-week absence, the assistant pastor was unexpectedly called to another church. The opposition lost their leader. Barriers began to tumble. The spirit of division began to disappear. The vicious undercurrents that had threatened to carry them all off to sea dissipated, leaving harmony in their wake. With harmony came energy, and the desire to build bridges—a desire that has never left Bob nor the Garden Grove Community Church. He felt a renewal of purpose, a fresh surge of enthusiasm, and busied himself with the search for property. Now that he had the go-ahead from the congregation, his dreams were unimpeded by the negativity that had surrounded them. His dreams were soaring so high he even had difficulty controlling them.

When he found ten acres near the center of Garden Grove, he thought it was perfect. It wasn't for sale, but he felt confident that God would make it available. One Sunday afternoon he took his Bible and walked the site, claiming it for God's work and quoting "Ask whatever you will and it will be given to you." He was wearing his best Sunday suit, but he knelt down in the dust, his finger on the verse of Scripture, and prayed, "Please, God, let the owner sell us this property." Then he arose, stretching to his full height, brushing the dirt from his pants. He left feeling secure. God would answer his prayer.

But when the answer didn't come right away Bob grew impatient. Didn't God care? Didn't He know how important it was? Bob didn't realize at the time that God was thinking ever so much bigger than he was, looking to answer many more prayers than just his.

As Bob paced the floor in Garden Grove, a young Indonesian refugee, Maurice Wiggers, was asking God to please help him to be able to come to America and live and work in freedom.

In Singapore, an elderly missionary by the name of Henry Poppen was praying that upon his return to the United States he would still be able to serve God in the ministry.

Peter DeGraaf, a young Dutch immigrant in Canada, prayed for the opportunity to come to America and begin his own business.

Across the country, a new minister, Harold Leestma, asked God for the chance to reach more people with the good news that Jesus loves them.

Kenneth Van Wyk was a ministerial student in Holland, Michigan, praying for God to show him where to go to use his special talents and training in youth and Christian education.

In Southern California, LaVon and Vern Dragt were suffering through Vern's bout with polio. When he recovered, they went into the Tupperware business and became enormously successful. They decided to move into Orange County to be closer to their office, and were praying for the right church.

Soon, a ten-acre walnut grove became available at the corner of Lewis and Chapman Streets in Garden Grove. It wasn't as centrally located as the other property Bob had wanted. It seemed like God was giving him second best. However, as new freeway plans were unveiled, he realized that it was at the hub of three different freeways. Instead of placing him in the center of a city of one hundred thousand, God had given him the heart of a county of millions!

The price was sixty-six thousand dollars. It might as well have been a million, for all the ability the church had of raising it. But Bob was undaunted. It was right. He knew it. Somehow they would raise the money. They had a savings account of eleven hundred dollars; Bob withdrew a thousand and opened escrow on the property. They gave him one hundred twenty days to raise the additional eighteen thousand for the down payment. The little congregation gave and gave, many sacrificially because they believed in Bob and the dream God had given him. The Schullers cashed in their insurance policies. All resources were exhausted. But at twelve noon on the one hundred twentieth day, they were still three thousand dollars short.

Bob came home for lunch, throwing himself despondently onto a kitchen chair. For a minute or so, he just sat there, cradling his head in his hands, a look of resignation in his eyes, the fight all gone. Bobby was perched opposite him, one foot on the floor, one leg draped across the chair, his little foot wiggling. He was stuffing a peanut butter and jelly sandwich into his mouth with his chubby, jelly-smeared fingers. Arvella snuggled baby Jeanne, feeling her soft baby hair against her chin as she paced back and forth across the kitchen floor. No one spoke until Bob blurted out, "It's all lost." Silence.

Arvella continued to pace. She opened her mouth as if to speak, then she pursed her lips together, her chin quivering. Finally, she turned toward Bob, fastening her eyes on his so intently that he was forced to look away. "Bob," she began, "I think you should call Warren Gray."

"But he's been so good to us already," Bob interrupted. "And he's old and sick; cancer could take him any day now, you know that."

"I know. But you've got to call him. We can't let this opportunity slip away; the Lord wouldn't want us to. I know He wouldn't." Arvella's voice was filled with determination as she unconsciously kissed Jeanne's smooth forehead.

Bob knew enough to listen to Arvella. She was deeply committed to him and to their ministry. She was levelheaded, much more so than he sometimes was, and he respected her judgment. He got up slowly from the chair and walked toward the phone, forcing himself to take each step. His hands were big, and he had to squeeze his shaking index finger into the appropriate openings to dial the Grays' number. He listened as the phone chimed, counting the rings. Arvella deftly swooped down with her free hand and washed Bobby's face with a wet paper towel, shooing him out of the room, never taking her eyes off Bob's face.

"Warren, I've got good news for you; I can give back the two thousand dollars you donated for the land. Escrow closes today and we're three thousand dollars short. We're going to lose the property."

The old rancher's voice was weak and worn with many cares. It had been an effort for him to even reach his hand out to answer the telephone. He looked over at Rosie who was propped up in her favorite chair, her useless body twisted from years of paralysis, her eyes pleading. For what? He didn't know. For a second, he let his mind slip back to the first time he had seen those violet eyes, rimmed with dark lashes all around. He had thought them the most beautiful he had ever seen. He still did.

He cleared his throat. "Bob, we can't let that happen. I can do more than I have. Meet me at the Bank of America office on Main Street in Santa Ana in about an hour. I'll draw the three thousand out of my savings and give it to you." Bob closed his eyes. "Bless you, Warren. I'll be there." He put the receiver back in its cradle and walked over to where Arvella stood, sweeping both her and baby Jeanne into his arms and drawing them close. He buried his head in Arvella's hair and drank in the fragrance of the two of them, his heart full of gratitude, his eyes swimming.

He arrived at the bank early and waited in his car, nervously tapping his foot against the floorboard. When he saw the stooped rancher climb gingerly from his car and slowly straighten up, he winced visibly at the suffering which always tore at him so. Bob bounded from his old Chevy and embraced the rancher warmly, wishing he could impart some of his own youth and vitality to him. Mr. Gray transacted his business and handed Bob a cashier's check for three thousand dollars.

"Thank you, Warren. I can never repay you, but God will."

"I know," the wizened old man said, a smile warming his pale cheeks and lighting up his hazel eyes. "I know. God wants those ten acres, and Rosie needs a church."

Bob walked down the street to the Orange County Title and Trust Company, arriving one hour before the one-hundred-twenty-day deadline. He went to the escrow desk, took eighteen thousand dollars from his pocket, and placed it on the desk. God took title to His ten acres.

But Bob was left with the challenge of coming up with four hundred dollars a month to make the payments. As he was weighing the possibilities, all of which looked hopeless, a new family was joining the church. God had at last directed LaVon and Vern Dragt to a church home; and this couple, who had been penniless only a few years before, began right away to tithe. Four hundred dollars a month.

As God worked out His timetable, everyone's prayers were answered in the new property on Lewis Street. Maurice Wiggers came from Indonesia to become the custodian. Henry Poppen became the Minister of Visitation after his illustrious career as a foreign missionary. Kenneth Van Wyk became Minister of Youth and Education, and Harold Leestma became Minister of Evangelism. From Canada, Peter DeGraaf came to be the church gardener. The little stained-glass chapel on Chapman Avenue was sold at a forty-thousand-dollar profit to the Southern Baptists, who had been praying for their church location, too. Bob wasn't surprised. "Good architecture is always an excellent investment."

With that in mind, he sought the very finest architect he could find to design the new walk-in, drive-in church on Lewis Street. It was a novel idea, one that he knew could draw a lot of criticism. If done incorrectly, Bob was well aware it would come off looking tawdry and cheap, no matter how much it cost. He wouldn't let it become an insult to his God, nor to the intelligence of the unchurched people he hoped to attract. He wanted the entire project to be executed in such a way that it would draw praise from all quarters for its excellence in architectural design.

He selected one of the most famous and respected architects of the twentieth century, Richard Neutra. The two of them spent many years working together on the total plan for the church complex, and Neutra became another big influence on Bob's value system. His doctrine of biorealism captured Bob's imagination and fit in perfectly with his own beliefs. According to Neutra's theory, God has provided human beings with a built-in tranquilizing system which is triggered by a response to nature. The beauty of nature produces a deep, satisfying relaxation experience for people of all ages, making them more able to receive outward suggestions.

Bob wanted the church to function as a medium which would help provide an effective communication between each individual and God, and between the individuals themselves. He wanted it to be a place where people would be receptive to God's ideas, God's dreams, where they would be able to respond to these and to make commitments to them.

The entire concept went back to the knowledge that had been revealed to Bob as he rang all those doorbells. He knew what most unchurched people wanted. They were looking for a refuge from the hectic pace of Orange County's pressure cooker. They wanted some place where they could relax and feel at home, some place beautiful. They longed for the simplicity of nature—gardens aflame with flowers, the tranquility of still pools of water, and the pleasant tinkling of waterfalls.

Bob Schuller understood this longing completely. Hadn't man originally been created to live in a garden? Wasn't that his natural habitat? Wasn't he as much out of place in the city as a tiger in a cage at the zoo? No wonder people were tense and irritable, no wonder they were nervous and frustrated. They were out of their environment. He had lived on a farm, had experienced the contentment of uninterrupted vistas of green grass and waving corn stalks that melted into the pale gray horizon as they met the dome of bright blue, unpolluted sky that stretched all the way to eternity. He liked to remember the peace and wonder of preaching sermons on the banks of the river, under God's canopy. And in his church, he wanted as much of this feeling as he could possibly get. He wanted a place where the secular and the sacred could be integrated together in architecture.

The Christian life isn't just relegated to Sunday mornings in church, but is a vital part of a person's every living moment, no matter where he is, no matter what he is doing. Bob wanted this message to be sublimated in the church building, so that experiences there wouldn't be recalled as separate from everyday life. He wanted there to be a continuity, a link between them; feeling that if a person could see an airplane dart across the sky at a time when he felt especially close to God, or cars making their way down a busy thoroughfare as he accepted Christ into his life, his spiritual dimensions would take on an added significance and beauty.

They deliberately designed one entire wall of glass so that people could look out and see the world, so that the sanctuary would be flooded with the light and the beauty of the gardens. One has only to look at churches down through the ages to know that this is a relatively recent arrival in ecclesiastical buildings.

"Why, do you suppose, have churches always been built to restrict people's views of the outside world?" Neutra questioned Bob one day.

"I don't know. I guess I've never really thought about it. Maybe it has to do with God being in the sanctuary."

"No," Neutra countered. "Remember that the earliest Christians worshiped God out of doors, on the mountaintops, by the sea. I think centuries of church design have been influenced by the catacombs. For generations, Christians were forced underground, their only safe places of worship being the dark underground caverns. One group of children after another had their religious experiences by the light of flickering candles, safe from the world in the damp darkness of the caves. Even the altars where they knelt to pray were usually coffins or niches in the shadowy corridors.

"Then, at the end of the great persecution, when the Christians were at last free to ascend from the catacombs and begin to build their cathedrals, they sought to recreate what to them had become a religious atmosphere. They constructed cavernous, dark buildings of stone, gloomy places where little light could penetrate, with cheerless, candle-lit altars."

Bob knew at once that he was right. He even went farther, realizing that today when the average building committee sets out to design a church, they are trying to recreate their own childhood impressions of what a religious building should be like. "My gosh," he thought, "they are unconsciously planning a building that will appeal most to those who were raised in the church and who had happy experiences there. They're automatically tuning out the mass of secular, unchurched Americans."

Bob feels that these churches stimulate negative emotions of darkness and gloom and would settle for nothing less than the perfection of a beautifully designed building that would let in the sunlight and bring light, joy, hope, and peace with it. He determined in the beginning that his church would be designed to attract the unchurched, that it would be modern and give the impression of a progressive, exciting program. It was to be centered around all vertical lines, symbolizing man's uplifting relationship to his Maker. Even the stones in the walls around it would be set vertically. It had never been done before; but the international style of architecture, with its massive sheets of glass, its straight, honest lines of steel and aluminum, demanded it.

Richard Neutra designed a superb network of buildings, centered around the long, narrow, glass-sided sanctuary. Constructing them all at once was out of the question financially, so the little congregation decided to first build the fellowship hall and Sunday School rooms. About a hundred cars braved the searing September sun that day in 1959 when groundbreaking ceremonies were held. Long ribbons on stakes snaked through the walnut trees, marking the outline of the new building. Photographers were on hand to capture the moment on film. History was being made. All because of one woman who could neither speak nor walk.

The joy of the day was overshadowed, though, by the funeral Bob had to perform the next day. Rosie Gray was dead. As he stood alone with Warren high up on a windswept hill looking down at the unobtrusive little grave in the country cemetery, Bob paraphrased an old proverb, "They also serve who only sit and wait."

The long, low fellowship building was built with all-volunteer labor and took an entire year to construct. The men, pastor included, would be on hand early each Saturday morning with their tools and would work all day, laboring to build the first installment of a dream. The women would show up later with a pot-luck dinner for their hard-working husbands. Men who held top professional jobs—executives, doctors, teachers—worked right alongside skilled and semiskilled laborers. Together they built a church to glorify the God they all loved. During this year of labor, a sense of community was forged among the members, a feeling of family developed between them and their pastor that couldn't have happened any other way.

In the fall of 1960, the congregation, which now numbered around seven hundred, gathered for its first services in the new fellowship hall. Robert and Arvella Schuller had much for which to be thankful. It had been only ten years since Bob had graduated from seminary and the two had married; their joint accomplishments during that time had been remarkable. In their five years at the Ivanhoe Reformed Church, they had built it up from thirty-eight to four hundred members. In the next five years, they had taken the Garden Grove Community Church from nonexistence to seven hundred members. They had built two different sanctuaries in two different locations and had now unified the walk-in and drive-in churches into one congregation. Sheila, eight, Bobby, five, and Jeanne, one, were there to share in the pride at what God had accomplished through the hard work and charisma of their parents who, despite Bob's gray hair, were still under thirty-five. Many might wonder, and rightly so, about the amount of sacrifice a family would have to make in order for the parents to have accomplished so much in such a short span of time. Bob firmly believes that you can be a super success in your profession, but if you neglect your family to the point that you are not successful at home, then you have failed in the most important task God has for you to do. So let's stop right here and take a look at Robert and Arvella Schuller, husband and wife, and the parents of three small children.

6

Family Order— Ruling with Love

Establishing a new church, especially one that grew as fast as Garden Grove Community, made raising a young family at the same time an awesome challenge. And the Schullers were away from their roots. Both their families were back on the farms in Iowa, so there were no grandparents to babysit or give advice. Bob and Arvella were alone. In typical Schuller style, they just simply worked harder at it. They are a very detail-oriented, people-oriented couple, a pair who prize excellence in everything, and marriage and parenthood are no exceptions.

Bob, the powerhouse, is tempered by Arvella, who is also energetic, but more even-keeled; they are a couple paired by God to complement each other in their ministry, and in their home as well. Each of them had the opportunity of being raised on farms in middle America by hard-working, God-fearing parents who loved each other and their children. Their parents respected traditional values and passed these on to their children. They taught them love of God and love of country, love of their fellow-men and love of themselves. Surely, anyone who brings such a legacy into his own parenting experience is several steps ahead of someone who has not had the benefits of such an upbringing.

Bob says that theirs is an autocratic family. He is the head of the house, the king. Arvella is his queen and each child is a prince or princess. He is quick to point out that it is a benevolent autocracy, where the king and queen rule their subjects together in love and in consideration for each one's best interests. The children have always received a great deal of love and lots of touching, which both Bob and Arvella feel is of the utmost importance. From an early age the Schuller children have also been taught that they are representatives of their monarchy when they are away from home and that they should reserve their very best behavior for those times.

Notwithstanding, somehow Sheila and Bobby had the distinct impression that since their Daddy was the pastor they had the God-given right to do anything they wanted to at his church. They have been known to steal sugar cubes from the kitchen and play cowboy on the stairs. They always enjoyed Sunday school where they frequently knew all the answers, and in the drive-in particularly loved to sneak away and swing on the swings. If they were caught, though, and usually they were, the Queen Mother meted out swift and terrible punishment to their royal highnesses' wiggling little bottoms.

One of Sheila's favorite tricks was to stand at the back of the church while her dad shook hands with the congregation after the service. As he extended his big hand and spoke cordially with the people, Sheila would put out her own small fist and vigorously shake each one's hand. One time she even hid under Bob's flowing black robe. As the next woman reached out to shake the pastor's hand, she was surprised to see a little dimpled one dart out from under his robe about waist high. Unappalled, she shook first one and then the other. "Good morning, Reverend Schuller. Good morning, Sheila."

Since the Schuller home was furnished by the church it was often used for church functions, even after the little chapel was built. Arvella always tried to have the children put to bed before choir practice or Bible study, but Sheila, who especially loved music, would creep out of her bed and down the hall, crouch behind the door, and listen to the choir's singing far into the night. The Schuller home was also always open for visiting clergy, who often dropped in unexpectedly and stayed for a day to a week at a time.

One time when the president of their denomination was coming to visit, there was a flurry of activity as they rushed around trying to get their modest home ready for such a distinguished visitor. Wouldn't you know that this was at the time when Bobby was going through his cigarette phase. He loved to pretend that he was smoking an imaginary cigarette. Anything would do—pencils, pens, toothpicks. Arvella had already taken television away from him for a week, but he still persisted in maddening four-year-old fashion. Finally, Bob, afraid that he would embarrass them in front of their important guest, called Bobby into his room for a man-to-man talk. He carefully explained to him the very real evils of smoking cigarettes, finishing up with what he thought would certainly be the real clincher. "Bobby," he warned gravely, "smoking cigarettes can give you cancer."

The little tyke looked up at his father, his eyes as round as saucers. "What's cancer?"

"It's the very worst disease you can think of," Bob related truthfully. Bobby was aghast, and fortunately the little discussion cured him of his predilection.

Within a few days, Dr. Hagaman arrived. He was everything you would expect the president of a conservative Dutch denomination like the Reformed Church in America to be. He was stately and quite magisterial and very Dutch. Everything went quite well until he pulled a pack of cigarettes from his pocket, took one out and lit it. He took a deep drag and let out a long sigh of immense satisfaction, sending a spiral of smoke through the air.

Bobby sat staring at him for a moment or so, a quizzical expression playing across his open countenance. Finally, he could stand it no longer. He walked over to the good Doctor and planted himself squarely in front of him, gazing up into his imposing face. When he wasn't acknowledged, he reached up and tugged at the gentleman's suit jacket.

"You shouldn't smoke, you know," he spoke the words with the dignity of someone who knows what he's talking about.

Dr. Hagaman paused in his conversation and looked down at the lad, unwittingly blowing a faceful of smoke in his direction as he did so. "Why not?"

"It'll give you a terrible disease," the little boy said, drawing himself up and standing as straight and tall as his four-year-old frame would allow.

"Oh, really? And what might that be?" the Doctor questioned in a condescending tone.

Bobby stood there, hesitating for a second, thoughtful. All of a sudden his face brightened into a big smile. "Diarrhea."

Bob sees the family as the original small therapy-group and feels that this is one of its God-ordained purposes. It should be a place where communication flows easily from one to another, where no one should be ashamed to speak his mind and share his feelings. Family members should love each other with accepting, nonjudgmental love, no matter what. He and Arvella have always been deeply committed to each other and to their children, and even though they have had their share of arguments, which Bob insists are good for a family because they clear the air, there is still the knowledge that regardless of occasional anger, the love is always there.

The Schullers have tried to pattern their family life after those of other successful ministers who have also been successful in raising their children. Couples like Ruth and Norman Peale and Ruth and Billy Graham have been enormous inspirations to them as they have sought to juggle demanding public and private lives and have them both succeed. Bob has never forgotten the time he was in Dr. Peale's office when Norman interrupted their conversation in order to speak at length with his daughter by phone when she needed her father's help, and has tried to carry this tradition on into his own family when possible.

That's not to say that there weren't conflicts. Bob believes there will always be problems in family life on this planet, that constant harmony among family members is impossible. The main thing is commitment to each other, regardless of these conflicts.

There was the time early in their ministry in California when Bob wanted a fishing pole for Christmas in the worst way. He has always loved fishing and wanted one he could use in salt water. He admits to having made rather a pest of himself, even leaving notes on Arvella's pillow and clipping ads out of the paper and posting them conspicuously around the house. Arvella was getting quite annoyed; there was no way she was going to give him the coveted deep-sea fishing pole.

She began saving the empty rolls from paper towels, hiding them from Bob. On the night before Christmas Eve, she taped them all together into a long, thin tube. In the last one, she placed a can of shaving cream. Then she wrapped her creation up in bright red Christmas paper and tied a big bow around it. A tag read, "Merry Christmas to my wonderful husband. With love, from Arvella." It looked for all the world like a fishing pole tucked in at the back of the tree.

Later that afternoon, Bob returned home from his little office at church. He had spent hours preparing for Christmas Eve services and was really exhausted. One glance at the tree, though, and he really sprang to life. His whole face lit up brighter than the sparkling tree itself, and he had to restrain himself from running into the kitchen. Instead he sauntered in, swaggering just a bit, his eyes twinkling, looking like the cat that just swallowed the mouse. Arvella was stirring stew on the stove and purposely ignored him. "There's a new package under the tree," Bob began in a menacing tone. "It's awfully long and thin. What do you suppose is in it?"

"Now Bob," Arvella glanced up at him with an annoyed look, "you'll just have to wait until tomorrow to find out what's in that package."

He looked at her for a moment, trying to appear blasé but puerile curiosity got the best of him. "I can't stand it!" he cried. "I'll never be able to wait that long!" His mind was racing. Then he paused, composed himself and looked expansive. "I'm starting a new Schuller tradition. From now on each of us gets to open one gift on Christmas Eve." Then he gave her such a pleading, pitiful look that Arvella was helpless to protest any longer. "All right, Bob. You may open one present."

He rushed to the tree, snatching the pole-shaped package from its spot at the back and began to rip the paper off wildly, his hands shaking from excitement. He didn't even take time to read the tag, but just demolished the wrappings in his mad scramble to hold the long-desired pole in his hands. All of a sudden, he stopped, his hands poised in mid air, his expression frozen. He glanced up at Arvella, in fear and disbelief. "Where is it? Where's my pole?" Then his optimism took over. "Aw, I know, you're teasing me. I bet you've got it hidden in the garage?" Arvella shook her head. Bob swallowed hard. The veins in his neck began to protrude. He raised his expressive eyebrows. His voice was very small. "Under the bed?"

"No Bob. This is it. That's all there is."

It was a crushing blow. He just stood there, looking from that can of shaving cream to Arvella's remorseful face and back again. How could she have been so cruel?

"Oh Bob, I'm sorry. I really am. It's just that you were so sure you were going to get that pole, and you were so darned irritating about it.

I couldn't get it for you. Christmas gifts are supposed to be surprises." As soon as she had spoken, Arvella began to inch away from him warily. His eyes had become narrow slits.

"Surprises, huh? You like surprises, do you?" In a flash he had that can of shaving cream open and began squirting its frothy white contents all over Arvella, while Sheila and Bobby looked on in undisguised delight. She was screaming as she shot off the couch and ran through the house, but Bob followed her in hot pursuit, emptying that can of shaving cream all over her, from head to toe. When at last they collapsed in a puddle of suds, laughing breathlessly, he caught her close and pressed his forehead against hers. "Don't you ever do that to me again."

With three small children in the home, there was bound to be sibling rivalry. Bobby had a favorite pair of cowboy boots and took impish delight in chasing poor Sheila, kicking her in the shins with the pointed toes of those boots until she was black and blue. There are so many other ways that have been used universally by little boys to drive their sisters crazy, and the typical responses they evoke only seem to intensify their quest. The teasing, the stuck-out tongues, pinching, tattling, and squealing; Bobby, Sheila, and Jeanne ran the gamut.

At one time, Sheila was so undone with her brother that she decided to run away from home. She left a note in the napkin holder at the dinner table saying that she loved her parents very much, but that Bobby was just too mean for her to put up with one more day. Bob found the note before she had made her escape. He used the opportunity to tell Sheila how very much he loved her, how much he and her mother would miss her if she went away. At the same time, by his example, he taught her the value of commitment and nonjudgmental love. No wonder she buried her head in his arms and vowed never to run away again.

But there were other times when Daddy could be so pigheaded. How infuriating it was to a child who had gotten up on the wrong side of the bed to be told to change his dial from mad to happy as if he were as emotionless as a radio. Bob instilled the value of positive thinking in his children at a very early age. He believed it and he lived it and that's all there was to it. Sometimes he could be maddeningly insistent that it be put into practice, whether the little prince and princesses felt like it or not. But there were other times, when he would remember how annoyed he becomes when he has his own positive material thrown at him when he is not in the mood, and he would relent in his drive for completely positive natures in his brood.

Summer vacations were an exciting time for the children, three little suburbanites transported back in time and space to the wonders of an Iowa farm. Bob always began vacations by leading the family in a prayer that God would keep them safe on their trip. But an old car full of three kids for several days in the heat of summer is not necessarily safe, surely not among siblings, neither is it relaxing for parents. That drive through the deserts of Arizona, New Mexico, and Texas can sap the strength of anyone, even the positive preacher from California. The year when Jeanne was an infant, Arvella hung diapers over the windows in an effort to keep the hot sun from burning her tender skin through the glass.

Those weeks spent on the farm were times of family togetherness, times of renewing ties with relatives on both sides, all of whom still lived within miles of their original homes. Bob and Arvella's children had cousins to play with, grandparents to spoil them, and an array of farm animals to fascinate them.

It wasn't always the domestic animals that brought excitement to the little Schullers though. One morning enroute to Iowa, after Arvella had prepared a beautiful campfire breakfast in Yellowstone Park, a big black bear came rambling into their site, frightened them all away and ate their meal, every bite.

Since Bob and Arvella never had a new car, the trips were always plagued by mechanical difficulties of one kind or another. Once they had a flat tire out in the middle of the desert. Of the many talents God has given Bob, mechanical abilities are not one of them. He got out of the hot car and into the hotter sun, confident that he would be able to put the spare on with little difficulty. But it soon became apparent to everyone that he didn't know how to work the jack. He tried it this way and that, getting into some positions that were definitely unclerical, and finally blew up in exasperation. He was angry with everyone; the family, the car, the tire, the heat, the jack. But mostly he was frustrated by his own ineptitude.

He strode angrily back to the car, slamming the door hard as he threw himself into the driver's seat, muttering under his breath. Then he threw it into gear and pulled the car off the road until the flat tire was well inbedded in the sand. Not quite as angry now, he resignedly got out of the car and sat down in the burning sand, the tire resting in between his knees. And he began to dig. Clawing at the shifting sand with his bare hands, he started to dig a hole under the tire. After half an hour, he was dripping with sweat, his clothes and face and hands filthy from his labors. And he had hit a rock—that whole expanse of desert full of sand, and Robert Schuller had parked over a big, immovable stone! Arvella, Sheila, and Bobby crawled out of the car, and the four of them struggled with that rock, wriggling it back and forth until at last Bob could lift it out. Finally he had gouged a hole underneath the tire large enough to maneuver in, and was able to change it so that they could be on their way again.

In order to make time for Arvella in his busy schedule, Bob instituted a weekly date night. This is held sacred by both of them and practically nothing is allowed to interfere with it. It may have been only a trip to McDonald's for a hamburger and walking hand in hand to window shop during those lean years, but it didn't matter. It was the fellowship that was important, the time of being just two instead of five, a time to remember that they had married each other because they loved each other for themselves.

Bob and Arvella place their relationship to God first, their relationship to each other second, and their relationship to their children third. Bob has often said that the greatest thing a couple can do for their children is to give them a good mother-father team. That's something he and Arvella have always tried to do. They are both 100 percent committed to a permanent marriage, and their children have that base on which to build their own relationships with each other and with those outside the family unit.

While Bob was counseling a woman one day, she told him that all she really wanted from her husband was that which he willingly gave to the family cocker spaniel. She explained that the dog is waiting for him when he comes home from work, waiting for him to look at her. When he does, she begins to wag her tail, waiting for him to speak to her. And finally, she wants a touch. She wants him to reach down and pat her. "That's all I really want from my husband," the woman said, "a look, a word, and a touch." Bob never forgot the woman's words and has tried to incorporate them into his own relationships with Arvella and the children. Another set of words that has helped Bob define his communication both at home and in the world are those an old missionary once told him: "Be friendly. Be frank. Be firm."

Arvella, of course, was in the home with the children for the majority of the time, but Bob was not. So he made a special effort to create a time when he could be alone with each child on a regular basis. A time when he would really listen to them and really share with them on a deep, personal level. He also tried to find moments when he could pray with each one individually. He's been the kind of father who would teach his children a positive Bible verse and sing with them as he drove them to school in the morning. And he's never been ashamed to say "I'm sorry." He's pulled some bloopers, there's no doubt about that. There have been those times when he wasn't paying attention to their needs, wasn't listening—times when he was too caught up in his own driving pursuits to consider those of his family. But, usually sooner than later, he's apologized.

One thing that Bob and Arvella instituted early in their married life was the extended Lord's Day. Much as the Jewish Sabbath begins with sundown on Friday night, the Lord's Day gets started at dinner time on Saturday in the Schuller household. Saturday night and Sunday are strictly established as a time for Bible study, prayer, worship, and family togetherness. Right after dinner, they hold their weekly circle of prayer, laying each one's needs before the group and praying for each other, both silently and out loud in conversational style. The whole family loves to sing, and Saturday night often found them with voices and hearts raised in joyful choruses like "Surely goodness and mercy shall follow me all the days of my life" or in hushed tones praising their God with the hauntingly beautiful strains of "Alleluia."

Sunday mornings, of course, were set aside for church, but the remainder of the day was considered an extension of the worship experience. As much as is possible in a household of small children, tensions and interruptions were kept to a minimum. It was a day set apart from all the rest, a time to recharge those spiritual batteries and get ready for a new week. The children were not allowed to play with their friends, nor could they watch television or go to the store. They were expected to pursue quiet activities within the home. For the little ones, that might mean coloring or playing quietly with dolls; as they grew, they looked forward to these peaceful days when they set aside time to read or write or think and dream. Often they took rides together out into the country, anything to get their minds off the hustle bustle of their lives and in tune with the peace and creative power of God.

Quite likely, it was the tranquillity of the Sabbath that buoyed the family up and gave them all the boundless energy they had for the work week. Surely, in 1960, none of them had any idea the great things God had waiting for them just around the corner. . . .

7

I Will Build My Church—God Expands the Dream

THE NEXT TEN YEARS would be ones of staggering growth, with the congregation of the Garden Grove Community Church burgeoning to more than five thousand members.

I once heard the pastor of a small church speaking on church growth, which he was hoping to stimulate and in fact has. He looked out over his congregation, smiling broadly, and said, "I am your pastor, the shepherd of the sheep. My job is to take care of you sheep and see to it that you are well fed and healthy and maturing in your faith. You are the sheep." Here he paused and winked. "What is the responsibility of the sheep? Sheep are supposed to give birth to more sheep, they're supposed to multiply. If you will get out there and share the transforming power of Christ with your friends and neighbors, we'll have more sheep than we'll know what to do with."

The dynamic enthusiasm of Robert and Arvella Schuller and the programs they offered were a magnet that attracted the lonely, mobile, rootless people of Orange County. Bob adopted in the beginning of his ministry the slogan that even more than "Possibility Thinking" has been the hallmark of his ministry: "Find a hurt and heal it, find a need and fill it." These simple words and the philosophy they represent built Garden Grove Community Church from 718 people in 1960 to 5,188 in 1970.

But people are funny; quick as they are to jump on the bandwagon and go with a winner, they can also be critical of success, especially in the field of religion. A church down the street with seven hundred members is a nice little place, one with five thousand members is a threat. It threatens the unchurched because they are afraid they are somehow going to get snookered into the place by the same vacuum cleaner that swooped up the other five thousand. It threatens other ministers because it makes them feel inadequate or guilty. It threatens the secular world because they see a growing religion which they feel powerless to deal with, unless you count the vitriolic cynicism of the editorial press in some papers.

During these ten years, Robert Schuller was to come nose to nose with what I call the "Salk Theory." Jonas Salk, that great doctor of medicine who pioneered polio research and discovered the Salk Polio Vaccine, had a legion of critics he dealt with over the years. At one point, he made an interesting observation about the nature of criticism which seems to hold true for any person who is successfully innovative.

"First," he said, "people will tell you that you are wrong. Then they will tell you that you are right, but what you're doing really isn't important. Finally, they will admit that you are right and that what you are doing is very important; but after all, they knew it all the time."

Bob Schuller took little heed of criticism; he was too busy working to accomplish his ever-expanding visions. The first assistant he added to his staff was to be his Minister of Evangelism. The job description for this position has never been altered from that day to this; it remains, "To recruit, train, and motivate laymen and laywomen to be lay evangelists of the church." The main goal was then and is now to continue to add new members to the church. But just new members wasn't enough for Bob. He wanted to attract new members from the unchurched community—people who have never been active in their faith or in a church. And these people must first be won to a vital new relationship to Christ. From that commitment would stem excitement about becoming an active member of Garden Grove Church.

"We will have failed if the only people joining this church are those transferring from other churches," Bob told his young assistant quite emphatically. "Your task is to so inspire and train the laity of this church to share their faith with the unchurched in such a meaningful way that new persons will be accepting Christ all the time. Then there will be so many new people joining this church that you will be conducting classes year-round. Just the continued training of new Christians in the faith will be a full-time job for you."

He was right. An average of seven hundred new members each year have been added to Garden Grove Community Church, two-thirds of whom have never been active church members anywhere else.

With all the new members being added, there was need for more Christian education. The next position to be filled was that of Minister of Education. Bob set up his goals to recruit, train and motivate lay people to be the teachers in the church. He firmly believes that an inspired congregation must first be an informed congregation. He had always admired those who believed in the church of the laity, and had decided early that a church with involved, trained lay people was the healthiest church. However, as he studied the experts in the field, he could not find a working program anywhere to really train the laity.

There was no material available to teach lay people how to become what Bob calls "ministers in residence" in the local church. It appeared that for all the talk, no one really took the training of the laity seriously. "I want a theological seminary for the laity," Bob demanded from his new minister. "Christian education requires more than just Bible study. We need courses in church history, theology, philosophy, psychology, comparative religions, practical theology like counseling, witnessing, teaching as well as courses in the Bible itself."

The new pastor was intrigued with Bob's vision and made it his own. He organized what was possibly the first seminary for the laity, CALL, Center for Advanced Lay Leadership. They gleaned a faculty of experts from all over Southern California and set up a truly comprehensive course of study, requiring 220 units for full qualification.

Bob's third assistant minister was someone who would be in charge of caring for the daily needs of the congregation. His Minister of Family and Parish Life was to recruit, train, and motivate the laymen and laywomen to do the pastoral work in the growing body of believers. He didn't want any member to ever be alone in tragedy or in need. There must be a network of caring people to show Christ's love to each one in a positive and practical way, so the new minister organized the congregation into geographical zones of eight families each. Each group has a lay pastor who watches over the other seven families and each eight groups in any given area form a division with another lay pastor who leads the larger group. That way the entire growing congregation is organized with lay people trained to care for them.

The Garden Grove Community Church never waited until money was available before hiring the ministers. Wilfred Landrus, who had written that first motion to move forward in uniting the two congregations, explains it this way: "If we'd have been negative thinkers and waited until everything was just right, we'd never have done anything! We'd still be back at the Orange Drive-in. That's where Bob's faith was so essential, spurring us on and giving us the courage to dream. We felt it was God's purpose to build a great church here in Garden Grove. We thought Bob could really go places, and we were behind him, supporting him. We wanted to give him a platform from which to speak."

And going before all were the words of Jesus as recorded in Matthew: "I will build my church. . . ."

With the rapidly growing number of people who crammed into the little fellowship hall every Sunday, everyone could see that they wouldn't be able to delay the construction of the main sanctuary for very long. The combination of the drive-in and walk-in congregations had been an enormous success and the entire group had formed strong family ties.

They played records for the drive-in services, with the sound man inside the fellowship hall waiting for his cue. He couldn't hear anything of the service from there; in fact, he couldn't see anything but Bob's backside, so he waited for Bob to give him the signal, his hand reaching behind his back. But Bob, with all his dramatics, would sometimes get carried away and flick the cord from his lavaliere mike with a quick backhand stroke. Whenever that happened, the conscientious volunteer with the record player would blast the congregation with the next hymn, often in the middle of the sermon. These sorts of things, for the perfectionists Bob and Arvella, were all the more reason to forge full steam ahead on the sanctuary.

The money required to build such a magnificent structure was beyond the realm of the local congregation, so to help with the expenses, they sold promissory notes across the country to people in the Dutch Reformed community who had means and wanted to help. Between the notes and the increased giving of the members and a couple of short-term bank loans to get them through construction, the church was built. It wasn't the sort of thing that could be built by amateurs as the fellowship hall had been. This project required the skill of a professional crew. And in just ten months the new structure was completed.

It was a beautiful building, long and narrow and very modern, rather like a giant rectangle, and it seated one thousand people. It had originally been designed with a balcony holding seven hundred more, but due to lack of funds it was decided to add it on later. Richard Neutra, the architect, had been horrified at the prospect of omitting the balcony from his design. In a heated consistory meeting, he had blurted out in frustration, "You can't just chop it off like a piece of bologna!" But chop it off they did.

Nevertheless, the overall effect of the building was stunning. At the North end, four modernistic bell towers containing twelve bells soared into the cloudless Southern California sky. A long wall of stone continued the lines of the glass-sided sanctuary; and in front of that long expanse of glass and stone were Bob's twelve fountains—one to represent each apostle—a reminder to the people of the Garden Grove Community Church that God took twelve ordinary men and used them to turn the world upside down. They were rigged, in the true tradition of Schuller showmanship, to a switch in the pulpit so that he could turn them on and have them shoot twelve feet into the air so that their shimmering arcs could be seen easily from either the sanctuary itself or the half circle of four hundred cars parked in the drive-in portion of the church.

It had taken two years, but they had done it. The ten acres had been graded, paved, and landscaped. Ten miles of wires, pipes and sewers had been installed underground; streets, gutters, and curbs had been developed; water and gas lines had been brought into the property. Bob has been criticized by both liberal and fundamental Christians, not to mention the secular press, for the "extravagance" of the lavish layout, but he's always felt that criticism was a small price to pay in order to follow the dream he felt God had given him so he could reach more of the unchurched with the good news that God loves them. Some have felt that the pools and grass and flowers were a great waste of money, that the grounds should have been done austerely in concrete. As one man complained, "You certainly can't eat them."

"You're wrong," Bob corrected him. "We'll eat them. We will feed emotionally on the beauty of the sunshine, the quiet waters and the green pastures. And as we are filled with the wonder of their beauty, something beautiful will happen to us. Beauty is never a luxury. Beauty is a necessity."

The ultra-modern sanctuary was dedicated in November 1961, just six short years after Bob and Arvella's arrival in California. Dr. Norman Vincent Peale came out to preside over the joyful ceremonies. I can just see his eyes sparkling as he saw what his positive thinking concept had done for the young minister a continent away. It must have given him a great sense of pride, but a feeling of smallness too, to know that the God he served had used him and the ideas he had pioneered to bring success to others as they sought to spread His love to a hurting world.

At last, the walk-in and drive-in services could be held at the same time. No more trying to pipe records out to the cars in the drive-in. In the massive floor-to-ceiling windows on the east side of the sanctuary, there were giant twenty-five-foot tall doors of glass which opened at the touch of a finger from a control center in the pulpit, allowing Bob to stride out onto a little balcony where he could see and be seen by the people from their cars. He developed a style of pacing back and forth in his indoor-outdoor pulpit so that he could be seen alternately by first one congregation and then another.

The drive-in was equipped with a sound system enabling people to tune to AM-54 on their car radios to hear the service, and the music and words were also piped outside by means of one hundred high powered loud speakers. "Blink your lights!" Bob boomed to the cars. "You Baptists can honk your horns, if you want to." He was invariably answered by a cacophony of honks and bleeps. "Sorry about the birds," he quipped. "Their favorite pastime nowadays is picking up walnuts from the grove over there and dive bombing them on the cars in the drive-in."

The dream had become a reality, a giant indoor-outdoor sanctuary where both congregations had flowed into one, uniting people in cars with people in pews.

But to Bob Schuller, it wasn't enough. As he would say later, when you are climbing a mountain and reach the peak, it only gives you a peek at the peak of the next mountain waiting for you to ascend its rocky precipice. "The moment you stop dreaming and growing, a church begins to die."

There were still all those people out there, people who needed the love and hope that Christ could bring into their empty lives, people who were tired of struggling and needed the inspiration of a positive faith. Bob was committed to the logo which he had printed on his business cards, The Garden Grove Community Church . . . "Putting strong wings on weary hearts." And he knew that within a small radius of the church were thousands of weary hearts, just waiting for their set of wings—if he could ever get them to come for them.

As always, his answer was ministry, mission programs to reach out and love the people to Christ. Southern California, with its proximity to Mexico and the rest of Latin America, was filling up with Spanish-speaking persons whose lack of English was keeping them from finding adequate jobs. Bordering on the Pacific, California had also become a mecca for displaced people from the Orient. With thousands of people unable to read or write or speak English, Orange County had an urgent need for a good language program. Bob had Dr. Frank Laubach come to describe his "each one teach one" method of literacy training.

Dr. Laubach, who had originally developed programs for teaching illiterates to read and write in hundreds of different languages, had been a missionary to the Philippines for many years. His literacy training was used by governments in many countries. His program was adapted to teach English as a second language, and the Garden Grove Community Church set up a Laubach Literacy Training Center and began to train instructors, all of whom were volunteers. After a twenty-five-hour training course, each instructor takes a small number of non-English speaking persons, usually one to five, and begins to take them through literacy skill books. They are taught grammar and pronunciation as well as how to speak and read and write English. In three to four years time, the student can read and write English at about a sixth-grade level.

Then there was the matter of church music. God put quite a team together in Robert and Arvella Schuller: Bob the dreamer, the innovator, the orator; Arvella the planner, the musician, the orchestrator.

For the first few years, she had played the little organ, led the choir, everything; but as time went by, she was able to turn the direction over to volunteers and, eventually, paid ministers of music. But she never lost her first love—the organ. In May of 1962, partly because of her interest and drive for perfection, the church's first pipe organ was installed, a 1,530-pipe, 23-rank Wicks. Virgil Fox, famed organist at Riverside Church in New York City, played the dedicatory recital.

Arvella, having abandoned her own dream in favor of Bob's, used her own vast musical talents in setting the overall theme of excellence in music at the church, in planning the service, coordinating the pieces to be performed and creating the unity of harmonies and words and styles that have made Garden Grove Community Church one of the most highly respected in the country for the quality of its music. She added harp, trumpets, and violins to the services as soon as possible, and they have been a mainstay of the spiritual, musical experience of the church ever since.

Bob and Arvella, whose personalities drive them to keep on searching for new ways to improve both themselves and whatever is under their direction, continued to strive toward greater heights in every area of church activity. Neither of them has ever been content with the status quo, no matter how great it may be.

Once after returning from a summer vacation, Bob drove onto the church grounds. He was struck by the beauty of the glass sanctuary, the perfection of the fountains and the quiet reflecting pools. The towering trees tossed in the breeze, and sun drenched the entire scene in breathtaking light. He thought back over the years of doorbell ringing, the dark years of inner turmoil, the church split. They had made the right decisions; he knew it now. The magnificent sanctuary had been featured in scores of international architectural publications, and had won awards for excellence in design.

His three staff ministers were waiting for him, anxious to share their reports of increased ministry. New members were being added and their spiritual lives were being fed. Everything was great; membership now stood at just under two thousand.

He walked into his office and slumped down into a chair, suddenly very tired. As he looked out onto the little garden, a deep depression, worse than he had ever known, assaulted him. There were no problems. There were no worries. There were no challenges. Everything was going according to plan. He had no more goals. "Oh God. How can I stand it? My work can't be finished. It just can't be." He knew then that the "is" should never catch up with the "ought." What he needed were new goals, new visions. "Oh, Lord, give me a new dream."

Almost immediately, he was given two dreams at once. Architecturally, the proportions of the church buildings and property required a tall tower to complete the symmetry. Bob began to envision a two-hundred-fifty-foot tower silhouetted against the skyline of Orange County. "But," he grilled himself, "would it be a monument or an instrument?"

He presented his idea to the board, and immediately someone jumped up saying, "We cannot justify such a tall tower. It simply is not practical." Bob smiled, "What if we put elevators in it? We could put a chapel on the top floor. What an inspiration it would be to worship high above the sights and sounds of the world."

Different ones began to nod, catching the vision.

"We need more space for classrooms," Bob continued. "And offices; you know our office space is limited now. We could put a board room in it. Our vision wouldn't be restricted like it is now. When we meet, we will be forced to look out on all those hundreds of thousands of cars, all those homes and offices. We'll be forced to see far, think big, aim high, reach wide. We could even put in a psychological clinic, a Christian counseling center."

Suddenly the project was practical, inspirational, pace-setting, and—it excelled. The idea was accepted, the plan approved. It would be a moderately ranged goal, but it was a goal.

Shortly thereafter, Bob received a phone call from a sculptor in Los Angeles. Henry Van Wolf was an internationally known sculptor who did a lot of designing along religious lines. Some years earlier he had been inspired to sculpt a statue of Christ, the Good Shepherd. He had labored three years, putting in a total of six thousand hours of work and investing thousands of dollars in the statue. First he had made a small scale model, then a larger one in clay, and finally the plaster mold. He had crated and shipped the mold from his studio in Van Nuys to Munich, Germany, where Jesus with his shepherd's staff and four sheep were cast in bronze. By then, the seven-foot

Christ weighed a ton and a half. Next the bronze statue was shipped by boat to New York and then transported by rail across the country to California, where Mr. Van Wolf lovingly cleaned and polished the figure, finally coating it with twenty-two carat gold leaf.

The artist had visited the church and thought it would be a perfect resting place for his beloved statue. The description of it alone captured Bob's imagination, and he lost no time in driving out to the San Fernando Valley to have a look at it. It was exquisite. The strength, the tenderness, and the love of Christ the Good Shepherd were captured forever in precious metals. The little lambs about His feet were perfectly at home under the watchful gaze of their Master.

As soon as he saw the perfectly-chiseled face of Jesus, all Bob could think of was acquiring the piece of statuary for the church. He was convinced that this tender portrayal of Christ, the Good Shepherd, was created for what his church members called the Garden of the Twenty-Third Psalm which was located in front of the glass-sided sanctuary, where twelve fountains burbled. The fountains themselves were set in a long reflecting pool which made the members think of a verse from that eloquent psalm, "He leads me beside the still waters."

"A famous actress is coming by the studio today," Mr. Van Wolf said, dashing Bob's plans. "I feel quite certain that she is going to buy the statue."

"Wait one week, please," Bob pleaded. "Give me a chance to call the church board together and give them a chance to buy it."

"I'm sorry, Reverend Schuller. But I just can't wait. I need the money and I need it now. I can't take a chance."

Bob's mental gears began racing. "I'll take it. I'll give you seven hundred dollars today." (That was easy—he knew he had that amount in his savings account.) "And I'll pay you another twenty-three hundred for a total down payment of three thousand dollars over the next two months. I'll pay the balance down over the next three years at five hundred seventeen dollars a month, including interest."

The sculptor smiled. "Reverend," he said, "I'm convinced God wants you to have the statue. I know I want you to have it. It's a deal."

The bylaws of the church's corporation state that six day's written notice must be given in order to call a special board meeting. And exactly six days later, Bob walked into that board meeting all smiles. Long-time members of that venerable board say they can always tell Bob's mood and what he hopes to accomplish in a meeting by his attitude when he arrives. He may come in all business, with a thousand other things on his mind, and be quite aloof and unassuming; but when there's something he wants, it's a different story. Friendliness and charm exude from every pore, and the eloquence that is such an integral part of Bob Schuller is used to the utmost. That day, with his most extravagant adjectives, he described the beauty of the outstanding statue to the men who were gathered, painted them a verbal picture of exquisite design as he explained how it would be the finishing touch to the Garden of the Twenty-Third Psalm. And what a bargain—only twenty-one thousand dollars for a lasting work of fine art that would bring inspiration to thousands for years to come.

But all the showmanship and possibility thinking in the world couldn't budge the decision of the consistory that day. Their answer was "NO." Bob was flustered, to say the least. He had to have that statue. I think had he had the personal capability to pay for the Good Shepherd, he would have bought it himself. But he didn't. However, Robert Schuller doesn't bow easily to defeat. If he can't climb over, he'll tunnel underneath.

Bob was determined to raise the twenty-one thousand dollars. He took a hundred dollars from his personal savings as the beginning donation. Then he went before the congregation the following Sunday, describing his dream for the beautiful statue and telling them that an anonymous donor had given one hundred dollars to start the ball rolling. He then took a special offering, and the congregation gave above their regular tithes to purchase the Good Shepherd that would become such a symbol of their church. Bob had raised the twenty-one thousand dollars. The Good Shepherd had at last found a permanent home.

Bob, with his ever-present flair for the dramatic, unveiled the ethereal statue and his plans for the Neutra-designed Tower of Hope at the same time to his flock. In his sermon that day, entitled "How to Make Your Dreams Come True," he expounded on the high-speed glass elevators that would whisk people from the ground floor up into the floors of classrooms, the counseling center, the twenty-four-hour telephone hotline. And then, as only Bob can, he kindled their excitement as he promised them "a little chapel at the top of the tower that would be a twinkling diamond of hope in the night sky at the freeway hub of this great county. It will truly become a tower of hope, saying to the public that there is an eye that never closes, there is an ear that is never shut, there is a heart that never grows cold."

It took a year and a half of growth and fund raising and planning before ground was broken in July 1966 for the fourteen-story tower. In the meantime, a preschool building was completed to accommodate the growing number of children involved in the ministry as well as to reach out to the community by providing a loving, Christian preschool and day-care center. Dr. Norman Peale was again on hand to preside jointly with Bob over the groundbreaking festivities and man the shovel for that ceremonious first turn of dirt.

Believing that people love pageantry, Bob has always done everything with a great deal of drama and ceremony. Had he not gone into the ministry, he surely would have made a terrific Hollywood director or promoter. And, despite the claims of critics that he has gotten wealthy from the church, he would doubtless have made a lot more money in a secular vocation. But making money has never been one of Bob's goals in life. From childhood, his one burning desire has always been and continues to be the building of one great church to the glory of God.

It took twenty-six months to build the Tower, and during its construction the sanctuary was finally enlarged to the size Richard Neutra had originally designed. More pews were added to the ground floor and the graceful balcony was put into place, adding an additional seven hundred seats, bringing the total seating capacity of the sanctuary to seventeen hundred. This type of expansion is typical of both the Garden Grove Community Church and Robert Schuller Ministries. Even though they think big, dream big, and "possibilitize" a lot, they never take a step until they are sure it is really needed and that God's timing is right.

One thing that Bob had insisted on in the design of the Tower of Hope was that it must have a tall, illuminated cross on top. He seems to know instinctively what advertising executives go to school to learn—you've got to keep your product before the public. You must have visibility. It's not that Bob equates the gospel of Jesus Christ, the very power of the living God, with everyday household products such as toothpaste or toilet tissue. It's just that people are people, and they are very predictable most of the time. The same principles that work to sell toothpaste also work to reach the unchurched for Christ. Remember, these are the unchurched we are talking about. The ones who would call themselves unreligious. If you want them to pay attention to what you are trying to tell them about the saving love of Jesus, you can't do it by keeping your little church buried under a cloud of pious superiority. Didn't Jesus Himself tell us not to hide our light under a bushel? How does the children's song go? "This little light of mine, I'm going to let it shine."

In 1967, Robert Schuller had a light, the light of a risen Savior, and he wanted to share that light with a hurting community. And so he insisted on that cross. It was to be ninety feet high and perched atop the 252-foot tower; it would be the highest point in Orange County. It would be one of the major landmarks in an area rife with landmarks. As one journalist in an especially corrosive article caustically emphasized, it was even more prominent than Disneyland's plaster replica of the Matterhorn.

As the Tower of Hope was nearing completion, the superintendent approached Bob one day. "I've checked, Bob," he began to broach what he knew would be a difficult subject. "It can't be done. It's impossible to put a ninety-foot cross on top of that tower. We'd have to brace it, put wires. Even then it would act as a tuning fork in high winds and destroy the whole building. I'm sorry."

"Impossible?" Bob bellowed. "It can't be impossible! You just haven't talked to the right people, that's all. When there's a job to be done, you must talk to the right people. I know that at NASA there's bound to be someone who knows enough about aerodynamics to tell us how to get that cross up there. They can balance gigantic booster rockets on those tall silos. If they can do that, we can certainly put a cross on our tower."

And that's all there was to it. Bob wanted a cross and he was going to have a cross. And on November 20, 1967, high atop the brand-new Tower of Hope, a ninety-foot cross became a lighthouse, a beacon of hope and love to all of Orange County. All because one man refused to say "It's impossible." Later that night, after all the pomp and ceremony were over, a car could be seen cruising back and forth from the Santa Ana Freeway to the Garden Grove Freeway. Crammed inside that car were eight people—Bob and Arvella Schuller, Sheila, now sixteen; Bob, thirteen; Jeanne, eight; Carole, four; baby Gretchen, who was only two; and an eighty-three-year-old man who had ridden the train all the way from Alton, Iowa. As Tony Schuller gazed upon that cross, its arms outstretched to call the lonely and downtrodden to its bosom, Bob noticed that a gentle smile played around the corners of his father's wrinkled mouth. And as Bob felt tears wet his cheeks, he couldn't help but praise the God who had answered an old man's prayer to let him live to see this day; he praised the God who would draw all men to Himself and, like Tony had done with Bob's toys, take the broken hearts and make them whole again.

Less than a year later, Anthony Schuller went home to be with his Lord. He had been ill, and was going into the hospital. As Jennie helped him out the door, he took a careful look around the house, noting each table and chair. When his eyes had drunk their fill, he turned slowly to Jennie, leaning on his cane. "I'll not be coming back, you know," he said. "I'm going home."

With the opening of the Tower of Hope with its two-story chapel in the sky on the top floor that overlooked all of Orange County, another ministry opened its heart and its ears to a hurting world—the New Hope Telephone Counseling Service. It was one of the very first twenty-four-hour telephone hotlines in the country, the only one run by a church; and it was staffed entirely by volunteers from the church who had been trained to help the callers, some of whom were suicidal, all of whom were lonely.

Then in 1968, thirteen years after that first sermon on the tarpaper roof of the drive-in, the Garden Grove Community Church won the *Guideposts* Magazine Outstanding Church Award. It was a tribute to the faith and drive and spirit of its founders, Arvella and Bob Schuller, and to the thousands of unchurched people who had found the living Christ there and stayed to give of themselves and their time to help make the Schullers' dream a reality.

By 1969, the continued growth of the congregation had made it necessary to take a realistic look at the church and where it was going. The building projects had generated so much publicity and attention in the community that attendance soared. Others have cast a jaundiced eye at this. But it's true. The church expanded rapidly during its campaigns for money. Not because they were asking for money, but because they were selling a wonderful new idea. They were offering people an opportunity to share in the creation of something exciting, something noble, something bigger than themselves. And people always respond positively to a project that makes them feel important and useful. Bob, now a polished, silver-haired gentleman of forty-two, had moved his own offices up to the twelfth floor in the Tower of Hope. He loved to look out the walls of glass at the panoramic view of Orange County. From his ultramodern office, he could see the source of his continuing drive and inspiration—the cars and homes and businesses of millions of people who still needed to hear about the wonderful possibilities Jesus could bring into their lives. Each Sunday found him there in his office before and between services in the great glass church. Coffee, juice, and his favorite bran muffins were brought up to him and his family as they shared the brief moments together in the midst of their hectic schedule. It was here that he prayed and made last minute changes in his sermons.

But each Sunday he became more and more distressed. From his aerial vantage point, he had a perfect view of the parking lot of the church. He shook his head in amazement as he remembered arguing himself red in the face when the Garden Grove City Council had insisted he provide one off-street parking space for every three seats in the church. It had seemed such an outrageous demand; but in the end, they had won. He had lost. The acres of concrete had been poured and dutifully scored.

Each week found him witnessing a sight that was becoming more and more familiar with the passing of time. The parking lot was full with rows of cars lined up like so many dominoes. And then it would happen. A car would drive into the lot and begin to circle through the maze of shiny chrome. Up and down it would serpentine through the lot until at last it would turn around and drive out and down the street, away from the church and the touch of God its driver sought.

Bob couldn't help agonizing to himself. "Who were those people? What were their hurts and needs this morning? Perhaps they have just lost a job or a loved one. Maybe their marriage is on the skids. Maybe they were seeking a reason not to commit suicide. And we let them down. We let them down because they couldn't find a place to park their car. My God, we're strangling in our own success!"

Bob went to work on his church board once more. "Growth can

either lift you or level you," he expounded. "It can either propel you forward or knock you down and grind you into the ground. The choice, gentlemen, is ours. We've got to have more parking." As he saw it, they only had two alternatives. They could buy more land or they could construct a high rise parking garage on the current property. This prospect was ludicrous to Bob. It was shoddy. It would ruin the beautiful architectural lines he had established. And, he pointed out to the board with a frown, it was expensive, maybe as much as five to seven dollars a square foot. They certainly didn't want to put that kind of money into an eyesore, did they?

They didn't. Fortunately, there was an adjoining ten acres to their property that had yet to be developed. A large syndicate held the lease option to the land; and the church approached them, offering them more than the fifty thousand dollars an acre which was their original option. But they were turned down flat. The property wasn't for sale at any price.

Bob and his board prayed. They possibilitized. They believed God for a miracle.

One day, in a conversation with his banker, Bob learned that the syndicate that owned the land had been taken over by Edgar Kaiser. He prayed some more. And somehow, from the recesses of his memory came an intriguing tidbit. Bob remembered that twenty years earlier the *Reader's Digest* had carried a condensation of a layman's sermon delivered by Henry Kaiser (Edgar's father) at Marble Collegiate Church in New York—Norman Vincent Peale's church.

Bob immediately called the prominent theologian who had been so supportive of him in the past. "Do you know Edgar Kaiser?" Yes, he did. "Could you write him a letter in my behalf?" Bob asked, explaining his need. The kindly pastor agreed to help, requesting that Bob write the letter he preferred, then he would make any necessary changes and send it on to the industrialist. Shortly thereafter, Edgar Kaiser received this letter:

> Dear Edgar:
>
> How fondly I remember seeing you seated between your father and mother in the fourth pew of the Marble Collegiate Church. You may not

be aware of it, but you and I have two exciting projects going across the street from each other. You are developing the City Shopping Center and I'm developing a church. Actually, one of my cohorts, Bob Schuller, is in charge of the operation. You have ten acres of land we need to buy for parking. Will you sell it? Name your price; we'll buy it.

Sincerely,
Norman Vincent Peale

Within forty-eight hours, Kaiser's head man Charles Cobb was on the phone to Bob inviting him to come negotiate for the land. Their price? One hundred thirty-five thousand dollars an acre or a total of one million three hundred fifty thousand dollars. Even for Bob Schuller, it was impossible. He countered at a million. Mr. Cobb was thoughtful. Yes, they could let it go for that price, providing a five hundred thousand dollar cash down payment could be made within six weeks.

There was another of Bob's famous emergency board meetings. "This is the one and only time we will be able to buy this property," he launched into his sales pitch. "It's a once-in-a-lifetime opportunity. We can buy it for one million dollars—that's only two dollars and fifty cents a square foot, less than half the price of a parking garage. And it will give us full frontage rights on Chapman Avenue. We get all the air rights too." He beamed. "It's a bargain." Then he laid his bombshell. "We will have to come up with five hundred thousand dollars in cold, hard cash by March 31."

There were audible gasps throughout the room. But Bob was right; it was a once-in-a-lifetime opportunity. And they knew they had to try. So they passed a resolution. "To give God a chance to work a miracle, we would have Dr. Schuller announce on this coming Sunday our intention to raise this amount of money and buy the property."

Bob hired a professional fund-raising organization to come in and recruit and train church members to help them raise the money. It was the most concentrated money campaign they had ever waged, an urgent financial appeal to the people to care enough about their neighbors to make room for them in their church. The congregation responded unselfishly and poured out what they could into the project. Bob's banker called to say he would lend him half of the amount if he could raise the other half himself. But try as they might, three days before the deadline found them still ninety thousand dollars short.

Just when he thought the situation was without repair, Bob received a call from one of Kaiser's lawyers. They were going to be unable to complete their part of the paperwork before the March 31 deadline. Would Bob mind postponing the date three weeks? "Well," Bob hedged; he didn't want to appear too eager. After a few minutes consideration and smiling broadly a silent "thank you, God," he returned to the phone. "Yes, that will be just fine with us. No problem at all."

By the third week in April, the necessary money had been raised and they took over the option to buy the property. When the papers had all been signed, Bob carried them jubilantly back to his office and began poring through them, wondering where he was going to find the remaining five hundred thousand dollars to complete the purchase by July when it was due. He graduated into the fine print of the contract and there found the answer to his prayers. "This offer will hold firm for the next five years; one hundred thousand dollars down and the balance to be paid over the next ten years at 6 percent interest." In less than two months time, the entire one million dollar financial package had fallen into place. Bob knew it was God's blessing on the venture. He could see His hand in it. The additional parking was created, bringing the total parking spaces up to the ability to park seventeen hundred cars. Just as Bob had predicted, attendance at church went up proportionately.

Quite a bit of discussion centered around the possibility of enlarging the beautiful sanctuary by covering the courtyard which stood between it and the Tower of Hope. They could already see that the lovely building, which they had thought would be their permanent church home, would not be able to keep up with the increasing numbers of people who wanted to become part of their fellowship. But the idea was finally tabled. It was too impractical; God must have a better idea. They would wait for his timing.

Bob was at last able to open the Christian Counseling Service in the ninth floor of the Tower. It had become apparent that there were some calls received in the New Hope Counseling Service that would require much more intensive counseling than could be handled by a volunteer on the telephone—problems of such intricate natures that the services of a professional therapist would be needed. Often the people wouldn't know where to go and would be frightened to go if they did. Good Christian psychologists were hard to come by, so it seemed that to fill the need, a counseling center right there at the church was what God wanted.

Bob has always sought to fill the needs that he has seen all around him. He has three questions he always asks himself. Would it be a great thing for God? Would it help people who are hurting? Is anyone else filling this need? If he gets positives on the first two questions and a negative on the third, then he generally tries to step in and fill the void.

And there were so many voids that needed filling. When the census reports came out showing that two fifths of the region's population were single, he moved in the direction of starting a singles ministry. Garden Grove Community Church was one of the first churches in the country to have a full-time minister to singles on its staff. The size of the church made it possible to divide the department into age groups, right away eliminating a problem that has burdened other attempts. Positive Christian Singles has been innovative in its approach toward helping this growing portion of the population handle its own unique set of problems. With one marriage in every three in the county ending in divorce, Bob was one of the first ministers to really get in and try to discover creative new ways of making these disillusioned people happy in the church. He saw early that ostracizing them for their failures and treating them as sinners would never attract them to the church or help them to find the forgiveness that Christ offers. He realized that they, too, needed nonjudgmental love in an atmosphere of acceptance if they were to be able to turn their lives around and become the people God intended them to be.

The bars of Orange County were full of singles trying to meet each other, looking for companionship, searching for meaning in their lives. He gave them an alternative—a caring, sharing fellowship of people who were all seeking to build each other up in Christian love, a way of meeting other singles in a moral, uplifting environment. Through potlucks and small groups, these people now have a way of social interaction that doesn't have to take place in smoke-filled rooms where the music is so loud they can't even hear each other, but where the atmosphere encourages dialogue and the building up of friendships.

This program has been so effective that men and women often come looking only for companionship and end up finding the eternal presence of God. And frequently they find another marriage partner from the same fellowship and are able to build a fulfilling, lasting marriage relationship.

The Garden Grove Community Church also looked at its community and saw great financial needs. Sometimes people would arrive at its doorstep completely destitute, with nowhere to turn for food or clothing. So the Helping Hands program was started. It eventually required a full-time staff to maintain the building full of food and clothing that was continually donated by church members. Bob has always believed that when a person in need comes for help to a church, that the church has a moral responsibility to give that person more than just advice and prayer. When needy people arrive at Garden Grove Church, they are met with actual practical aid. Just as Jesus told His disciples to feed the hungry and give drink to the thirsty, the truly helpless are never sent away empty-handed.

In that same passage of Scripture, Jesus enjoins us to visit those who are imprisoned. Bob set up a prison ministry at the church, with a full-time minister to the local prisons. In addition to counseling and visitation, they have also established a special tradition at Christmastime each year. Some ten thousand homemade cookies are baked by the congregation and friends and packaged in bags of six. Then on Christmas Eve, assortments of cookies, cards, and words of encouragement and love are distributed to every prisoner in nearby prisons, bringing them the forgiveness and beauty of the infant King.

The Garden Grove Community Church has also been especially caring of senior citizens. Realizing the needs of this large segment of the county's population, Bob formed a senior citizen's ministry, complete with its own pastor. Called the Keenagers, its current minister is none other than Bob's own beloved Uncle Henry, now well into his eighties. His missionary days completed, he serves his Lord even in his retirement years, and keeps a sharp eye on the nephew he inspired to follow in his footsteps. Henry Beltman is a real old-time, Bible-thumping preacher who can really whip Bob into line and is the resident expert on keeping him humble. In addition to helping them find a new life in Christ, the Keenager department aims to stimulate its members, helping each one to see that no matter what his age, he can be a vital, exciting person with much to contribute to his world.

Along those same lines, under Bob's direction, the church built a twenty-story apartment building for retirees, a Christian retirement home. It was financed through the federal HUD program and is located just down the street from the church. A little mini-bus is always available to take the seniors, most of whom do not drive, back and forth to services and also to transport them to do volunteer work which is a great challenge and stimulation to them. The goal again is to give them a sense of worth and to give them dreams and hopes and even excitement in a peaceful Christian atmosphere.

Arvella instituted a women's department at the church, with constant activities designed to excite and instruct the women of Orange County and beyond. Regular Bible studies are conducted, along with luncheons and fashion shows. Renowned speakers are brought in from around the country to bring new creative ideas to women of any age or career. There is the yearly Day Extraordinaire held in the fall of the year and a Women's Conference that meets the week before, drawing women from all walks of life across the country. Valuable seminars help each one discover more of her self and the person she can become with God's help. They leave stimulated and with a new sense of self worth based on God's love.

Arvella has labored tirelessly for many years in the women's ministry she founded, working quietly behind the scenes in many cases. It is a sorrow to Bob that she so often doesn't receive more of the recognition for her many accomplishments. He has only the highest praise for his ''first and only wife'' as he likes to call her and credits her for helping him to see and appreciate the full beauty and dignity of women.

Bob doesn't approve of male chauvinism. He doesn't believe that God approves of it either. Jesus never spoke or acted in a way that demeaned women. Rather, he raised them up to a level of equality that was unknown in that day. Bob agrees that we see some male chauvinism at work in the New Testament Church, but points out that it was not a sinless church. It was influenced in that area by the pagan society of its time. He believes that every person is to be treated equally before God.

God has given Robert Schuller a big dream, one so big he had been prepared to spend his whole life in its accomplishment. Neither he nor Arvella had expected the work, on which they had planned to labor for forty years until their retirement, to be completed in just fifteen years. They were still young in 1970; Bob forty-four, Arvella forty. I guess that's when they came face to face with the realization that Alfred North Whitehead had been right when he said, "Great dreams of great dreamers are never fulfilled, they are always transcended."

Bob could look all around him and see little churches struggling and failing in the great commission Christ had given them to go into all the world with the gospel. Jesus had been quite explicit that the work begin at home, and that's what Bob had tried to do with Garden Grove Community Church, his mission outreach into Orange County. He developed a burning desire to share the principles that had worked for him with other pastors so that their churches could reach more of the world for Christ. It was frustrating to him that he was so often misunderstood—that the large churches of the country were misunderstood.

If Christians are doing what they are told to do by their Savior in the Great Commission, they will be telling the world about the wonderful news that Christ died for them to bring them new life and new fellowship with God. And if they are doing this, then the people who listen and accept what they say are going to want to go to worship this God and learn more about Him. They are going to ask their friend or neighbor or business associate, who told them about God in the first place, where they go to worship Him. Then that excited Christian is going to tell his friend about his own particular church, perhaps even invite him to services there. And what is going to happen to that church? It's going to grow. Because a very happy, vicious circle is created when members are excited enough about their relationship to Christ to articulate that faith to others, and those who hear in turn become so turned on that they go tell others. A church with a congregation like this could easily mushroom into gigantic proportions. New Christians would be added to the flock regularly, not just people who already knew God and moved into the area, but ones who never knew Him before at all.

Isn't this what the Bible means when it says that God doesn't want anyone to perish but that all should come to a saving knowledge of His Son?

Robert Schuller feels that a church should be staffed to serve. It shouldn't just be a place where the Word is preached and prayer meetings are held, youth societies meet, and the women get together and sell cakes to pay the bills. A church's job is to attract and minister to those people who don't know God in a personal way in such a manner that they want to get to know Him better. Its job is to provide all the programs and services to the community that it needs so that the unchurched persons of that community will want to become involved in it. They are not asking for heavy sermons on Sunday mornings, nor do they want to attend a Wednesday night prayer meeting. They need help with their self-esteem, with their finances. They don't want a Bible study; the people who want to study the Bible are already in church.

Unchurched people often have deep problems within themselves. They have trouble maintaining their relationships with others. Bob feels that the pulpit is not the place to carry on a teaching ministry. It's the place for spiritual therapy.

Through salvation, he feels that a person's deepest emotional needs are met. He says that man requires a sense of identity, security, and stimulation. He can receive these in a relationship with God through Christ and the Holy Spirit. And Bob believes that this kind of personal relationship with God gives the person a positive self-image.

Garden Grove Community Church is a mission station. It uses the same principles to reach unchurched people as are used in India or China. It delves into the community and finds out why people are hurting, and then develops a program to meet that need. Just like Christ, Garden Grove Community Church tries to meet people at the source of their greatest need and show love in action. It's not enough to stand in a pulpit and say "I love you" and then not care enough to provide a program at the point of need.

It is a mistake to just preach and teach. Bob says, "The church fails unless it is a mission, and a mission fails unless it is a church." Worship services should create an opportunity for an authentic experience to take place individually between each person and God.

One of the problems churches face is that of creating an atmosphere where people feel free to mingle and speak to each other. You often walk in, sit down, and there is an invisible barrier. No one will talk to you. At Garden Grove Community Church they labor to break down that barrier. That's why Bob initiated the widely emulated practice of having the people of the congregation turn around and shake hands with each other and say "God loves you and so do I." He is often criticized by the seeming isolation that the drive-in church affords just by its physical logistics, but says he has those persons smile and wave at those who are parked nearby, even honk their horns if they so desire. But he stresses that the drive-in is just a funnel, it's not the bucket itself.

He admits, though, that the immensity of the size of the church has taken away many of the personal joys he once had as a pastor of a smaller congregation. The actual pastoring of the people on an individual level he now leaves to his large staff of ministers; not because he doesn't want to do it, but just simply because it is not possible for him to do it along with his other duties. He misses the personal fulfillment a pastor receives from the interaction with members; laughing with them, crying with them, the hospital visits, consoling the family at the death of a loved one, the joy of watching a radiant bride (one that he may have watched grow up and blossom into a young woman) walking down the aisle on her father's arm. Even so, he doesn't wish for the old days of the little chapel again, because he knows the total program offered now is doing much more good, bringing so many more people to Christ, helping so many more people who are hurting. Sometimes, when he really thinks about his distance from the congregation, it tears him apart inside, but he purposely chooses to put these feelings aside. He can't afford them. He has to answer God's call, and that is not what God has called him to do. There are eight other men on staff who have that privilege, that calling. About the only ones that Bob still pastors personally are those he has known for a very long time, original members, close staff members and close personal friends.

Though he isn't involved down at the grass roots level any more,

Bob doesn't see this as a deterrent to his preaching. He knows the universal needs present within all human beings. One thing he is dogmatic about is the fact that the unchurched don't want or need to have a sermon preached to them by a minister who feels he is superior, one who stands up in the pulpit with the attitude that he is better than his congregation because he has studied Greek and Hebrew and they haven't—he graduated from seminary and they didn't. He feels that a person preaching with this attitude is emitting emotional vibrations that do not build spiritual relationships between pulpit and pew. Rather than preach like that, Bob prefers to share experiences, to witness to them of the power of God as he has known it and seen it in others. As he sees it, "When you witness, you create an experience; when you preach sermons you produce polarization." Robert Schuller and the staff of the Garden Grove Community Church endeavor to generate a climate of acceptance, an atmosphere of nonjudgmental love.

Bob believes that where growth stops, the seed of decay and inevitable death is planted. He calls that a nonnegotiable universal principle that is true for every organism, whether it be an individual or an institution. He speaks not necessarily of quantity growth, but does feel that such growth is an inescapable outcome of quality growth unless the market is saturated. He thinks that growth should be related to basic goals, and that roles should be defined before goals are set.

Bob sees the role of the Garden Grove Community Church as the Body of Christ in the community of Orange County, California, and as that body it is to be actively involved in the business of living and loving and lifting up the loads of those people who live there. His hope is that these people will be unable to escape the authenticity of that caring, sharing, and accepting love; that they will see it as a pure, nonmanipulative acting-out of the love of Christ in the lives of the church as a whole and of each member individually; and that they will be drawn to make that Christ their own. This is the role of a mission church, actively engaged in ministry to the unchurched.

The size of a church, says Bob, should be in relation to the size of the unchurched population living within a reasonably serviceable radius. Within such a fifteen-minute driving distance from the Garden Grove Community Church there are five hundred thousand unchurched people, who do not know the saving grace of a God who loves them with all His heart. Obviously the main goal of the church is to reach out to as many of these people as possible in such a way as to touch their hearts with the Savior's love. Obviously then, the church could have a maximum possibility of a two hundred fifty thousand membership. However, realistically he would hope and expect to be able to reach 10 percent of that number for Christ, eventually having a maximum membership of twenty five thousand. At that point it would be a matter of revitalizing the membership with constant new life, new excitement. As members moved away or passed away, there would be the challenge of winning new people who would take their places. When you remain a mission, Bob says there should always be changes in focus in relation to the changes taking place within the community.

Dr. Schuller likes to tell the story of the man who was fishing off the pier one day. The fish were really biting, and he was reeling them in. Each time he caught one, he would take out his ruler and measure it carefully. The larger ones he threw back into the water, the smaller ones he put away in his creel. A young couple was watching him intently for some time, and finally their curiosity got the better of them. They asked the man why he was throwing the biggest, best fish back in the water. He looked up and smiled. "They were too big to fit into my frying pan."

Bob says, "The shoe must never tell the foot how big to get. Never surrender leadership to the shoe." He feels that many churches are restricted in their effectiveness by manmade obstacles that keep God from coming in and doing the really great things He would like them to do. He uses the example of the little church that doesn't even think of bringing in a Christian rock group in hopes of attracting a couple thousand teenagers because they know that their property is so small. He says that leadership is the force that sets the growth goals for an organization, and that too many churches have surrendered leadership to property, often without even being aware of it.

The question is often brought up that a large church is an unfriendly church, that by virtue of its numbers alone it must be impersonal and uncaring. To this, Bob shouts an emphatic no. He feels that interpersonal relationships that demonstrate authentic caring are not necessarily related to size. He points out that the optimum size for dynamic group therapy is about twelve people, and if you're concerned about size then maybe you should limit your church to that number. He thinks that the concept that a small church means greater care and love for the individual is completely false. Garden Grove Community Church, for example, has a membership of over ten thousand, and the comment Bob hears most often is that it is a church with an atmosphere of extreme friendliness—a place of caring and camaraderie. "It's not a matter of size, it's a matter of spirit," he reiterates.

Bob doesn't feel that it is any more or less difficult to accomplish a spirit of community in either a large or a small church. He merely points out that it doesn't exist to the full extent in many of the small churches in the country. How does he know? "Well," says he, "if it did, then the churches wouldn't remain small for very long; they'd be growing, because the people are so hungry."

Bob Schuller is quick to point out that the biggest doesn't necessarily mean the best. He quotes an old Chinese proverb that says, "Dragons are food for shrimps in shallow pools." He feels that the difference is that it be superlative—it must excel, it must be getting progressively better. Bob is a self-confessed incurable progressive; he thinks there must always be a better way to do a given task. The status quo must not be maintained, you should never be satisfied with yourself and what you are doing but always be striving to do it better.

These have always been the driving forces that have urged him on to new adventures, new possibilities, and in 1970, there was an incredible excitement-generating idea ready to explode over the horizon—the "Hour of Power."

8

THE ELECTRONIC MINISTRY

IN THE EARLY DAYS of the Garden Grove Community Church, Bob had derived a great deal of inspiration and enjoyment from a local television program sponsored by the National Council of Churches. Entitled *Great Churches of the Golden West,* it featured the worship service of a different California church each Sunday. He felt it was really serving a need in the community, especially for those who, for one reason or another, weren't able to attend church personally. Those with handicaps or illnesses that kept them home bound, those in the hospital, those with infants or sick children, those with no transportation, could turn on their TV sets and hear an opening hymn, a scripture, a prayer, and be uplifted in their spirits.

After several years, *Great Churches of the Golden West* went off the air. It collapsed because there was no sustaining consistent quality; some of the church services were beautiful and inspirational, others were mediocre at best. To Bob Schuller's way of thinking, the cancellation of the program left a terrible void. True, there were religious programs on television, but none of them were in the form of a regular, mainline church service. Being first and last a churchman, he felt keenly the loss and what it must mean to the shut-ins who were left without a source of encouragement.

It frustrated Bob; it grated on him, probably because he felt there was nothing he could personally do to remedy what he saw as a grave gap in local television programming. But Bob Schuller is not the sort to take ineffectiveness lightly. He is a man of action; when he sees an area of need in his community, he wants to step in and fill it.

Billy Graham planned a large crusade in Anaheim for the fall of 1959. Bob had always admired the noted evangelist, who had had a profound effect on his life and ministry. He had come to Hope College during Bob's student days there, and it was during his sermon that Bob felt God's call on his life in a new and more intense way. He rededicated himself to Christ that day and received a fervor for evangelism at the same time. He credits Billy Graham with being used of God to urge him to further commit his ministry to evangelism. From that day on, he has always had as a focal point the bringing of his followers to the point of a personal commitment to Jesus as Lord and Savior.

It seemed to follow as a natural course of events that Bob would serve as the vice-chairman of the Anaheim Crusade. Billy always has a school of evangelism associated with his crusades, in which he instructs and encourages local churches in evangelism and church growth. This time, it was held at the beautiful campus of Garden Grove Community Church. Bob was pleased to be able to have a short time to speak personally with his esteemed colleague, and one of the things they spoke of was television. The crusade was being taped for TV, and Bob took the opportunity to ask Mr. Graham a little about it; most notably the big question: "How much does it cost?"

Billy put him in contact with his producers, Fred Dienert and Walter Bennett. They were most encouraging to Bob about his long-time dream. As the years passed, Garden Grove Church had grown and prospered, and still there was no locally televised church service. Bob Schuller saw the need, and the time was right to fill it. He knew it would be a great thing for God and that it would help people who were hurting. No one else was doing it, and God had laid it on his heart. He felt it; the time was now.

Mr. Dienert and Mr. Bennett said it would work, but Bob wasn't sure. It was a great challenge and a great risk, and there was much at stake. The three had figured it would take a total of four hundred thousand dollars to televise the program for a year in the Los Angeles area. It was a fortune, and to Robert Schuller, the conservative Dutchman, it was nearly out of the question. But he couldn't shake the pull; he knew it had to be done.

He decided to do something he had never done before. He put out a fleece. Thousands of years before, in the land of Israel, a young man named Gideon had placed a fleece on the threshing floor of his father's barn. "If you, Lord, are with me and will deliver Israel through me, then make the dew to fall only on the fleece tonight. Let the floor around it remain dry, and I will take it for a sign from You." God had answered Gideon's prayer. The next morning, the floor was dry, but the fleece was soaking wet with dew. The practice of asking God for a sign, which is fairly common among fundamentalist and evangelical Christians, was not the custom in the Reformed tradition of Bob Schuller. But he so wanted to be certain that he was within God's plan for his life in taking his church service on television, that he embraced the doctrine.

Fred Dienert, at home in Philadelphia, and Bob Schuller and his business administrator, Frank Boss, in Orange County, entered into ardent prayer in an attempt to ascertain the will of God. It was another "if-then" arrangement. "Lord, if You want us to begin televising our church services, then let the congregation pledge two hundred thousand dollars above and beyond their annual tithes for this purpose." It would be done with no professional fund raising, no preparation, just the gentle nudging of the Holy Spirit on His people, if that was His desire. Were there even a dollar less in pledges, Bob agreed to accept that as God's indication that they were not to televise.

One Sunday in November, he went before the congregation in the big glass church. Each person in attendance was given a blank sheet of paper and asked to indicate how much he would be willing to pledge during the coming year to support the televising of their church services. There was little else said, other than the sharing of his dream. Later that afternoon, when the pledges were all tallied, they totaled one hundred ninety-six thousand dollars; four thousand dollars short of the agreed upon amount. Bob wasn't sure whether to be relieved or disappointed. But within the next couple of days, mail began pouring into the church. Lots of people had gone home and prayed about their commitment, sending their pledges in the mail. When all was said and done, the pledges from the congregation amounted to two hundred eighty thousand dollars; eighty thousand more than the necessary amount.

Looking back on that day, Bob said it was one of the scariest of his life. Was it really God's guidance or not? He knew, like Gideon and his fleece, that he would have to take God at His word. He had to trust Him, and he did. He contacted Channel Five in Los Angeles and purchased air time beginning on February 8, 1970. Money was donated by the congregation to assist in the preliminary expenses; and Bob, with the support of his people, plunged both feet into the icy waters of religious television.

Two weeks sped by; everything went smoothly and according to schedule until two weeks prior to that first pacesetting Sunday. High-powered television lights were being installed high up in the top of the glass sanctuary when the treasurer came into Bob's office atop the Tower of Hope. "Bob," he began breathlessly, "we need new electric transformers, and they won't install them until we pay the cost of ten thousand dollars in advance."

Bob peered at him, and for a second he was silent. "Are you telling me that we need ten thousand dollars by tomorrow?" It seemed impossible.

"That's right, Bob" he replied.

Both of them knew that they had no money. "Frank, you're the treasurer. Where are we going to get that kind of money in a day?" Bob's voice was tinged with panic.

Frank answered, "Yes, I'm the treasurer, but you're the pray-er," and walked out.

Had they misunderstood? Didn't God want them to bring a worship service to Southern Californians who couldn't get out to church? Bob's head was swimming that night in an endless fog. The next morning, he was afraid to face Frank. He knew he'd be asking whether they were going to cancel all their plans. Could they go on TV or not? Had Bob prayed up the ten thousand dollars?

As the morning wore on, an air of gloom seemed to descend and take up residence on the twelfth floor of the Tower. Bob went through his meetings and paperwork mechanically. At eleven o'clock, he had an appointment with a couple for what he understood would be marriage counseling. He didn't recognize their names; and sure enough, when they walked shyly into his room, he had never seen them before. He braced himself emotionally for the recital of problems that was sure to come.

"Dr. Schuller," the man began, "you don't know us, but we've been listening to you speak. A few months ago you challenged everybody to give 10 percent of their gross income to the Lord's work, and we thought it was a great idea. Right then we made a pledge to God that we would give Him 10 percent of our corporate profit for the year. It being January now, we just got our accountant's report. We showed a profit last year of one hundred thousand dollars, and we've come to give you our tithe.'' With that, he reached into his breast pocket and drew out a check for ten thousand dollars.

Bob gasped audibly and closed his eyes tightly as tears fought their way out and began to make patterns down his cheeks. He embraced the generous couple and they prayed together. And then, just as quickly as they had entered his life, they were gone, like phantoms in the night. He had never seen them before; he has never seen them since. He doesn't even know their names. What other dimensions inhabit the universe with us, never leaving a clue as to their existence? And how often do they emerge from the shadows and take on human form, walking into time from eternity? Are they angels?

When the first worship service from the Garden Grove Community Church was aired in Los Angeles, no one, including Bob, had any idea of the far-reaching effects it would have on his life and on that of the church itself. Bob's original idea had been only to provide a mainline, inspirational church service for Southern California residents. But in a little time, the dream expanded.

For nearly a decade, the only clerics seen on television always seemed to be those getting hauled away in the paddy wagon from some protest march. The latest Gallup polls all indicated that the church was dying. It was unthinkable. Christ's church, His body of believers for nearly two thousand years, with so much good news that never changes in its portent and in its capacity for good, couldn't be dying. And yet, Bob had the horrible feeling that a hundred million Americans were being programmed to believe that Protestantism was in its death throes.

Bob saw in his television program, which he called the ''Hour of Power,'' the possibility of saying to an entire generation of Americans, ''Hey, we're not dying. We're very much alive and if you would join us, you'd be more alive than you have ever been in your life.'' In that first year of the ''Hour of Power'' telecasts, the congregation of the church grew by one thousand members; and each time they took in new members, Bob took great pains to see to it that it was recorded faithfully in the program. The cameras would pan the faces of each new member, most of whom had never belonged to a church before, and show the wonder, the joy that was mirrored there. Every week, the cameras recorded for the television audience the growing numbers of people worshiping in Garden Grove. Bob felt that it would subliminally give the impression that the church was vibrant and growing, which it was. He wanted to give the impression that the church in America had a great future after all; that it was an exciting place to be. His hope was that the attitude of his viewers would spill over into their attitudes toward other churches, not just the one they saw on television.

He began a custom which he has not altered from that day to this. Every six weeks, when a new pastor's class is taken into the membership of the church, he stands up and looks directly into the camera at the faceless numbers who are watching on TV. "No matter where you live," he explodes, "there is a church not far from you. Maybe it is a little wooden building with stained glass windows, or maybe it is made of brick or stone. If you look for it, you will find it; and when you do, you will find a group of people who are emotionally and spiritually healthy human beings. You will find wonderful, beautiful people like the ones you see here today. Go out and find them. You'll be glad you did."

The term *electronic church* hadn't been coined yet back in 1970; but if it had, Bob would have been just as emphatic in his denial of it then as he is now. He says, "There is no such thing as the electronic church. A television program can never be a church." It was never his intention that the "Hour of Power" take the place of the local church in the lives of its viewers. Quite the contrary. He hoped it would generate interest in the local church and has done everything within his power to see to it that this has been accomplished. Together with his Institutes for Successful Church Leadership, Bob has endeavored to work toward the advancement of the neighborhood church across the country and the world.

To Bob, "the church is ecclesia. It is a community of committed people who have created a colony of caring for one another. A church is a community of people who touch each other, who care, who see eyeball to eyeball. It is people who call on others when they are sick or in the hospital, people who prepare food and take it to those who are unable to do so. A church is baptisms, weddings, funerals. I am the pastor, we are the church. But the church is not the building; the church is not the television program; the church is the people. What the viewer sees on television is not our church. God forbid. It is our electronic ministry, but it is not our church."

One of the criticisms leveled at what the press calls the electronic church is that it lures churchgoers from established local churches into the seclusion of a TV set in their home. In most cases this is quite erroneous, taking place perhaps only 6 percent of the time. A much more frequent occurrence is when a nonchurched person, who has never thought much about God, is turned on to Him through a television ministry and then goes and joins a local fellowship of believers.

As an electronic ministry, Bob sees the "Hour of Power" as having certain inherent limitations as well as possibilities. He feels that it cannot be used to fulfill what some people would call the "prophetic" role of the church. It is an instrument, but you must understand the limits of the instrument. Don't try to perform brain surgery with a butcher knife. If you aggravate people, if you provoke them, they will simply switch their dials. You cannot bring about meaningful change by insulting or preaching down to people. Bob still feels that the best way is to put people in a classroom situation where the teacher can get down on their level, where he can treat them with respect by allowing a dialogue between equals rather than a sermon by someone who appears superior.

He also sees television as severely limited as an educational medium, even as he has always viewed his own pulpit. Immediately, all sorts of academic barriers are present in a situation where it is not possible to set up prerequisites. In an audience where only God knows where each person stands in his knowledge of the Bible and other spiritual areas, it is impossible to give adequate instruction. You are bound to bore some by presenting facts that are too basic for their superior knowledge and confuse others by teaching concepts that are above their current understanding. In either case, it is all too easy for these viewers to turn off their TV sets. Then you have lost them altogether.

Bob believes that television is a limited vehicle at best for the propagandizing of denominationalism. He thinks the average person intuitively knows when he is being given a snow job. And he doesn't like to be indoctrinated by a front man. Bob loves his denomination, and likes the idea of being accountable to a higher power, but he is so committed to church growth in all the denominations, Catholic and Protestant alike, that he doesn't want to narrowcast.

Even though it has its limitations, Bob understands television to be a powerful medium and, when used properly, one which will make important contributions to society. In order to utilize its possibilities to the fullest, one must first comprehend its nature and the mentality of the twentieth century. He believes that today we are dealing with a graphic mentality as opposed to a logic mentality. He admits this is tragic, but that does not change its reality.

Prior to the emergence of the visual age, people received most of their knowledge from books. There was a topical sentence and a paragraph that explained it, then another topical sentence and explanatory paragraph, and so on. Of course, people still read books, but proportionately they spend far more time engaged in electronic visual pursuits, whether it be television, movies, or even video games. More than written sentences and paragraphs, communication today is likely to be in the form of a picture and a couple of words. As a television preacher, Bob understands this and builds his programming around it. He knows that if he doesn't throw in a picture or a story, people are going to get bored and turn him off.

He sees religious television as a powerful tool for what he calls pre-evangelism. It should never be thought of as a substitute for the local church, but it can give the secular person a new awareness of what a spiritual dimension could mean in his life. It can give him a new concept of what a church is and what his own neighborhood church can offer him. It can give him the impression that it is fun to go to church, that church attendance can be a happy and joyous experience. It can stimulate his God-consciousness and give him a hunger to learn more about God and His people.

Bob is not so quick to assume that electronic ministries can be effective channels for actual conversions to Christianity. He knows what some electronic ministries claim, and he doesn't deny their figures. He also doesn't deny the thousands of letters he receives testifying to life-changing conversions through the "Hour of Power"; there are too many to ignore or discount. Bob just feels that the electronic ministries have more success in the field of pre-evangelism. He believes that if he can stimulate his viewer to be excited about God and to start looking for God in his everyday life and to begin attending a local church, then through that close community of caring and sharing, he will come to accept Christ as his Savior.

Bob is excited about the possibilities of mass counseling through the vehicle of television. On an airplane one time, he sat next to a psychiatrist from upstate New York. She worked in a large mental hospital, and Bob asked her what ratio existed between doctors and patients there. When she replied that it was one doctor to every seven hundred patients, he was horrified. What could they hope to accomplish? "Oh, you'd be surprised," she explained enthusiastically. "As I walk through the ward, I speak to each person with whom I come into contact. I touch them and ask them how they are; I smile at them. Never underestimate the power of a look, a touch, and a smile."

Bob has seen firsthand how these principles literally turn people from suicide toward a new commitment to live. He is adamant in his belief that television, when it consistently provides a positive input, can be very effective in mass therapy and bring about infinite changes for the better in its viewers.

Religious television can also provide its viewer with real, healthy entertainment, and Bob doesn't feel this side of TV ministries should be necessarily played down. He sees entertainment as a vehicle to help bring about relaxation and tranquillity, and believes tranquillity to be a conditioning for creative communication. Creativity occurs when the mind is relaxed and tensions are removed. Bob sees television as an instrument for relaxation provided that the programming is designed to consciously or subconsciously uplift the emotional health of its viewers.

Since its unobtrusive beginnings in 1970, the "Hour of Power" has become a driving force in Christian television. It is currently seen in more than 176 cities and towns across America as well as having a large audience in Canada and Australia and the Virgin Islands. It is also carried by satellite over the three big Christian television networks: Trinity Broadcasting, Christian Broadcasting, and Praise the Lord Broadcasting. It is televised over the American Armed Forces Television Network, which beams to all of the country's ships at sea and military bases in other countries. Dr. Schuller attributes its phenomenal popularity to the fact that it gives the people what they need in a way that makes them want it. "We give people something they can grasp, a religion they can put to work in daily living. They can measure their own progress and see the results.

" 'The Hour of Power' is positive and psychologically helpful. It offers Christ-centered solutions to the problems of today, and my messages are easy to understand and apply. There is a great need for evangelical Christianity wrapped up in possibility-thinking terms." Bob believes that there will be a national resurgence of faith through the churches of America and that the "Hour of Power" will be a force in communities across the country to help build the local church.

The expansion of the "Hour of Power" was slow and conservative when measured by the standards of some of the other Christian programming. Six months after its start over KTLA Channel Five in Los Angeles, it began televising over WOR in New York City. By the time I came on the scene in 1973, the service was being shown in eighteen markets, mostly in large urban centers.

I'll never forget the day Bob offered me a full-time job with the ministry. It was spring, and Donna and I had just had our third child, a beautiful little girl. I was sitting on top of the world, and as I drove over the freeways of Orange County, I could see the giant cross perched atop the Tower of Hope. Bob and I had an appointment to discuss the work we had been doing on worldwide religious freedom, but I could hardly make my mind concentrate on such matters when the beauty of Southern California assailed me from every direction. Suddenly, out of nowhere, a thought popped into my mind. "Bob is going to offer me a job today."

Later, esconced on the twelfth floor of the Tower, Bob popped the question. Even though I had been halfway expecting it, it took me by surprise. I liked my job as assistant to the president of a large California-based fireworks firm. My boss Pat Moriarity had been exceedingly kind to me, and I was very fond of him. But during my seven-month acquaintance with Bob Schuller, I had come to love and respect him very much. It was a difficult decision, one that took me two weeks to make, but one I have never regretted.

In the ensuing years, Bob has been more than a boss to me. He has been my father, my brother, my best friend. I have experienced mountain peaks with him, and there have been times when I have been so low, you'd have had to raise me up to bury me. I've been angry with him, oh so angry; and he has hurt me deeply, too. But those things are always part of any human relationship that is conducted on a deep, personal level. Any time you open yourself up and make yourself vulnerable to another, you run the risk of being hurt. But it's worth it.

That first summer, before I actually began my job in September, I made many visits to the Schuller home. Bob has always taken the summer off from his hectic schedule at church, and this one was spent landscaping his new home. Ever since their arrival in California some eighteen years earlier, the Schullers had lived in a series of tract homes much like everyone else in the sprawling suburbs of Orange County. Now they had taken the big plunge. They bought an old farmhouse near the church which came with two and a half acres of ground. The house was small, only three bedrooms with no family room or den. It was old and in bad repair, with antiquated bathrooms and kitchen. But to possess a yard larger than a postage stamp in Orange County is no less than a feat of magic. It was overgrown with weeds, there was practically no grass at all, certainly no flowers or shrubs. But it did boast some lovely trees.

When Bob Schuller looked at it, all he saw were possibilities. The first time I pulled down the long driveway, I could hardly believe my eyes. Robert Schuller, my boss, dignified cleric and television personality, was wielding a shovel. He was literally covered with dirt, and the sweat was flying off his bare back, his hair plastered to his head. Right alongside him worked his son, Bob, who had just graduated from high school, his six-foot-three inch frame topping even that of his tall dad.

Bob landscaped that entire two and one half acres himself, from the design to the finished product; and each time I visited, I could see the progress he had made. Bob, the lover of beauty in nature, transformed his property from a bed of tumbleweeds to one of the most beautiful parks I have ever seen. By the front door of the little rundown house, he dug and installed a natural-looking waterfall which played gently over the rocks and into a dark pool. In the rear of the property, he built more pools, with a wooden deck cantilevered out over them.

To the side of the house, a swimming pool was built, set in the middle of rolling green grass. He planted bushes and flowers, and even bought a couple of koi fish to swim in the pools. It was the culmination of a dream for Bob, to have a retreat from the congestion of Orange County, an oasis of tranquillity in which he could relax and create.

It has taken Bob and Arvella years to renovate the old house and add on more rooms a little at a time, but the results are breathtaking. When visitors arrive now at what seems to be a gracious country estate, many are critical of the extravagance of the beauty, not realizing that it was not so much money as the creative genius and hard work of Bob and Arvella Schuller that produced the lovely home and grounds.

I reported to my first day of work as Dr. Schuller's executive assistant on September 15, 1973. My office, if it can be called that, was in a little cubbyhole near the restrooms on the twelfth floor of the Tower. It was a small operation then, and very close-knit.

Right at the outset, I got more than I had bargained for. Ed Arnold, a sports announcer for the ABC affiliate in Los Angeles, had been the announcer for the "Hour of Power" from its inception. A devout Christian, he had done this on a volunteer basis and had never missed a Sunday in three years. This year he had been elected President of the California Junior Chamber of Commerce and was required to do some traveling, some of which fell on a series of Sundays that fall. Imagine my chagrin when Bob called and asked me to stand in for Ed on the program. All this, and after only a week of work.

"It doesn't pay anything," Arvella had said, "but we will buy some pastel shirts and suitable ties for you to wear on the air." I was in desperate need of shirts and ties at that time; but what with Tara's medical bills and a new baby, there just wasn't any money with which to buy some. I have always wondered if she knew my situation and came up with that plan to help me out at a time when I really needed it. Certainly God used her to provide for a need in my life. It was the beginning of my limited announcing career, which lasted for several years. Any time Ed couldn't make it, I took over for him, and eventually I was able to conquer camera fright. Ed and I look somewhat alike, and some viewers probably never noticed the difference, but my family loved it.

As can often happen, internal problems developed between Robert Schuller Televangelism and the Walter Bennett Agency which produced the program and purchased the air time for it across the country. I wasn't privy to all the details at the time, but knew a break was imminent about six months into my employment. Then one day, Bob called me into his office unexpectedly. He started telling me details about the beginning of the "Hour of Power," all of which I already knew. I braced myself. I knew Bob well enough to know that when he began giving me a history lesson, I'd better watch out. Something big was in the offing, whether good or bad.

He worked his way through the four years, finishing up with a sentence that just about blew me skyhigh. "So Mike," he smiled, "now that we have severed business relations with the Bennett Agency, I'd like you to take over the job. You can produce the program and buy all the air time." They had set up an in-house advertising agency which would provide the same services as the Bennett Agency had, and that day I was made its president. I couldn't believe it. Here I was, a thirty-one-year-old kid, being handed the job of a lifetime. I would be running an agency with a gross expenditure of six hundred thousand dollars annually.

I'm not normally a blusher, but my face turned beet red. I could feel the heat creep rapidly up my neck and face, right into my hairline. "But Bob," I sputtered, "I don't know the first thing about television production. I don't know how to buy air time."

He was impervious. "I know you don't, but you'll learn. In the meantime, it's management by objective. You just go out and hire the people who do. Make sure you get the best. You'll do fine."

The first year was baptism by fire. I had no choice, really. It was do or die, sink or swim. And I sure learned a lot—fast. I have always been committed, as have the Schullers, to quality. When Bob made the decision to go on television, he knew he would have to compete in the marketplace. If you are going to do television, you had better be television, you had better give the viewer what he has come to expect from television.

Television is not the route to go if you want to project the poor, humble Christian image. You may have a wonderful message to communicate, but no one will listen to you long enough to find out what it is. Americans have already been preconditioned to what television is like. They expect it to be fast paced, entertaining, and colorful. And I had to step in and continue to create that kind of an atmosphere of excellence and expertise, when I actually had no expertise at all. With God's help, we pulled it off, and I completed that season a wiser man in many ways.

It has now been nine years since I began in the exciting field of TV production. I has gotten more sophisticated each year, as technology has created better equipment, and each week we at the "Hour of Power" have endeavored to provide a program of the highest quality possible. We've had our share of critics; one reporter said the program was too slick, too professional. "What's the alternative?" I asked him. "Do you want one that is black and white and stapled?" Neither Bob nor Arvella nor I nor any of the "Hour of Power" staff would demean our God by turning out a program about Him that was anything less than the best we could do. He gave us His best when He entered human history and gave His very life for us. We feel that a slipshod, unprofessional program would be an insult to Him and to our viewers as well.

To put together a program that excels every week is no mean task, and requires the cooperation and industry of a whole crew of people. I guess the first person to enter the picture is Arvella. Ever since their marriage, she has always planned the worship service from beginning to end, even in their days in Ivanhoe. She now holds the title of Program Director, even though she has never taken a penny for her services. She is assisted by her oldest daughter Sheila, and both of them have at their disposal vast musical backgrounds which are reflected in the content of the service.

Now that the church has a full-time professional minister of music and a large music department, he makes recommendations to Arvella regarding the musical selections for each Sunday's services. But the final decisions rest with Arvella and Sheila. They select and coordinate the music, scriptures, and prayers for the program so that it will portray one central theme. Arvella has always put in more than a forty-hour work week for the church, most of which is behind the scenes. Her relentless drive for excellence is readily seen in each program, yet she seems content to remain the unsung hero most of the time. Donna and I marvel at her stamina and her energy. Anyone who has been able to raise a family of five children and endure the pressures of the Schuller's accelerated lifestyle, work long hours daily at a job, and still not have even so much as a cleaning lady in to help her in the house on a regular basis, has got to be some special lady.

By Thursday each week the content of the program is set, and I call our production meeting. The whole staff gets together to go over the order of worship for Sunday. In attendance are people like myself, Arvella, Sheila, the television director, people from the sound department, people from the music department, people from the production staff and people from the Crystal Cathedral management. Together, we literally go through the entire service as it will be done on Sunday. We listen to all the music on tape and decide on the staging, meaning we determine where the different people will stand during the program.

That night, a full rehearsal is held in the sanctuary. The choir is on hand, and sometimes the soloist, and they physically rehearse and stage the worship service. The director is there so that he can decide on his camera positions; and between then and Sunday morning, he has pretty well mapped out his strategy and the shots he wants to get for television.

The "Hour of Power" has never owned its own television equipment. The state of the art changes so rapidly that TV equipment becomes obsolete often before it is even paid for, and we have never felt we would be responsible stewards of God's money by owning it ourselves. We have always rented it on a weekly basis and had it brought down to the church from Los Angeles on Sunday mornings in what is called a preset. We used to use a large truck full of television equipment, but now have a room designed for that purpose in the basement of the Cathedral.

It arrives in the early hours of the morning each Sunday and must be brought down into the bowels of the church in the darkness. Part of the crew arrives as early as two o'clock to begin setting up for the shoot. They bring in the cameras and the recording equipment and all the TV monitors and the switching devices and install them temporarily in the television room. Then, around four o'clock, more of the crew arrives. Grips, among whom is my son Mark, begin to drag the heavy television cables and cameras. The cameras are turned on and technicians start aligning them. It is important that the proper color gets onto the recording machine, and there is some technical fine tuning that must be done before the video taping is begun.

The television director meets with his six cameramen to tell them how he has laid out the program and to go over which cameras will be used for which parts of the service. Five of the cameras are stationed at various locales inside and one is placed outside on a crane. The director literally goes through the entire service again with the cameramen around six in the morning. Then at eight, we have a rehearsal so that the cameramen can actually see the program through their cameras and finalize their angles. It lasts about an hour during which all the musical numbers and solos and anthems are performed, unless the choir is singing one of their old standbys and the crew is already familiar with it.

At this same time, Dr. Schuller and the other ministers who will be taking part in the service, as well as the guest for the day and the soloists, are in the make-up room being readied for their part in the program. At first, this seems a bit much, overly theatrical and all that. After all, it is a church service. But with the high-powered lights that are necessary for television and the nature of color TV itself, people without proper make-up end up looking washed out and sick. It just wouldn't make for a very attractive program. Who wants to look at a ghostly white apparition trying to speak to them about important matters? Every other television program uses the appropriate make-up, and the viewer isn't used to seeing people on TV any other way.

Finally, everything is in readiness. The sanctuary is full of people. The minister of music comes out and teaches the congregation the songs that will be sung that morning. This is something that everyone really appreciates. It is so frustrating to be in the middle of a meaningful worship service and to have your heart in tune with God, only to have your communion shattered by having to try to master a new song.

Down in the television room, a staff of people are ready to actually produce the program. It is a series of three small rooms that are joined together by glass walls and doors. You would never guess the mammoth size of the Cathedral just by looking at the tiny rooms delegated to TV production, and I guess this is in keeping with Bob's original premise that it is the church and the ministering to people that are really important, not the television production per se.

Above the ground, in the sanctuary, thousands are gathered to worship God in community together. There is a lot of talking and hugging and smiling, a lot of rustling of papers as they look over the schedule of worship. As the minutes tick away toward 9:30, everyone begins to quiet down and listen to the organ swell as they prepare themselves for worship and prayer.

Below the ground, in our production room, a relatively small group of people is gathered. There is very little talk here, not much smiling and no hugging. We are also going to worship God, not in the traditional sense like the people upstairs, but in a way that is almost deeper. We are going to worship Him in service, giving Him the very best that each of us has to offer. We are going to offer up to Him our talents, our creativity, our skills, our knowledge, in the welding together of a television program dedicated to His glory.

It is very quiet in the trio of rooms; each of us is concentrating on one thing, that of doing our own particular job with excellence. Arvella and I, along with any guests that may be present, are seated in the producer's room, which is the one closest to the hallway door. It is a tiny space, actually, with a long gray couch along its rear wall where visitors may sit. It faces the glass partition that separates this room from that of the director. Built in along the glass is a long wooden console, maybe eighteen inches deep, which also faces into the next room; recessed into the wood are three small television monitors. Each produces a black and white picture; the first is the program screen, which carries the images that are actually going onto the master tape. Next is another that shows the same pictures, but also has a time code that runs continually through the taping so we can tell what is happening at each exact second. This is invaluable in the editing we will do later. The third screen is what we call an Iso reel, where we can study isolated pictures from the various cameras. The room is dark but for the flickering images on the three screens, and Arvella and I are seated at two chairs before them.

We can look into the control room, which is where the directors work. There are three of them; the director, the technical director, and the assistant director, and they are all sitting on chairs just in front of another large built-in console unit. The entire wall in front of them seems to be covered with television monitors of different sizes. There are six small black and white screens that produce the shots taken by each of the six cameras, each one reproducing a different scene or angle from the sanctuary above. To the right are two larger screens; one marked "program," the other "preview." These show the actual shots that are going onto the master tape. The one labeled "program" has the same pictures that appear on the producer's screen that Arvella and I study. The "preview" screen shows the director what the next picture will look like before it actually appears on the "program" monitor. The console beneath all the screens is equipped with various levers and switches, which are used by the technical director to cut from one scene to another or to fade from one angle to another at the command of the director.

To the right of the control room, again separated by a glass partition, is the monitoring room. As in the other rooms, one is amazed that so much technical equipment can be crammed into such a small space. This one holds all of the video recorders and the devices used to monitor the various signals coming in from the cameras and sound equipment. There are six consoles which are for the adjustment of the technical accuracy of the cameras before they can be recorded on the video tape machine. This room is manned by two men, the video operator who physically adjusts the knobs to insure that the proper picture is getting on the video tape machines, and the video tape operator who actually runs the machines—all three of which are one-inch machines that record high quality, high-band color pictures. One of them records the master tape, which is the actual program. One records what we call the submaster, which is basically a protection copy in case there is a failure on the master. The third machine records the Iso reel. It pulls isolated shots from the taping to be used later in future editing.

So on any given Sunday morning, there are seven of us packed into these small, dark rooms. It is much the same as the production of any television program, and it would be an illusion to think it is not. The only difference is that we are taping a church service. What the viewer eventually sees in his home is pretty nearly identical to what our congregation is seeing above us in the cathedral. Because it is actually a recording of our real worship service, we've got to take it as it comes. We can't call "cut" and start over again if we make a mistake, so we've got to really concentrate and make sure we get it right the first time.

While the congregation upstairs is settling down and beginning to learn the songs for the morning, all of us are getting down to the business of taping the service so that people all over the world can worship with them. Arvella and I study our notes, the director studies the monitors as the pictures zoom in and out and refocus on new angles as the cameramen set up for new shots. Speakers pipe in the sounds of the music above. Dr. Schuller appears on the screens, greeting the congregation personally before the actual service and taping begins. In our rooms, it is quiet but for the sound of his voice. The director signals to his assistant and the crew in the monitor room as the low countdown is begun. "Five, four, three, two, one." At that instant the trumpets in the cathedral sound the triumphant, clear notes of the opening fanfare, the organ begins to soar, and the choir bursts into joyful song. The program has begun.

Immediately, the director springs to life. He is in constant contact with his cameramen through the headphones he wears, and his eyes are glued to the eight monitors before him. It's a fast-paced job, requiring him to be concentrating on many different things at once. He must be ready for the next segment as well as know what pictures are on his screens at all times. He decides which camera will be utilized in the master tape at each split second and tells the cameramen which angle he wants.

All the while he is gesturing to his technical director telling him which shots he wants and how he wants them. The technical director must move with lightning speed; he's got to know how to interpret the rapid body language of the director and be ready to push the buttons and pull the levers before him, switching first one camera and then another onto the screens. The entire procedure is reminiscent of the precision grace of a conductor with his orchestra. The director's arms and hands fly through the air, pointing at first one monitor and then another, tracing invisible arcs from one screen to the other while the technical director dissolves and cuts his cameras back and forth, their images appearing and disappearing on the color screens. The assistant director, meanwhile, is taking timing notes as to what physically is going onto the screen, recording the minutes and seconds of each segment of the program.

Arvella's and my responsibilities seem few at this point in time. We are studying the actual program, the shots that are going onto the master tape. We note mistakes, areas we would like to change. We are looking at it with editing in mind. How can we improve the flow or cover up a blooper? Bob will want to know our impressions in between the two morning services so he can make any adjustments in his message, so we view the service with that in mind, too. If there is a problem of sufficient magnitude, we will decide whether or not to retape a particular segment or even the entire program during the eleven-fifteen service.

By the time the hour is over, we've got an entire television program video tape. As the congregation files out of the church, we replay any portions that may be questionable and make the decision as to retaping. Fortunately, this is not usually necessary. Most of the time, within fifteen to twenty minutes after the conclusion of the service, we know our work is sufficient. The words we've all been waiting for are passed from one to another. "It's a wrap."

By this time, my job is pretty much finished for the day. I usually go on into Bob's office and visit with the family or any guests that might be present. There's coffee and juice, fruit and rolls for everyone. By eleven o'clock in the morning, we've all put in a full day's work and are more than ready for a bite to eat and a little relaxation. Bob, of course, must now go back up into the cathedral and conduct yet another service. Before long his voice can be heard booming over the sound system, "This is the day that the Lord has made, let us rejoice and be glad in it."

Back in the television room, grips are busy dismantling all the equipment for its return journey into Los Angeles. The master tape is sent over to the house of the Schullers' daughter, Sheila Coleman, where she and her mother will review it and make additional notes for editing. And Bob and I, and probably a lot of the twenty-two-man crew, head home for a well-deserved nap.

On the following Wednesday, the director, a film editor, and I go into an editing studio in Hollywood, which we rent by the hour, to edit the program down to the fifty-eight-minute-thirty-second length which is standard for television. This can take us anywhere from an hour or so to all day, depending upon the number of changes we must make. When we're through, we'll take the completed master and send it to Ann Arbor, Michigan, where it is dubbed, or reproduced, onto separate tapes which are then shipped out all over the world.

station that airs the "Hour of Power" receives its the program each week, and this is what they project waves into the TV sets of their area. All this takes time, so am that is seen on television was usually taped about three earlier.

is is only a small part of the Hour of Power operations. Most of the remainder is spent in handling the mail, which is really a monumental task. The Hour of Power building is rectangular, modern, and about half its construction is in gold-tinted glass. It's located just across Chapman Avenue from the church and is joined to the church parking lot by an overhead footbridge that spans the street. We haven't always had such a nice building for our business headquarters, but have enjoyed this one for the past five years. We thought this three-story structure with its thirty thousand square feet of working space was going to be the answer to our prayers, uniting all the facets of the television ministry under one roof and giving us enough space to work efficiently. However, possibility thinking put an end to those plans right away. Bob decided he wanted to open up a Christian school devoted to excellence in education and the musical arts. He fired up enthusiasm in his Minister of Education at the church; and before we knew what was happening, teachers were hired, curriculum was planned, students were enrolled—all before a suitable location had been found in which to hold classes.

Believe me, a situation like this is not all that unusual around the Hour of Power and the Garden Grove Community Church. After all, one of the basic premises of possibility thinking says that you make the decision first and then solve the problems. If I've heard Bob say it once, I've heard him say it a thousand times: "Never bring the problem-solving phase into the decision-making phase."

So here we were with an entire grade school and nowhere to put it. In keeping with his basic priorities of service to the community first, Bob decided to take the first and second floors of the Hour of Power building and turn them into a school. While he was at it, he went ahead and moved the church nursery and day-care center over to the new building, too. So we ended up with only the third floor devoted to the business of the Hour of Power.

Soon the Crystal Cathedral Academy was in full swing; the first floor windows were decorated with the children's water-color paintings, and the back parking lot was partially fenced off to provide for a playground. The academy is now in its fifth year, and the Hour of Power is still limping along on the third floor. That is, except the shipping department which is across the street in the old youth building at the church. We have a warehouse, too, where we store the gifts that we offer to our television audience.

Around a hundred and fifty people are employed at the Hour of Power, corresponding to approximately the same number over at the church. Most of them are women, many in supervisory positions. We also employ many retirees. The main business at the Hour of Power is definitely to turn the mail around. We receive approximately forty to fifty thousand letters every week, and the answering of these is a job of stupendous proportions. For most of us, it is the hardest part of all to deal with, but it is really inescapable.

With such a heavy volume of mail, it is a real challenge to handle each letter on a personal level. It would really be wonderful if Dr. Schuller could sit down at his desk each morning and open his mail, read it, and answer it personally. I know that is what he would like to do, but it is simply impossible. There is no way he could personally attend to his mail, even if he did nothing else all day long for the rest of his life.

So we have developed quite a complicated system in an attempt to give our viewer the best service possible. First, the letters are taken into letter processing, where they are opened by machines. After the letter is opened, it is personally handled by a staff member, one of whom is my own mother. The staff member separates the letter from any donation that may be included and forwards it on to the reading department.

In the reading department it receives its most personal attention. Each letter is read by one of our readers in its entirety. About 80 percent of our mail is merely requesting one of our offers or maybe Bob's printed sermon material. When this is the case it is coded to that effect by the readers and sent into the next department. However, when a letter is expressing a need, the readers are responsible for seeing to it that the need is met.

In that case, they send the letter over to the counseling department where we have trained counselors who handle it personally. If it is requesting prayer, they save it together with others and bring them to the Wednesday morning prayer meeting. Here the Hour of Power staff meets to pray for the needs of the viewers. Each staff member is personally handed his own small stack of letters for which he prays individually and specifically during the service. When a letter is requesting some answers to spiritual questions, the counselors use the Bible as well as Bob's material on the subject to formulate an appropriate reply. We also have on hand paragraphs that Bob has already written that deal with many of the more common problems that people have.

I wish I could say that every letter that goes out from the Hour of Power has been hand-typed by one of our staff, but that just isn't the case. It would be impossible for us to employ a staff large enough to personally type all our letters. In addition, it would not be economically feasible. We take our stewardship of God's money very seriously at the Hour of Power, and to pay for the enormous facility and the huge staff that would be needed to personally answer the mail would be a blatant misuse of His resources.

Bob fought computerization for years but finally had to admit that it was inevitable. We have used an outside computer service for some time, but have now come to the point where we realize that even this is not good stewardship. By owning and operating our own computer, we can cut our cost by 50 percent, and that means a 50 percent more effective use of our donor's money. Our own in-house computer is dedicated solely to serving our viewers. It enables us to answer our mail just that much faster and more efficiently. When our people write in with serious problems, they need answers right away. They can't afford to wait several weeks while their letter is going through time-consuming hand-operated channels. Our computer allows us to serve them more effectively, and we feel that is what we have been called to do.

Many ministries only send out receipts for their donations, but Bob has always felt that a letter should be sent, so that's what we do. It is true that we keep a big mailing list, about nine hundred thousand names, but that is nothing new to Robert Schuller. Even when he preached from the rooftop of the snackbar at the Orange Drive-In Theatre, he maintained that a mailing list was the first line of publicity, the way to build a church. He hasn't changed his mind.

Even so, we run the Hour of Power on much less operating capital than do many other ministries of comparable size. Big crisis mailings and begging for money over the television just aren't Bob's style. We are probably one of the most popular religious television programs in the country, and yet we receive one of the smallest amounts of revenue from our viewers. It doesn't bother us; we planned it that way.

Most of our letters are requesting whatever offer Bob has just spoken of on the program. These we try to send out as soon as we possibly can, and over the years we've gotten much better at serving our viewers in this way. Some have complained that we shouldn't give the gifts, that it is too commercial; and yet Bob is always emphatic that the gifts have a message, that they be a source of ministry and inspiration. They are not chosen lightly; a committee meets periodically to discuss them. Bob is always present and has an uncanny knack of being able to tell what is going to be the most helpful to his audience.

We have had some blunders, though. Once we offered a little palm tree at Easter time. We thought it was a great idea, because of the significance the palm played in Jesus' last days on earth. But we had a serious packaging problem. It was one of those times when we made the decision and never could get the problems solved. The dirt that surrounded the rootball of the little palm kept falling out of the container. It got into the machinery at the post office; you can imagine how popular we were with them! And by the time it arrived at the homes of the viewers, the poor little plant was nearly dead, with no dirt around its roots to nourish and protect them. I'm afraid a lot of our possibility-thinking Christian viewers did not respond particularly positively to this problem. Many categorically refused to even try to turn it into an opportunity. However, we did get some letters from dear souls who used it as an opportunity to nurture the little plant back to life, and many of them succeeded.

Another time, we offered a little silver-colored metal statue patterned after our own beloved Good Shepherd. It was about four inches tall and really quite attractive. Most people liked it very much, but we did get one extremely irate letter from a woman in Florida who really thought big. She was anticipating two exact replicas of the seven-foot-tall Good Shepherd statute as it stands on our grounds and had had pillars prepared for them on either side of her driveway.

Most of our viewers really appreciate the gifts, some of which end up playing very important parts in their lives. One woman wrote in to say that she was wearing one of our crosses when she and a friend were held up in a store. She just held on to the cross and prayed during the entire ordeal. Her companion was shot and killed, but she escaped unharmed. Most of our offers are faith-builders, and in more instances than not, I think our viewers realize the spiritual aspects of them. Often they are just a concrete, physical reminder of God's love, something they can look at or read and from which they can receive a lift. Our yearly publications of Dr. Schuller's Daily Devotion Books have been especially helpful to many, as have the other books he has written, and most of our audience really enjoys the printed copies of his sermons that we send them.

It's a funny thing about Bob's preaching. People either like it or they don't. He has often been criticized for his flamboyant, dramatic style, but it comes very naturally to him. It really isn't put on for show. I don't think there is a preacher or public speaker of any kind who doesn't have his own style of communication. Even those of us who don't usually speak publicly have our own way with words, our own usage of our hands and facial expressions that come naturally to us, and Bob is no exception. He is no different on television today than he was in the drive-in years ago.

People who have known him since his first years in the ministry joke good-humoredly about his theatrics and the fact that he loves to talk. Even his mother used to fret over his seeming lack of sermon preparation and study, and he often used to complain despondently to his old friend Raymond Beckering on a Saturday night that he didn't know what he was going to speak on the next morning. Invariably, however, he always got up and did a fantastic job. It is far easier for him to get up and speak, even when he feels that he is not prepared, than it is for him to sit passively and listen to someone else speak. Speaking is easier for him than listening, no matter what the situation, and that is a definite plus when it comes to pulpiteering.

Back in the late sixties, when the charismatic movement was just coming into its own, Bob was quite concerned that he have whatever gifts God wanted Him to have. He called another pastor of the Reformed tradition, Harold Bredeson, and asked him to come over and pray with him about the baptism of the Holy Spirit. Harold, long a leader in the charismatic movement, spent an entire day in prayer with Bob. At last, he told him he didn't feel God meant the gift of speaking in tongues for Bob. They prayed for his infilling of the Holy Spirit, and Harold prophesied correctly that Bob would be given the gift of sayings, that he would be able to speak English in a way with which people could identify and understand. Often he will get in the pulpit and words will come out that he hadn't planned to say; after the service, he won't even remember having said them.

Bob always begins with his heart when he preaches, never with his head. He is not out to manipulate people, but simply to share with them what is in his own heart. He feels that if he doesn't speak from the heart, he won't be sincere. "People say I am persuasive," he says. "I am persuasive because those whom I persuade are convinced that I am sincere. If they are not turned off by my looks or my style or my church, if they really listen to me, they will know that I sincerely believe in what I say."

Bob never chooses his sermon topics by the ecclesiastical calendar. He would never say, "Well, this is Pentecost Sunday so I think I'll speak on the Holy Spirit." What if he doesn't feel like it that day? Then he wouldn't be effective. He would rather speak from what God has shown him that week, from what is fresh on his mind. That's not to say that he doesn't teach spiritual truths; he does. It's just that he chooses to share them in a more oratorical, parabolic style, much as Jesus used to do.

He has often said that if he ever preaches a sermon on adultery, you will know what his problem is. He feels ministers deal most often with those subjects which mean the most or give them the most trouble personally. He admits that since the main thrust of his ministry is self-esteem, it is a clear indication that he has difficulties in that area himself; inferiority complexes that probably have their roots way back in his childhood as a shy, overweight, nonathletic, not overly attractive farmboy in Iowa.

He will not speak on a subject that he is not completely sold on, so in this way it is easy for him to be sincere. He is committed to an orthodox, evangelical, historical Christian theology. He believes in the Apostles' Creed, the virgin birth of Christ,the physical resurrection of Jesus, the second coming of Christ. Anything that he doesn't completely comprehend himself, he doesn't deal with, either in print or from the pulpit. He feels that by not dealing with it he is showing respect for it as the Word of God. He assumes it is true, but would not preach a sermon on it if he were unsure of his own ability to treat it as God would have him do so. He deals with issues that he can personally feel; things like the reality of an indwelling Christ by the power of the Holy Spirit, God's healing power at work in people's lives. If he can feel the reality of a spiritual truth, he will talk about it.

Admittedly, a lot of Bob's rhetoric is unabashedly corny. He is a genius at creating little slogans and loves to make words rhyme, whether he is planning a sermon or not. But, you know, it's amazing the power that God generates through some of those corny, seemingly shallow little sayings. Once he did a series entitled "Alter Your Altars," asking people: "Who sits upon the throne of your life? Is it yourself? Your possessions? Pleasure?" He finished by challenging them to change that, to alter their altars and let Christ sit upon the throne. A catchy little phrase, but God used it to bring a prominent Boston lawyer to his knees in an acceptance of Christ into his life.

A Kentucky woman wrote to us about the loss of her little girl to brain cancer. "Praise the Lord," she continued, "through it all I found Him on a very deep, personal level which has changed my life so completely. When I heard Dr. Schuller speak, I realized even more how the Lord has moved in my life and, as he says, 'turned my scars into stars.'"

Another letter came from a man in Chicago who has one of our 'bloom where you are planted' pens. He wrote, "The other night I came home from work tired and discouraged. As I took time to pray and thank God for His love and wisdom, my eyes fell on the pen lying on the dresser. There was my answer. 'Bloom where you are planted.' I went back to work the next day with love in my heart for the one who had hurt me, and I asked God to help me show that love and to bloom where I was planted."

A man in Washington told us of the death of his wife. "She loved God, Dr. Schuller, and she was a possibility thinker. It helped me to realize she was in heaven, and I placed your medallion with the possibility thinker's creed on it over the cross at her grave."

A woman wrote in to say how much she enjoyed Bob's messages. "I heard your 'Gateway to the Greatway' first, and it was at this time that I rededicated my life to Christ."

And in another letter the writer says, "I am a Roman Catholic Sister, but it gives me great joy to hear men like you preach the message of our Lord Jesus Christ. I pray to the Heavenly Father and the Holy Spirit to grant you a continued outpouring of love, peace, and joy. And may your program be blessed in every way."

A child writes, "I am ten years old. Our family watches 'Hour of Power' every Sunday. We have accepted Jesus from listening to you."

A man in Texas writes to say, "One year ago, my marriage was on the rocks, but through your beautiful messages every Sunday, I have a good home now."

One letter explains, "I cannot find words to write down on this sheet of paper the way your closing prayer for the people moved me. I felt as if Christ touched me personally to let me know that all was forgiven between me and Him."

Still another letter reads, "You have been a source of inspiration to me ever since I discovered your program on the TV a year ago. I was so despondent about life—I had lost confidence in everyone and had forgotten that there was a God and that I should give thanks for the heartaches I was experiencing. You helped me to find myself again and return to God."

From a Methodist minister, we got this word, "I want to thank you for bringing the gospel message in the 'Hour of Power" to our nation's capital."

It is not uncommon for us to receive comments like, "I want to thank you for helping me. If it hadn't been for you, I think I would have committed suicide this past year. Your power of positive thinking is wonderful. I now truly believe in God."

Or, "Although I am of the Jewish faith, you have helped me to realize that through God and love all things are possible."

Here is another one, "I came from India; before I had a Hindu religion, but after hearing your speech, I became a Christian and I accept Jesus Christ as my personal Savior."

In another letter from a Catholic nun are these words, "It was beautiful and cheerful and dynamic this morning. You, Doctor, are always so orthodox, so authentic, so Catholic."

These are only a sampling of the letters we have received here at the Hour of Power, but they are quite representative. I know Bob wishes that he could read every one over and over personally, but he does receive a random sampling of the mail every week. I know it thrills and encourages him to hear of the work the Holy Spirit accomplishes through his ministry, as it does all of us who have the privilege of reading the letters we receive.

We also get a small percentage of negative mail. Most of it is either complaining that Bob doesn't preach the Bible or that the viewer hasn't yet received the item he had requested. Occasionally we will get complaints regarding a guest we have had in the pulpit or a guest soloist. There's not a whole lot we can do about negative mail other than check to make sure that the gifts have gone out. It is impossible to please everyone, no matter how hard we try.

Lots of people look at the Hour of Power, see the direct-mail pieces it generates, and figure that Robert Schuller is getting rich off of religious television. Nothing could be farther from the truth. In fact, he does not receive, nor has he ever received, a dime from the Hour of Power, even though he works long hours in his capacity there. Nor does he siphon money from it in other ways. He receives a salary from the church, as any pastor does, but it is nowhere near commensurate with the size of the congregation nor the income of the church itself. His books and his speaking engagements are the major source of his income, as well as an inheritance from his father. And from his personal resources, he gives back to the church each year more money than they pay him for his annual salary.

It is true, however, that the Hour of Power does generate a sizable income from its direct-mail pieces and from the donations sent in by its viewers. About 40 percent of the letters we receive contain donations. It must be remembered that "Hour of Power" does not have sponsors who pay for its television air time. It is a syndicated program and must pay each one of its stations individually for the time it spends on the air. Television air time costs increase yearly, and right now it costs six hundred fifty thousand dollars a month, or eight million dollars a year, to purchase time on the stations where we are seen. Add onto that the enormous costs of renting the technical equipment we use in the TV production and editing, and the costs of maintaining the building and paying the salaries of our employees, and even the purchasing of office machines and paper and other supplies, and you're talking about an incredibly expensive operation.

In an interview on the Phil Donahue Show one time, different members of the audience questioned Bob at length about the money that is generated by religious television. One in particular said that he just couldn't justify the priorities. In rebuttal, Bob said, "Let me be forthright about it. We have two choices: either to have a television ministry or not to have it. And believe me, I weigh that every year. If we have it it's going to be very expensive. The point is, we are reaching a lot of people for the dollars, and we can't do it any cheaper. The question, I guess, is, 'Is it worth it?' I think it is. The other day I received a phone call from Lee Beirning in Sioux City, Iowa. He's ten years old and he's dying of bone cancer. He watches me every Sunday, and he said, 'Dr. Schuller, I'm dying; but boy, thanks. Don't ever go off the air.' "

He is only one, but there are more. In an airplane recently, Bob was approached by a nice-looking young man. As he began to speak it was obvious that he had some sort of problem; perhaps he was drunk or mentally retarded. His words were very guttural and extremely slurred, but his smile was genuine. "Dr. Schuller," he began, "your ministry has changed my life and given me the desire to go on living. I had cancer of the mouth, and the doctors removed nearly all of my tongue. I was so depressed, I didn't want to live anymore. Then my dad told me to watch your program." Tears filled his eyes. "I've accepted Christ as my Savior, and He has given me back my will to live. Now I just take one day at a time, and I've got a brand new life." He beamed.

Each of the television ministries of our country, I'm sure, has hundreds, even thousands of stories like these of lives that have been touched through them. We are in a period of revival in some respects, and surely God is using the mass media to reach as many people as possible. He has chosen certain men and women to be used in this unique field of evangelism, and I personally believe that the choice is His. I am not about to question God's omnipotence in this matter or in any other. When I see people who were lost and stumbling in empty lives but who have come to a saving knowledge of Christ because of a television ministry, I know that God is blessing the electronic ministries.

Surely He is not willing that any should perish but that all should have eternal life, abundant life forever. God knows each of us so well. He knows what will appeal to us individually. He knows the number of people who can best be reached in their own little neighborhood church, and he is also well aware of the ones who would never set foot inside such a place, but who would watch a program on television. God knows that the needs of individuals are different and require different means to meet them. But the men and women who carry out His work here on earth are not perfect. We are all going to fail Him at one time or another. We're all going to be less than He would like us to be. And that goes for our organizations, from the tiny neighborhood churches all the way up to the massive television ministries.

Nevertheless, God is working through us, through all of us who are committed to His service. And even the weakness of our humanity can be used to His glory.

9

THE THEOLOGY OF SELF-ESTEEM

OVER THE YEARS, many people have been confused as to just where Robert Schuller stands theologically. He has a heavy following in liberal as well as evangelical circles and has been well accepted by Full Gospel Christians. This makes him everybody's target; the liberals complain that he is too conservative, the conservatives that he is too liberal. Most of them probably don't understand where he is.

It frustrates Bob that he doesn't feel respected by some of his peers, and it is true that retailing religion doesn't carry exactly the same connotation that evangelizing the world does. Possibility thinking doesn't sound quite as spiritual as faith, either. And yet the terms are synonymous. Bob Schuller believes in the total gospel, and his church tries to meet the mental, social, physical, and spiritual needs of the community it serves. He has a basic commitment to Christ and to reaching the unchurched with the good news of salvation through Christ, but adds that he is just as interested in the social gospel as in the gospel of saving souls. He is quite adamant that the whole gospel has not been preached when a man's soul is saved. He believes that the only way to self-respect and self-love is through creative achievement.

I feel that Bob would like very much to be accepted and respected by other pastors and theologians for his contributions in the areas of theology and church growth. He has written many books, some seventeen in all, but none of them have been on the level of the theologian. All have been directed, as has his entire ministry, toward reaching the unchurched. Perhaps he has felt in the past that he didn't have the age or the personal clout to be well received as the author of such a book. Whatever the reasons, they no longer are an obstacle, for his own personal theology is the subject of a recently published book entitled *Self-Esteem: The New Reformation*. Bob describes his theology as possibility thinking, the systematic theology of self-esteem. Only time will tell how well it will be accepted by his peers, but I know he is hoping it will start a reformation, that it will have a profound impact on theology. At the very least, he feels it will give more credibility to his work.

In a letter he wrote to the Reverend Jesse Jackson several years ago, after a chance meeting on an elevator in Chicago, Bob Schuller outlined his basic theological position in four points:

1. I am a believer in Jesus Christ, and have accepted him as my personal Lord and Savior. In that sense, I am of the Evangelical theological tradition.

2. I believe in positive thinking. It is almost as important as the resurrection of Jesus Christ. A negative-thinking Christian isn't much good to God or to his fellowmen.

3. I believe in the reality of the Holy Spirit. And I believe that I am a Holy Spirit-filled person. I pray for this. I believe in prayer. And I pray constantly for the "fruits of the Holy Spirit" as mentioned in Galatians 5:22.

4. I believe that the real fruits of the Holy Spirit, the reality of Christ, and the excitement of positive thinking come together as we create a world of brotherhood.

Bob feels that he has been called by God to take what he calls the systematic approach to theology rather than the more traditional Biblical approach. He contends this is because the people he is trying to reach don't accept the Bible. If he starts out by quoting heavily from a source that most of them don't consider reliable, he's not going to get to first base. He speaks with tongue in cheek of some fundamentalists who worship the Holy Quadrangle: Father, Son, Holy Spirit, and Holy Bible. For that reason, he doesn't consider himself to be a fundamentalist.

He believes that the Holy Spirit is the servant of the Lord, who is the incarnate Word. When he speaks of preaching the Word, he means he is preaching Christ. Christ is the Savior, the Bible is not. He believes that the Scriptures are meant to be the servant of Christ, not the master of Christ. By this, he doesn't mean to imply that he doesn't think God blesses all the many evangelists who use the Biblical approach to lead people to Jesus. He also acknowledges that there are those people who receive Christ into their lives just by reading the Bible. Bob accepts the Bible as God's revealed truth and knows that God speaks through it for the salvation of the world. He is only pointing out that the Book itself is not the Lord. He calls Jesus Christ the North Star, saying that if we keep our eyes on Him we will find life, salvation, hope, and healing.

Bob contends that the fact that his own theology is more systematically-based than Bible-based doesn't mean that it is anti-Bible. He knows it must be Biblical or it will not have integrity. He feels the systematic approach will communicate more effectively with the unchurched he is trying to reach; and he has developed quite an intricate system of theological concepts that undergird everything he does, even though he rarely speaks of them. The guiding premise of his theology is that the one basic, deepest, most profound need of human beings the world over is the need for self-esteem.

Bob likes to lead his listeners or readers through what he calls the infant and uncertain science of psychiatry because its great leaders have also sought to define man's greatest needs. He looks first at that great Jewish psychiatrist, Sigmund Freud, who said the ultimate hunger was the "will to pleasure." Freud felt that sickness and neuroses were the result of that hunger being frustrated. Another of the great Jewish psychiatrists, Alfred Adler, said Freud was too shallow in his thinking; the deepest human need, as he saw it, was the "will to power." He pointed out that people will forsake all kinds of pleasure to drive themselves to reach the top of the ladder, whether it be professional, academic, physical, or financial success. They will willingly go to war and risk death in the push for power and recognition. The third great Jewish psychiatrist Bob likes to mention is Abraham Maslow, with his theories on self-actualization. Probably his favorite, though, is Viktor Frankel, who said man's greatest need is more than pleasure, more than power, more than self-actualization. The ultimate hunger is the hunger for meaning.

Bob maintains that none of these concepts is totally wrong and none of them is totally right. Deeper than these is the need for self-esteem. Bob considers himself to be a historic Christian and a Calvinist. However, one of the places where his own theology differs from that of Calvin and the mainline church is in his conception of original sin. The reformed tradition believes that original sin is rebellion against God, but Bob sees this as shallow theology. He feels a distinction should be made between Adam's sin and original sin. Yes, Adam's sin was rebellion against God. He was created sinless, and he deliberately chose to rebel. Thereafter, he was overcome with feelings of guilt and ran and hid in the bushes.

Bob says that the rest of mankind was born in the bushes; they never had firsthand, experiential knowledge of the beauty of God like Adam and Eve did. He believes that rebellion is only an outward manifestation of an inward condition with which we are all born, the very core of which is a negative self-image. In other words, we are all born without trust. Why else, he asks, would a dying man rebel against salvation? Why else do lonely people run away from real love and friendship? That is why the building of self-esteem is such an integral part of Schuller's theology.

Dr. Schuller draws some of his authority on this subject from Erik Erikson, one of today's giants in the field of child psychiatry. Dr. Erikson believes that children are born without trust, which he says is a learned response. Bob cites accepted practices in neonatal intensive care units around the country, where nurses are instructed to stroke and talk to the tiny premature infants in their care. He equates this to his own pulpit strategy; he smiles a lot, makes people relax and laugh; he's giving them sounds and strokes because he believes that people who don't trust need to be stroked.

Unless trust is adequate, all kinds of defense mechanisms enter the picture. People don't trust, so they wear masks; at their deepest levels they find it impossible to be totally honest, even with those they love. Finally the whole personality becomes a series of tensions and worries and fears and guilts and ambitions and ego trips until at last you arrive at the exterior symptom of all these problems—rebellion against God. Bob Schuller is saying, "Let's look at the core; let's deal with the root problem, not just the symptom."

How do you change the core of a person? Do you go up to him and say, "You are a rebellious, dirty, rotten sinner?" Bob shouts an emphatic "No!" And yet, in seminary Bob was taught that the ideal sermon has three parts:

1. Tell the people what terrible sinners they are.
2. Generate a sense of guilt within them.
3. Give them the good news that they can be forgiven.

The three-part sermon is patterned, in part, after the Heidelberg Catechism with its three important things people need to know:

1. How great are my sins and miseries.
2. How Jesus can deliver me from them.
3. How I can show my true thankfulness to God for my deliverance.

Bob has no argument with any of these. It's just that he earnestly believes that this is not the best approach to take to win the unchurched to Christ. He likes to use just one point, "My only comfort in life and death is that I, with body and soul, am not my own but belong to my faithful Savior Jesus Christ." Then as Bob would say, "Wow! That feeds my self-esteem. If He is mine and I belong to Him, then I am somebody!"

He doesn't feel that there is anything that would provoke Jesus to wrath more quickly than ministers not communicating to sinners the grace of God. And he defines God's grace as God's love in action for people who don't deserve it. The theology of self-esteem is a theology of communication. You never communicate with people by insulting them, manipulating them, or intimidating them. You can't bring about effective change within personalities by continuing to batter their self-respect and insult their dignity and violate their self-esteem.

Of course Bob believes in the virgin birth of Jesus Christ and he believes in the deity of Christ as total God and total man. He believes that Christ died a vicarious death on the cross for the sins of mankind in order to restore us to a right relationship with God. He believes that in the resurrection of Christ all believers have eternal life. He believes in a literal heaven and hell and in a literal devil. He believes in the second coming of Christ. He believes in a final judgment of humanity by Christ based upon each person's relationship to Him. He believes in the doctrine of the Trinity, and in the work of the Holy Spirit in a Christian's life. He believes in the necessity of a single, life-changing conversion experience—a new birth into God's family through Christ. He believes in a life of holiness and purity that reflects the moral perfection of God. He believes and accepts all of the historic doctrines of Christianity, the Nicene Creed, the Apostles' Creed; and yet I doubt he would ever choose the words I have used to describe his beliefs. He speaks a different language entirely, which probably accounts for his popularity with the unchurched and the confusion he sometimes brings to Christian circles.

When Bob Schuller speaks of salvation, he is most likely to recite, in an ultra-dramatic manner, the last minutes of Miguel de Cervantes' *Don Quixote*. Done in the theatre as *Man of La Mancha,* it is far and away Bob's favorite story. He sees it as an analogy; Don Quixote is the Christ symbol and the harlot Aldonza symbolizes humanity. He believes that Cervantes had experienced an authentic conversion to a vital relationship with Christ during the Spanish Inquisition and that he wanted to communicate the truths he had learned, but was not permitted to do so due to the extreme religious climate of the day. So he chose to write a parable.

Bob sees in the foolishness of Don Quixote, tilting at windmills, what mankind sees in Jesus. There is a misunderstanding of the wisdom of God that sometimes makes it seem as foolish as an old man brandishing his sword at the blades of a windmill. "Am I crazy because I see the world as it could become?" asks the old knight. "Or are you crazy because you only see it as it is?" Bob does not see idealists as crazy; he tends more to think of people who see the world only as it is as crazy. They're not creative, they're not uplifting sources. They don't dream beautiful dreams, and because they're not part of the solution, they keep the world just as it is.

In the squalor of a wayside inn, Don Quixote discovers the prostitute Aldonza. He doesn't consider her vocation, is quite blind to it, in fact. When he looks at her, he doesn't see the filth, the unkempt hair, the torn clothes, the haggard face creased with years of sin. He looks upon her with eyes of love and sees only the beauty for which she had been designed, the queen of God's creation. "My lady," he calls her in a voice of utmost compassion and tenderness. "I shall call you Dulcinea," which translated would mean sweetheart or precious. Regardless of the contempt with which she holds him, regardless of the crudity of her language and her manner, Don Quixote keeps right on loving her. "My lady, Dulcinea."

In the last minutes of the play, the old man is dying, just like Jesus, from a broken heart. He has been despised and rejected by the people he had sought to help. Suddenly his room is transformed by the entrance of a beautiful, regal lady. She is dressed in mantilla and lace, like a Spanish queen; and she kneels at his bedside and prays. "My lord," she says, "you gave me a new name. You called me Dulcinea." She rises and stands proudly, "I am your lady." Symbolically, she has been born again.

It's not fair, says Bob Schuller, to be angry with people and to call them sinners. Like Aldonza, they are scared; they don't know how to face terror. Sometimes they don't even know how to face themselves. Jesus, like Don Quixote, once treated a harlot like a lady. Even though the mob's appetite for violence was almost out of control, His compassion prevented them from stoning her to death. He looked at her and saw not her shame; but from the depths of His love He said, "Neither do I condemn you."

Bob also has another way of looking at situations like this. He says:

> Suppose someone who is my equal invites me to have coffee with him. I will enjoy it, but it will not do much for my self-esteem, one way or the other. But suppose the President of the United States invites me into the Oval Office for a visit; that would give my self-esteem quite a boost. Of course at any given time, about 50 percent of the people are unhappy with the president, no matter who he is. Is there anyone who most everybody agrees is perfect? Who is accepted by all as the Ideal One? I say He is Jesus Christ, the Lamb of God without spot or blemish.
>
> What would I do if He called me on the phone and said, "Schuller, I want to meet you. Let's get together." I figure He is going to have a large crowd there, because really important people rarely have time for one to one relationships. But when I arrive, He is all alone, just waiting for me. He talks with me as if He really respected me, and I am thinking that if He knew me better, He wouldn't feel the same way. But then He comes over and puts His arm around me and looks right at me with His beautiful eyes and says: "You know Bob, I need you. I'd like to live my life through

yours, if you'll let me." Well, I'd probably look at Him and tell Him that there are imperfect things about me with which He wouldn't want to be associated.

"You don't deserve to be embarrassed by me," I would tell Him. "I'm not good enough for you."

But then He takes off His robe of righteousness and drapes it around me. "Here, wear it," He says. And I am declared righteous by the Person of God. The righteousness of Christ is imputed, freely given to me, as if I were perfect, as if I had never sinned, as if I had fulfilled all righteousness.

When you meet an Ideal One who knows you as you really are, but treats you as if you were as perfect as He is, you have a psychological, existential encounter with grace at the most profound level. That is when you are literally born again. That is when you begin to accept yourself. Real self-esteem comes, and you can dare to accept the Holy Spirit and become a channel for His fruits of love and joy and peace. Then you don't need your old defense mechanisms anymore; you can let go of the fears, the angers, the guilts, and at last the rebellion against God.

In order to lead people to salvation, Bob believes you must first introduce them to Jesus, the Ideal One. Jesus knows all of their sins, and they know that He knows; but He treats them as if they were perfect. In the light of that burning love, they experience saving grace; they are declared righteous by the Son of God. Bob tells his congregation, whether they are in the church or reading one of his books or listening to him on television, that they can experience new life by admitting that they need help, that they can't do it alone. He tells them to ask for the power of God, to be grafted into Jesus Christ.

Although Dr. Schuller takes a roundabout way of getting there, a way that many fundamentalists wouldn't approve, he eventually arrives at the same destination as they. Many of his messages are just going over different roads to that same terminus. While the fundamentalists' route may lead through the meadows, and attract a certain type of person, Bob walks by the seashore bringing others along. Those that he has brought most likely wouldn't have followed the man going by the more direct route. What speaks to one individual won't necessarily speak to another. But Bob is a genius at thinking up different ways to say the same thing. Sooner or later he hits upon the right combination.

Bob realizes that there are some people in all different denominations who claim to be Christians, who claim to have been born again, who love the Scriptures, who know all the right answers; but they are very short on kindness and forgiveness. They lack love and compassion. He believes that these Christians had the seeds of salvation planted in the soil of their soul's shame instead of in the remnant of their soul's self-esteem. It is his contention that the person who is converted out of shame still has his basic core of negative self-image.

When you appeal to a person's self-esteem as a strategy for conversion, you produce a different kind of Christian than when you appeal to personal shame and degradation and insecurity. Bob likes to tell people that God thinks they are wonderful; that He loves them so much that He would stop at nothing, not even death on a cross, to make them His friends again. That builds self-esteem.

Robert Ardrey, the famous anthropologist and behavioral scientist, once said that there were three fundamental, authentic human needs: identity, stimulation, and security. He went on to say that there was only one way for all of these needs to be met and that was through war. Bob Schuller, however, believes that these three basic human needs can only be truly met through salvation.

The Christian receives his identity in knowing that he is a child of God. He knows that he was created in God's image and that he was brought into God's family by God's own Son. He has a purpose, a direction for his life in living it for God. And he has the knowledge that he will spend eternity living with God in heaven. His is a life of faith, which is the natural air he was created to breathe. Stimulation comes from knowing God personally and from being involved with His people. To have intimate contact with the creator of the entire universe has got to be the very most exciting and satisfying relationship of all. Knowing that God is watching over us and accomplishing His plans for our lives brings more security than it could ever be possible to have any other way. As Bob puts it, God saves us from negative forces, negative thinkers, negative vibrations, and negative powers in the world around us. We are safe forever.

In his theology of salvation, Bob makes a distinction between self-esteem and self-will. Self-will is a sin, and he sees it as a result of not having adequate self-esteem. People who have low self-esteem are defensive and insecure, they are often pushy and rude. Bob understands self-esteem to be the fruit of salvation. He doesn't agree with other preachers who glibly drop words like selfish and self-centered, as if the ideal person were one whose self was dead. They often quote verses such as, "It is no longer I who live, but Christ who lives in me" (Gal. 2:20, RSV). Dr. Schuller, of course, is not about to argue with St. Paul; but feels that he is speaking here of the redemption of the ego, not the destruction of the ego. A person who no longer has any self-consciousness is no longer a person, but a puppet, and God did not create puppets.

In addition to self-love, Bob also speaks of three other kinds of love: (1) I love you because I need you is strictly a selfish love; (2) I love you because I want you is just another way to describe lust; (3) I love you because you need me is what Bob describes as Christian love. He feels that only those who have high self-esteem through Christ's transforming power can truly exhibit this, the highest form of love. Most pastors would call this agape love, from the Greek word for God's love; but Bob feels that the unchurched are not going to relate well to Greek, so he prefers to couch it in modern terms.

He often tells people to look only to Jesus for instruction about real love, the kind of love that gives itself away to others. Jesus is the authority on the subject, he says. Bob likes to relate a story about one of his travels when he stopped at an airport counter for Fannie Mae Candies. He was conversing with the clerk about the various kinds of chocolates and was amazed when a woman standing near him began to interrupt them. "You should try the creams. They're really very nice," she interjected. "Or maybe you might like an assortment with nuts." Every time the salesgirl tried to tell him about the candies, this woman would interrupt her and give her own opinion. Bob was really becoming annoyed with her. At length she left, and the clerk behind the counter let out a sigh of relief. "Okay, girls," she called to some other workers. "You can come out now. Fannie Mae is gone." Here Bob realized that he had been listening to the clerk when the creator of the candies was standing right there trying to give him advice. "We pastors and teachers are only the clerks," he reiterates. "When you want to learn about perfect love, go to the authority; go to Jesus."

People often think Bob doesn't preach about sin, and it is true that he hates to call people sinners. But that doesn't mean he doesn't deal with the gut issues of sin. He does, but in a unique way. He feels that most people already know that they're sinners. They don't need Robert Schuller to tell them. In fact, they don't want to hear about it at all, just like the fat man who doesn't want to step on the scales. Bob always tries to deal with sin in a positive way; when you attack sin negatively, people turn you off. They think religion is just a list of restrictions anyway; and if a minister is constantly enumerating their sins, they will never get to know Jesus and find out that Christianity is not so much a religion as it is a relationship. And it is the nature of the relationship that takes care of the sin problem anyway.

Bob has a series of messages entitled "Ten Creative Commandments for Constructive and Creative Living," which is just a fancy way to say the Ten Commandments. But it makes them exciting and interesting to the unchurched, most of whom would never subject themselves to a sermon on rules and regulations. In a positive way, he lets them know what is expected of them by God and that if they will meet these expectations, they will be better, happier, more fulfilled people. It hurts Bob that more and more Americans are rejecting God's commandments. He believes, with many others, that the country is not experiencing a rich outpouring of God's blessing because of its flagrant disregard for traditional values. He speaks of Jesus, who said you can't plant thistles and reap grapes; and says he fears America will be reaping bitter fruit in the future.

When he speaks of laws, Bob will often speak of physical, spiritual, and moral laws at the same time. With the current concern for physical fitness, people can easily identify when he says that we should take good care of our bodies. If we choose to abuse them by excess food, drink, drugs, or work, and give them too little exercise and rest, they are going to give us trouble. Likewise, he says our spirits need constant recharging. We need to feed our minds on God's Word, and our inspirational tanks can only hold a seven-day supply at best. If our spiritual batteries aren't kept charged, we start to sputter. To Bob's way of thinking, the moral law is encapsulated in the Ten Commandments. He says we must obey the physical, spiritual, and moral laws if we don't want to have trouble in our lives. He is quick to explain it is not a threat, but only a warning given in love.

In Possibility Thinking, though, Bob looks deeper than the classical definition of sin, embracing what he calls his theology of social ethics. He asks the question, "What makes an act right or wrong? Sinful or unsinful?" He believes that the answer lies in whether it builds self-respect or annihilates a person's self-dignity. He doesn't believe that any person has the right to use sarcasm or irony or insult to make a point. Communication should be done in such a way as to show respect for the other person, even though we don't agree with their position. An act is constructive if it raises the collective self-esteem level in a society. When anyone insults a human being by failing to treat them with respect, grace, or courtesy, he is violating that person's right to self-dignity and self-esteem. And in Schuller theology, that is a grave sin indeed. That's why you will often hear Bob speak out against preachers who use their pulpit as an authoritarian platform to condemn and induce guilt in people rather than to show them the way to forgiving love. He feels that in so doing, they are damaging their audience's right to self-respect. He has even been known to say that, in his opinion, that is the ultimate sin.

Most people know that Bob Schuller is extremely big on success, but his gospel of success is greatly misunderstood by many. He doesn't mean success the way the world means success. His idea of success is for you to fulfill God's plan for your life, to become the person God wants you to be. It is the worldly who measure success by material standards, but Bob has never espoused those standards. He thinks in terms of bringing a person back to a right relationship with God by the saving grace of Jesus—getting him away from sins that were destroying him before his conversion, ridding him of the guilt and lack of self-esteem that these sins brought upon him. He considers being successful the overcoming of difficulty; tribulation; physical, emotional, mental, and financial handicaps.

The Schuller's eldest daughter Sheila inherited from her parents a beautiful singing voice as well as a flair for the dramatic. In high school, she always played leading parts in school musical productions and plays. Once, as they were preparing to perform *Brigadoon,* her teacher made it known that she wanted her to audition for the part of Meg, the comedic "naughty lady" of the story. As she read over her lines, Sheila knew that as a Christian she could not in good conscience portray the character of Meg. Her heart sank as she realized she would have to disappoint her teacher and probably miss her opportunity to do something that mattered very much to her.

When the day of the auditions arrived, Sheila tried to sing for another part in the play; but her teacher refused her, making quite a scene. For a reserved teenage girl to be so humiliated before her peers was a crushing blow. She was so flustered, she barely knew how to handle the situation without bursting into tears; but she managed to stand up before a large group of students and teachers and explain that as a Christian girl, committed to moral excellence, she would be unable to play the role of Meg. As she had feared, she lost the chance to perform in the play. By the time her dad arrived to pick her up, she was consumed with feelings of failure and inadequacy, and threw herself tearfully into his arms.

Bob caressed her long brown hair gently, letting her sob. Safely in the car, the world shut out and far away, he turned her face toward his. "Sheila," he began, "I think you were wonderful, and I'm so proud of you. You did a fine thing today. Far from being a failure by losing a part in the play, you were a super success." At this his voice crescendoed. "You stood up for what you knew was right, even though it hurt. God used your pain to witness to all those kids and teachers about what is moral and good. They know where you stand now, and they won't forget it. You did what God wanted you to do—and that's success."

I am reminded of another daughter with long brown hair—my little girl. Her name is Tara; and unlike Sheila Schuller, she cannot carry a tune in a bucket, though she loves to sing. In fact, there is not a lot Tara can do that would compare with most little girls. I well remember the first time I brought Bob Schuller to my home to meet her. It was before I had come to work for him, but he already knew about Tara and had been anxious to see her. We drove the twenty-five miles from the church to our home in Mission Viejo, parked the car, and went inside. As we started up the stairs, we could hear the singing; two or three women's voices mingled with that of a tone-deaf child in a rousing rendition of "Jesus loves me."

We entered Tara's workroom; and I think Bob was rather shocked to see this dark-haired little girl with braids, dressed in a lavender leotard, grinning broadly from underneath a wheeled table to which she was strapped. She was delighted to see him and greeted him with peals of laughter and a soft hello. She was five years old at the time. And had been profoundly brain injured since the age of two. She had been working eight hours a day for the past three years in what proved to be a futile attempt to put life back into her useless limbs.

Bob strode over to her and cupped her small face in his massive hands. "Tara," he said, "you look beau-tee-ful. What are you doing?"

"I'm creeping in my turtle," she flashed her hazel eyes in his direction. "It's new."

I explained that since she was unable to get up on her hands and knees, her therapists had placed her underneath the table with legs that had wheels on the bottom. She was suspended there, where gravity couldn't drag her frail body down, so that she could get the feel of being three dimensional, so she could try to move her arms and legs and propel herself along.

Bob was fascinated. "How wonderful this must be for her self-esteem, to get her up off the floor and let her see the world from another angle. This is a peak experience for her, isn't it? And it gives her a peek at what it might be like were she ever to learn to crawl. It's marvelous."

He stood there for several minutes, watching her labor to move her limbs in a functional manner, struggling to move even one foot across the floor. I turned around and he was gone. He didn't return, so I went looking for him. He stood in a nearby bedroom, his face covered by his hands. He felt my presence and quickly dabbed at his eyes, which were brimming with tears.

Ever since that day, Tara has held a special place in Bob's heart. His theory on "Peak to Peek" was born in Tara's workroom, and he has included her on his list of super successful people. She has been the subject of many a sermon illustration. He loves her because she is an overcomer. Tara will never be able to walk or run or ride a bike or dance or lead cheers at a football game or get married or have children or hold a job. She will never be able to do any of the things that the world says are necessary to be successful. But she is successful in ways that many others will never be. She worked to achieve her potential, and she has achieved it against overriding odds. She has learned to be happy in all circumstances and some of her happiness rubs off on those around her. She loves God and serves him in patience and compassion. That's success.

Bob has given many different definitions of success. One is that it is a study of the flow of power—how to get it, how to redeem it, how and when to restrain it, how to use it, how not to abuse it. He sees the alternative to this as weakness. As he puts it, "In a world where there is so much sin and injustice and pain and death, God's people can use all the power they can get. To deliberately select the philosophy or the theological position that leads to weakness and inadequacy can never be justified."

He tempers these bold words with more of a revelation of what he thinks constitutes success. "In possibility thinking theology, you will never succeed unless you perform the servant role. And the servant role is inconceivable without the Cross. There is no way we can serve people without getting involved with them and their problems. In fulfilling the role of servant, we help people who are hurting; the bottom line is that we achieve our own self-esteem by building self-esteem in others.

Dr. Schuller likes to paraphrase John Calvin, who said that we are fallen creatures and like fallen creatures we are cracked cathedrals. The windows may be falling out and the tower may be leaning; it may be no more than an ancient ruin, but it's still a cathedral. Bob sees success as developing the possibilities within people so that they can discover their divine heritage and their self-esteem in the process. His theology of success is a belief that God communicates ideas that will help us discover our inherent potential, the outcome of which is that we will become the people we were created to be. And that's glorifying God.

In a world where churches and human values are declining, divorce is rampant, the family is ruptured, addiction to narcotics and alcohol is a part of everyday life, and suicide has reached epidemic proportions, Christians cannot afford to make room for failure in their thinking. Bob believes that anyone who calls himself a Christian and is interested in helping people who are hurting must be success oriented, unless he has a better way to solve these human conditions.

More than anything else, Bob looks at success as developing the God-given potential that lies within each human being. He doesn't necessarily mean financial success, but when he speaks to other ministers about church growth, he does say that if they really do succeed, the money will probably flow to their work. He objects to the hypocrisy he sees in some Christian circles, where there are those who object to professional fund raising and put down those who suggest techniques for increasing funds; yet these same people are often the first ones to ask for money to finance their programs. It also frustrates him when people criticize possibility thinking because it tells people how they can make money; then in their next breath they launch into a tirade about the evils of poverty.

Bob has his own way of combating poverty. It's not militant or political, it's not done through crusades or handouts or protest marches. He says, "The secret to solving the poverty problem is to develop possibilities within people to be creative so that they can become prosperous and develop self-respect in the process." He decries the fact that many have discarded the Puritan work ethic and feels that we can't expect to succeed and generate pride in ourselves if we don't develop our potential.

The solution does not lie in the redistribution of wealth. Bob has traveled twice to the Soviet Union and once inside Red China; he has seen firsthand what happens when you try to redistribute wealth. He was disturbed by the decay he saw in mainland China, comparing it to what would happen if the poorest of the poor in our country were to suddenly be given the governor's mansion. These poor, uneducated people, with no income, no job, no idea how to care for a fine home and property, arrive at the mansion where they will live for free. It's theirs. Within a month, a window breaks; they have no money, so they don't repair it. They can't pay the gardener, so he quits and the grounds soon become overgrown with weeds. They can't afford to have the house painted, so the paint begins to peel and chip. The plumbing needs repair and soon they are not able to use the elegant indoor bathrooms. After a few years, the mansion is nothing but a shambles. The decay he saw in China ate at Bob; he hated to see people living in these conditions when he knew there was a better way.

"Not to fight poverty has to be a sin, because poverty demeans people." Bob says, "It robs them of their dignity, it strips them of their self-respect; it makes them feel like pawns being manipulated." Bob feels that these people should be motivated; they should be taught that they have value, that it's possible for them to make something of their lives. At the deepest level, self-esteem and success are synonymous; therefore, Bob wishes that everyone could be successful.

Once on a trip to New York City, he was picked up by a black cab driver who had a large gold ring through his nose. When he realized the identity of his passenger, he began to speak animatedly, the ring wiggling with each word. "Dr. Schuller," he began, "I can't believe I'm really meeting you in person! You changed my life! I was born and raised in Harlem; I dropped out of school in the eighth grade. I was raised on welfare and I stayed on welfare. I didn't know any other way. I was angry and bitter about everything. Then one morning, my wife and I were flipping the channels on our television set, and there you were. You were smiling and waving your arms and bragging about everything being possible. It made me mad, and I turned to my wife and said, 'Sure. It's possible if you're white and live in California by Disneyland.'

"She said I was just the kind of person you were talking about—an impossibility thinker.

" 'You could get a job if you wanted to.'

"And that made me even madder. I told her I knew I couldn't; I couldn't do anything.

" 'You can drive a car, can't you?' She said. 'You could be a cab driver.'

" 'No, I couldn't; you know they wouldn't hire me; they don't want blacks.'

"But she wouldn't leave me alone. 'That's negative thinking,' she said.

"So the next day I called the cab company; sure enough, the first question they asked me was whether I was black or white. 'I'm black,' I told the man, and I figured I would never get a job.

"But he said, 'Thank God. We really need black cab drivers in Harlem.'

"I've been driving a cab ever since. My wife was so inspired that she went back to school and became a secretary. We both have jobs and it's great. We're even saving our money to buy a little house."

If enough people can be so inspired to see the contribution they have to make to society and so motivated to get out there and see what they can accomplish, the poverty problem would likely take care of itself in many instances. And I think people realize this. "The Hour of Power" is extremely popular with nearly all the ethnic and minority groups for this very reason; it inspires them to reach for their God-given potential. Like Ethel Waters, whom Bob loves to quote, they are learning, "God don't sponsor no flops."

If self-esteem breeds success, success breeds self-esteem. Bob's possibility thinking says it must be possible—somehow there is bound to be a way. It teaches people to believe in their own brilliance and in their own ideas, which come from God.

Bob deplores what he calls negative programming. He loves to say, "I am not what I think I am. I am not what you think I am. I am what I think you think I am." He believes that preachers can make people sin by constantly telling them they are sinners, and he feels strongly that it is amazing what people can do if they have not been programmed to believe that they can't.

Once on an airplane, Bob sat next to a meek little fellow who had his head buried in a book. Bob opened his briefcase to study for his Sunday morning message, and the man glanced over to see a copy of one of his books with a picture of him on the cover.

"Is that you?" he inquired.

"Yes, it is."

"Do you write books?"

"Yes."

"What subject do you write about?"

"Possibility thinking," Bob replied.

"I write books too," the little man said.

"Oh, really?" Bob was becoming interested, "What about?"

"Mathematics."

Bob knew then that they had nothing in common. Mathematics was the one subject that had always defied his mastery. But then he had an intriguing thought. "You know," he said, "in mathematics it doesn't matter whether you are a possibility thinker or an impossibility thinker. Two plus two equals four regardless of whether you are a negative or a positive person."

"Well, I'm not so sure about that," his seat partner interrupted him. "Let me tell you about myself. My name is George Danzig, and I am in the physics department at Stanford University. I've just returned from Vienna as the American delegate to the International Mathematics Convention, appointed by the President. I was a senior at Stanford during the Depression; we knew when the class graduated, we'd all be joining unemployment lines. There was a slim chance that the top man in class might get a teaching job, but that was about it. I wasn't at the head of my class, but I hoped that if I were able to score a perfect paper on the final exam, I might be given a job opportunity."

He paused to swallow, blinking behind his glasses. "I studied so hard for that exam, I ended up making it to class late. When I arrived, the others were already hard at work; I was embarrassed and just picked up my paper and slunk into my desk. I sat down and worked the eight problems on the test paper and then started in on the two that were written up on the board. Try as I might, I couldn't solve either one of them. I was devastated; out of ten problems, I had missed two for sure. But just as I was about to hand in the paper, I took a chance and asked the professor if I might have a couple days to work on the two I had missed. I was surprised when he agreed, and I rushed home and plunged into those equations with a vengeance. I spent hours and hours, and finally solved one of them. I never could get the other. And when I turned in that paper, I knew I had lost all chance of a job. That was the blackest day of my life.

"The next morning I was awakened by a pounding on the door. It was my professor, all dressed up and very excited. 'George, George,' he kept shouting, 'you've made mathematics history!' Well, I didn't know what he was talking about. And then he explained. I had come to class late and had missed his opening remarks. He had been encouraging the class to keep trying, not to give up if they found some of the problems difficult. 'Don't put yourself down,' he had said. 'Remember there are classic, unsolvable problems that no one can solve. Even Einstein was unable to unlock their secrets.' And then he had written two of these unsolvable problems on the blackboard. When I came in I didn't know they were unsolvable. I thought they were part of my exam, and I was determined that I could work them properly. And I solved one! It was published in the *International Journal of Higher Mathematics*, and my professor gave me a job as his assistant. I've been at Stanford for forty-three years now." He stopped and looked piercingly at Bob. "Dr. Schuller, I'm just going to ask you one question. If I had come to class on time, do you think I would have solved that problem? I don't."

Bob's own ideas on problem solving would be similar. His approach to problems is not to give in to them or to resent them, but to dig in and find a solution. He likes permanent solutions so that you won't have to deal with the same problem or a compounded version of it at a later date. He believes that possibility thinking means finding solutions to your problems; that with God it is possible for them to be resolved. He refuses to place the blame for people's problems on God, but maintains that they are always the result of free will. Someone has made the wrong decision, but that someone is never God. God never chooses to bring tribulation upon His people, but allows it in that He grants free will within His creation. By a gift of God, we are able to invent solutions to our problems, thereby exchanging our cross for a crown, our scars for a star.

Possibility thinking says that every problem is pregnant with possibilities. Every problem is an opportunity. Bob doesn't think he would have ever grown spiritually had God not pushed him into it through the various tragedies and problems in his life. He says ultimate security is boring. For stimulation you must look for adventure; climb a mountain, take risks. Possibility thinking turns him on with energy because it helps him escape from the road of security and commits him to the road of stimulation.

Bob says the Bible tells us many times that our human energy is determined by our relationship with God. Hard work doesn't produce fatigue, and real rest doesn't heal it. Most fatigue is psychological and emotional. According to Bob, that means it is also theological. After all, everything that happens to a person—every thought, every action—is tied inexorably to God, his creator. The human soul is a unity; it can't be sliced into sections like an orange. You can't divide theology from psychology. If it is a psychological truth, it must also be a theological truth, because all truth is ultimately united in God who is Truth.

God is the cosmic source of all energy, and when we are close to God and in tune with Him, we can tap into His boundless energy. Bob believes that the best way to get energy is to spend it. Energy is not a matter of age or physical condition; it's a matter of attitude. If you need more energy, you probably need more faith in God. You need a closer relationship to Him so that He will give you new dreams and you will be busy making those dreams come true. Dreams are always seemingly impossible when they come from God—He thinks so big. Anybody who loves and moves in the will of God is going to be a high-energy person. Great activity is not caused by great energy; great activity produces great energy.

For all his positive thinking, Bob is emphatic about commitments. He sees the two as going hand in hand. He doesn't feel you can enter into the Christian life without having a definite conversion experience, and a true conversion always includes commitment. He never tells people that life is going to be easy, never promises them perfection. In his own way, complete with corny sayings, he preaches just the opposite. "There's no gain without pain." "The tassle is worth the hassle." "Set your goal, define your role, and pay your toll." One of the main points he always makes is that a life-changing experience with Christ is always necessary for a successful life. He tries to illustrate that this causes a dramatic catharsis, making it possible to turn that symbolic mountain into a gold mine; and he's not talking about money. There is no psychologist, there is no psychiatrist, there is no therapy in the world that can change human behavior like the gospel of Jesus Christ and the power of God.

Bob tells us to expect trouble in our lives, but to commit ourselves to meeting that difficulty head on with the power of God, who will give us the victory. Trouble never leaves us the way it found us. It will change us; that is unalterable. But we can choose whether it will affect us for the better or for the worse. He tells the story of a man who became completely paralyzed. A friend who had not seen him for some time came to visit him, and was struck by the beauty of his bedridden friend's face and spirit. "Sickness and trouble really color a personality, don't they?" he asked. "Yes," the invalid replied, "and I decided that I would choose the colors and make them beautiful."

That is not to say that Bob doesn't believe in the miracle-working power of God to heal both circumstances and bodily infirmities. It is certainly one of the principles of possibility thinking. "All things are possible with God." "I can do all things through Christ who strengthens me." "With God, nothing is impossible." These are basic possibility-thinking verses of Scripture, as dear to any possibility thinker as they are to the most devout charismatic.

But in regard to miracles, Bob does have some fundamental beliefs. He believes that God willfully restrains His own power in three ways. First, His power is restricted by the very nature of the universe He has created. Secondly, His power is restrained by the nature of man; and third, His power is restrained by His own character and nature. God's decision to restrain His power only glorifies Him more. Power restrained is power improved. God respects the dignity of persons in such a way that He will not overpower their decision to act, even when the action breaks one of his own commandments and even when He knows it is going to be ultimately painful for that person. Bob sees a miracle as a beautiful act of God's providence moving in a life; he feels there are many of them happening everyday. We need to learn to see them, to look for the hand of God in our lives.

One of Bob's favorite miracles happened to two dear friends of his, Anne and Benno Fisher. They were Polish Jews during World War II. They were in their early twenties, engaged to be married, and very much in love. Both of their families were thrown into concentration camps; her parents and their eight children and his parents with their ten children. In the inhumanity of that time, neither knew the whereabouts of the other nor of their own family members. In God's mercy, both Anne and Benno survived the Holocaust, but every other member of their families was exterminated. Neither knew the other had lived through that black night of terror; each presumed his loved one dead. The years passed, but neither fell in love again.

Benno, who was living in his native Poland, went to Munich, Germany, in the hopes of finding an old friend in the war-torn city. To his delight, his friend was still alive and had just learned that his own mother was still living. She was in Stuttgart, and he could hardly contain himself, so anxious was he to see her. At this news, Benno let out a little cry. "Your father died in my arms in the concentration camp. Let me go with you so I can tell her about the death of her husband."

So Benno and his friend went to Stuttgart, Germany, and visited his mother. Benno was able to tell her of the tenderness he had shared with her husband in his last days of life. He then went to catch the bus which would take him back to Poland, this being the one and only trip to Germany of his life. There at the bus stop, he was attracted to a girl who looked familiar. As he paced back and forth, staring at her, he could hardly believe his eyes. She looked just like his dear Anne. Four years ago they had hoped to marry and build a good life together, but now she was gone.

The girl's face was flushed. She knew someone was staring at her, and she turned around to get a good look at him. As their eyes met, they rushed into each others arms. Today, nearly forty years later, they have been able to build the life together that they came so close to losing. Benno's eyes brim with bears when he reminisces about that day. "It was a miracle of God. That was the only time I was ever in Stuttgart."

Bob considers himself a bridge builder; he is always looking for the best in others. He also sees his strong sense of justice as a possible detriment to bridge building, but he knows that it is God's job to judge, not his. Instead, he concentrates on being forgiving, for he knows to forgive is Christlike. When Bob has been through an offensive experience, he looks for the possibilities for good in it. He also believes that to forgive doesn't mean to just clean the slate; it is to go farther, to interact and see the possibilities of helping the person who has offended you so that he or she can become a more beautiful person.

Theologically, Robert Schuller stands right in the center, boldly waving the banner of possibility thinking just under the cross of Jesus Christ. Like all those who hold extremely strong beliefs, I'm sure he would like all Christians to espouse his positive ideas; but he would much rather concentrate on the many issues in which Christians are in agreement than to argue over the few which are controversial. Bob dislikes negativity of any kind, and controversy is negative. It is also destructive, both to the interior workings of the church of Christ and to the witness it presents to the world. It is far better, Bob believes, to present a united front to the unchurched, exhibiting the true sign of the Christian community which Jesus commanded. "By this all men will know that you are my disciples, if you have love for one another" (John 13:35, RSV).

10

Two Guys with a Dime

THE FIRST TRIP I ever took with Bob Schuller was during the summer before I went to work for him on a full-time basis. We had known each other about ten months, and had been working on one of his pet projects at the time, Freedom of Religion, or FOR. It was 1973, and already there had been rumblings in Afghanistan. Bob intuitively sensed that it was only the beginning of worse things to come for the tiny country. Christy Wilson, the pastor of the only Christian church there, had been expelled, and even the church building was in imminent danger of total physical destruction.

Bob saw this as a major thrust of Communism into that part of the world, and as is typical of his nature, he decided to see what he could do about it. Even though most of the Afghan people were not Christian, the church in Kabul was a powerful force for good in that country. It provided a place for the many English-speaking people there to worship God, and it helped to maintain the status quo.

Bob has always been extremely concerned about the people imprisoned and mistreated for their faith, no matter where and when it has occurred down through the centuries. The great Holocaust of Nazi Germany was over before Bob was old enough to play a part in trying to stop it, but he has concentrated his efforts toward helping those persecuted for their religious beliefs by communist governments. In his own way, he has tried to be a part of the solution by standing up for the freedom of all religions throughout the world.

Even though he was only on seven television stations at the time of the Afghan situation, Bob was able to garnish fifty thousand letters of protest about the treatment of Christians and Jews behind the Iron Curtain. And one bright August day the two of us set off for Washington, D.C., to see what we could accomplish. It was not the same then as it is today. The "Hour of Power" was not being televised in Washington yet, and the name Robert Schuller was virtually unknown in that part of the country. Certainly, it carried no power.

Nevertheless, we managed to secure an appointment with Senator Charles Percy. He was on the Senate Foreign Relations Committee and was a specialist on that particular part of the world, and we hoped he could shed some light on the situation for us and maybe even help us to keep the church in Kabul from being destroyed. I think both Bob and I were a little nervous as we entered the Senator's ornate office, but neither of us would have admitted it for the world.

Percy greeted us most cordially, shaking our hands and offering us a chair. He listened respectfully to Bob as he shared his concerns about Afghanistan and admitted that he had a right to be concerned about the instability of the Afghan government. In fact, he was planning a trip there himself and promised us that he would look into the plight of the church there and let us know what he found.

As we left Percy's office that day, Bob gave me one of his mischievous looks. "How do we get into the Afghan Embassy?" he queried. "Well, if you're really serious," I replied, "you call them on the phone and ask for an appointment." We went to the nearest phone booth and crammed ourselves inside. I fished in my pocket for a dime and listened as it trickled down through the payphone. We had no clout with the Afghans at all, but possibility-thinking faith and quite a bit of individual and collective gall gave us the idea that it was possible. And it was. I thought then, and we have reflected on it many times since, about the power of a dime in a phone booth. We were only two guys with a dime, a dream, and a big God, but we were able to secure an appointment with the Afghan ambassador that day. He listened to Bob air his grievances, and, who knows, maybe it helped to forestall the destruction of the only Christian church in Afghanistan for a little while.

As it turned out, one of the reasons the Afghan government wanted the church razed was because it was taller than their Islamic mosques.

They understood this to be a threat to the people. Even though we tried, the church was eventually demolished and the Christian religion forbidden in Afghanistan.

On that same trip, we were determined to personally deliver the fifty thousand letters of protest to the Russian embassy. The embassy was an imposing place, and we could feel the negative vibrations that seemed to echo off its walls and down its dark corridors. We tried, but were unable to see the Russian ambassador directly and had to settle for a second-level secretary. We were treated courteously enough, but there was an undercurrent of hostility and obvious unconcern for the imprisoned Christians in Russia. Both Bob and I were saddened that our efforts appeared to be so fruitless.

Bob has been inside Russia twice and found it to be most enlightening. Once he went for the express purpose of making contact with the underground church there and imparting encouragement to some of its members. He had been strictly warned not to identify himself as a minister of any kind, and since he had spent the summer teaching on the Chapman floating campus, he was able to declare himself a teacher with a clear conscience. He had been told that there was no reason to fear for his own safety, but that for the sake of the well-being of the Christians with whom he hoped to meet, he must maintain a low profile during his visit to the Soviet Union.

The plan was that on Tuesday evening he would take a plane from Leningrad to Kiev and then on to Lvov, which is a city in the Western Ukraine. Between nine and ten Wednesday morning, a leader from the underground church there was to meet him in the lobby of his hotel, asking him if he knew the whereabouts of Garden Grove, California. He was to answer "yes" and follow the man at a safe distance for a few blocks until it seemed safe to rendezvous and attend a meeting of the church.

On Tuesday afternoon, his government-assigned guide was escorting Bob around the Museum of Atheism in Leningrad. There, in a rather large display, were pictures of the Garden Grove Community Church, including one of Bob in his robe standing in the pulpit. It didn't take long for the guide to ascertain the identity of his visiting teacher and it became obvious that Bob was being seen in a different light. He was horrified, mainly because of his rendezvous which was only hours away. Should he keep it or not? Selfishly, he didn't want to miss what was certain to be a great spiritual experience. On a caring level, he had really hoped to be able to bring some fresh inspiration to the oppressed church, but he sure didn't want to endanger its members and their families. He had no choice but to take the flights; Russian vacations are not given to quick changes in plans, so he boarded the plane at four and flew to Kiev.

There he was met by an Intourist guide who was waiting to assist him in transferring to another plane which was to leave for Lvov in thirty-five minutes. It surprised Bob when the guide indicated that the plane was to take off from another airport. He hustled Bob and Ike Eichenberger, who is director for the Institutes for Successful Church Leadership, into the nearest cab, spoke to the driver, and away they went. It soon became obvious, even in the gathering darkness, that they were heading out into the country. With only thirty-five minutes to make the connection, Bob was very uneasy. What if they were being called in for interrogation?

A half hour passed, and they approached the skyscrapers of a large city. But still they didn't stop. Soon it was pitch black, and Bob and Ike tried to make mental note of their journey as the headlights of the cab pierced the darkness, illuminating nothing but forests and an occasional farmhouse. They were becoming really frightened when the car careened through a formal entrance into a large compound of some sort. On either side of the road were large red stars, which they recognized as the symbol of the Red Army. It turned out to be an army airport.

Bob and Ike were ushered inside a large building and ordered upstairs and into a room. The door closed behind them, and they were ordered to sit down. Men and women in uniforms came and went, speaking Russian in low, gutteral voices. But no one spoke to Bob and Ike in any language; they were completely ignored. Two hours passed there in the night. They'd had no food, there was nothing to read, there was nothing to do but fidget in those hardbacked, rigid chairs, as rigid and unbending as the people who streamed in and out. Finally Bob's patience was gone. "We've got to get to Lvov tonight!" he demanded to anyone who would listen. But no one could understand. He drew them a picture of a little train with an arrow pointing from Kiev to Lvov. The Russians eyed him suspiciously and said, "*Nyet, nyet*" ("No, no").

By midnight Bob was furious, and everyone in that room knew it. In order to calm down the angry American, they finally located someone who spoke English. "You will not go to Lvov tonight. There is an unexpected thunderstorm. Listen, you can hear the thunder. We are not sending up any planes. We will put you in a hotel and send you to Lvov on the first available flight tomorrow." I wonder what would have happened had Bob not been so noisily insistent. They probably would have spent the entire night on those unyielding chairs. But as it was, they were taken to a hotel and eventually put on a plane for Lvov, arriving there at eleven-thirty the next morning.

It was too late for the rendezvous. In all his years of flying around the country and the world, Bob has been grounded because of bad weather only once—that Tuesday in Russia. God had intervened and prevented him from meeting with the underground church; God protected His people. From that moment on, Bob and Ike were kept under constant surveillance by the KGB. One of their agents was posted at the front door of their hotel and another one at the side entrance. A woman agent was stationed at the door to their room and she logged them in and out, keeping a record of their every move. Had not God stepped in, Bob would have surely led the friends he sought to prison. The thought sobered him. It terrified him. The awesomeness of God and His great power and love!

I soon learned that my new boss liked to try out his jokes and new story material on his aides before he shared them with his congregation. Many's the time I had to hold my sides with laughter as he entertained me as an audience of one with his hilarious accounts of ordinary events. What a gift he has of taking seemingly average situations and turning them around into illustrations of spiritual truths.

On one of our earlier trips together, Bob told me a story that he had never shared with anyone else, even though it had happened some years earlier. I guess he had never seen the humor in it before, but I laughed so hard I cried as he recounted the story of the bricks to me. We were sitting on a DC-10, trying to stay awake.

"You know," he launched into his story, "our first new home in California was very small, with about an eighty-foot-wide front yard. I'd never done any landscaping and wasn't very anxious to begin, but Arvella would not leave me alone about it. It had one of those park strips; you know, an empty space between the street and the sidewalk, and I didn't know what to do with it. I figured if I planted it with grass, people would step out onto it from their cars and crush it and it would never look nice. Then I got the idea of paving it with bricks. It seemed like a lot of trouble, but Arvella buoyed me up by reminding me that it would never need mowing or weeding or any upkeep at all. I liked that, but I still was hesitant to get started.

"Finally, one Monday morning Arvella handed me my shovel and a few of my favorite sayings, like 'beginning is half done' and 'inch by inch anything's a cinch.' I didn't like it," (he never likes it when he has his own material thrown back in his face) "but I knew I'd better get down to business. It was my day off and I knew I didn't have a good excuse. I figured it shouldn't be too hard. After all, it was just a matter of digging out some dirt from the space and filling it with sand and laying bricks in it and hosing it down. The sand and water would make the mortar.

"I was out there early with my wheelbarrow and shovel, and excavated a hole about twelve inches square by eight inches deep. It was discouraging, because I looked at my wheelbarrow and it was already nearly half full and I really hadn't thought much about what I was going to do with the dirt. About that time, one of my neighbors pulled out of his driveway on his way to work and asked me what I was doing. I told him and he reminded me about the dirt.

"'What're you going to do with all that dirt?' he asked in a superior voice.

"But I had a stroke of genius. 'I'm going to make a mound with it in the backyard.'

"He laughed. 'You're going to have an awfully big mound with all that dirt. My gosh, it'll take you a month of Mondays to get all that dug out.'

"My spirits sank, but I wouldn't let him know it. 'All I have to do,' I said, 'is practice possibility thinking, and it'll be out in no time.'

"He laughed again and looked like he felt sorry for me, then drove away to work.

"I went ahead and filled the wheelbarrow and pushed it into the backyard and dumped it. It made a big mound, bigger than I knew what to do with, and I'd only taken out a foot and a half square from the park strip. It was only nine o'clock, and I was already hot and sweaty and feeling sorry for myself. As I wheeled the barrow back into the frontyard, I looked up and said, 'Lord, there must be a better way to do this.' "

Bob was warming to his story and I was intrigued. We've landscaped three Southern California yards from scratch and I know how much work it takes. They're small, but their diminutive size demands that they be perfect, not like the acres in other parts of the country where the big old trees and native grasses and shrubs do all the work for you. Bob took a couple thoughtful sips of coffee and continued.

"Not five minutes later, a dump truck with a tractor and skip loader mounted to a trailer in the back pulled onto my street. It surprised me because it was a new street and not too many people had moved in yet. We didn't get much traffic. It came to a screeching stop right in front of my house, and as I glanced up I could see the letters printed on the side of the cab: 'Roy Thayer, Excavating and Hauling.' Roy Thayer, my center aisle usher at church. He rolled down his window and stuck out his head, squinting from the sun.

" 'What're you doing here, Reverend?' he asked.

" 'I live here,' I said and I told him about my project. 'What're *you* doing here?'

"He smiled and looked sort of sheepish. 'I'm lost.'

" 'Oh no you're not.' I told him, 'God found you.'

"Roy opened the door of his truck and climbed out, eyeing my dirt. He bent over and picked up a handful, letting it sift through his fingers slowly. 'Pretty nice dirt you've got here,' he said.

" 'Oh, the best,' I told him. 'This used to be an orange grove, you know; it's still got the fertilizer in it.'

"Roy was quiet for a minute, thinking. 'I could do this job for you in about thirty minutes,' he said, 'if you'd let me have your dirt. I could use this dirt.' So he dropped the gate on his truck and lowered his tractor and dug up that ten-foot by eighty-foot stretch of ground just as easy as you please. He threw all the dirt, and there was a lot of it, in the back of his truck and reloaded the tractor and took off.

"The job was done. I could hardly believe it. He'd left some dirt on the sidewalk, so I went inside and got a broom. I was just sweeping up the last of the mess when my doubting neighbor drove up for lunch. His mouth fell open. Boy, did he stare. I mean, I wasn't even sweaty or dirty or anything. You know what, he's a possibility thinker today!''

I thought it was such a good story that Bob was encouraged to include it in many of his speeches and sermons. He even tells it at the Institutes. He may pick a different moral each time, but it usually centers around problem solving: ''If you've got a problem, you can be sure that God has the answer for it. Just ask Him and trust Him to help you solve it.''

Bob has always fought with his weight and has devised some interesting ways of dealing with it. He found that he would continue to eat the airplane food even after he was full simply because it was still in front of him. So he developed a way of destroying it so he wouldn't be tempted to nibble while he waited for the stewardess to remove his tray. First, he mixes the salad, entrée, and dessert together. Then he empties all the salt and pepper all over it. Then he pours the cream and sugar on it and stirs it all up together, even emptying any leftover salad dressing on top. The results are disgusting. He's gotten many funny looks from the stewardesses as they come to take away his meal, but the funniest time was when he told one that there was something wrong with his soup. She looked at that concoction and just let out the most horrified gasp, her eyes as big as saucers. ''Oh my gosh,'' she wailed, ''I've served you the salad dressing instead of the soup.''

For all his care not to over eat, Bob does love sweets. One day many years ago we were in Chicago for the ''Phil Donahue Show.'' Since both Bob and I love to eat, we have a little routine we follow. We'll go up to someone at our hotel or maybe to a cab driver and ask them, ''If we never came back to this city again, where should we eat?'' This day after the Donahue show, we were on our way back into town to meet with radio newsman, Paul Harvey. We had a little time to spare, so we asked our driver where we should have lunch. He took us to a wonderful little restaurant in an old brownstone, and I noticed that they served soufflés.

''How long does it take for your soufflés?'' I asked, and the waiter answered about thirty minutes, so I ordered one for dessert.

''What's a soufflé?'' Bob questioned, his gastronomic curiosity piqued.

''Oh, they're delicious,'' I told him. ''Donna and her mother make them out of beaten egg whites and sugar and cream and flavorings. They're baked in the oven and puff up real pretty and soft and airy."

Bob was fascinated and ordered one for himself as well. They were lemon soufflés, the one and only ones I've ever had, and were they good! Steamy hot and subtly flavored with just the right amount of lemon and sugar. For Bob Schuller, it was love at first bite. One Friday afternoon after our arrival back in Orange County, Bob got a real craving for a soufflé. Arvella had never made one and couldn't find a recipe, so she called me for help. Donna gave her her sister's recipe for chocolate soufflé, which has remained Bob's favorite dessert for many years.

That first night, Arvella whipped up the egg whites and carefully folded them into the mixture of melted chocolate and sugar and cream. She buttered and sugared her new soufflé dish and gingerly folded the chocolate fluff inside while the family, led by Bob, stood over her and drooled. Just about that time, Sheila and her boyfriend went outside to get something from his car. They didn't return in the amount of time he thought they should have, so Bob asked twelve-year-old Carol to go check on them. Then the phone rang. It was the Orange police.

"There's been a robbery nearby," the authoritative voice related, "and there are some armed men that have escaped onto your property. We've got the place surrounded with a SWAT team, and you've got to get out of there. Please be very careful when you exit the house. Just come quietly down the driveway and duck behind our cars. You'll see them there. We've got your daughters with us, so don't worry."

Bob and Arvella and ten-year-old Gretchen bolted from the kitchen, abandoning the chocolate aroma that had begun to waft its way through the house, and quickly joined Sheila and Carol behind the patrol cars. They spent the better part of an hour crouched there in the dark before they were finally escorted over to the safety of a neighbor's house while the police continued to search for the bandits. It was around ten o'clock when our home phone rang. I was surprised to hear Bob's voice. "My soufflé is ruined!" he lamented as he told me about the night's escapades. I don't think he felt much better when the police were unable to locate the thieves in the dense growth of his yard. The next morning, they found out to their dismay that the thieves had spent the night up in one of their big trees. That was not the only time their yard has been the refuge for armed gunmen. Its central location and extensive grounds seem to make it a favorite.

The Schullers also have a modest little cabin up in our local San Bernardino Mountains. In fact, Bob and his son built most of it themselves. It sits on a steep mountainside with a magnificent view of Big Bear Lake and the sunset, but the very inaccessibility of the property rendered it nearly impossible to build upon. There were those who had abandoned it before, but Bob refused to give it up. "It must be possible." Being an amateur architect, he designed the cabin himself and figured out how to perch it up there on the top of the mountain just right.

During its construction, Bob fell from his ladder one day and had to be rushed down the mountain by ambulance. He had broken some bones and was bleeding from a ruptured kidney. As he lay there, flat on his back on a stretcher, feeling the ambulance sway from side to side as it raced down the steep, winding roads, he forced himself to talk to God through his pain.

"Why did I fall, Lord?"

And he heard God answer him, "Schuller, it's your own miserable fault. Why did you use such a rickety old ladder?"

"You're right, Lord," Bob answered, "but am I going to be all right?"

The reply was swift. "Yes."

Bob says he talked to his Lord all the way down the mountain for nearly an hour, and arrived in the hospital in such good spirits that the doctors commented on it.

The Schullers have enjoyed many family holidays up on the mountain. They water-ski in the summer and snow-ski in the winter. They like to take long walks through the pines or simply relax in front of the fireplace and gaze out at the mountain ridges that seem to go on forever, one right after the other.

One problem with resort areas and the vacation houses that populate them is that they are easy targets for vandals and thieves. The Schuller's cabin is quite rustic, full of old furniture and not much of value other than an occasional television set and record player, but one year they were robbed. Although the stolen items were never recovered, a teenage boy was tried for the robbery and put on probation. At the time Bob had been unable to come up the mountain for the trial.

The next Christmas was one of those miserable times when it rains and drips all week instead of blanketing the slopes with snow. By a few days after Christmas, Bob was really going stir-crazy. He was cooped up in that cabin with his two youngest daughters, who were bored and unable to go outside to play. Finally, he knew he had to get out of there, so he offered to take Carol and Gretchen down into Lake Arrowhead Village in the hopes of finding something to cheer them. It was dark outside and clouds were again gathering ominously. Each and every pinetree was soaked and dripping and the side of the road was engulfed with mud.

When they arrived at the village, it looked like it was in mourning instead of celebrating a birthday. About the only thing open was an amusement arcade. As soon as the girls heard its bells and whistles and saw the brightly blinking lights, they let out squeals of delight. Bob groaned. He hates loud, frantic places. But to placate his daughters, he escorted them inside and bought them tokens so they could play the games. He just stood there, feeling miserable and sorry for himself.

Soon he noticed that a young boy was staring at him shyly, and he gave him a slight smile. Thus encouraged he came over.

"I know who you are. You're Dr. Schuller, aren't you?" he asked. "I watch you on TV sometimes. I've had a lot of trouble. Sometimes it's so hard to be good," he continued, a sad look on his face. Then he brightened. "But watching you has really helped me. I'm trying real hard to do what God wants me to and to be a better person." Bob warmed to the boy immediately and began to encourage him. "I have to tell you something," the youth interrupted. "I know where your cabin is. You had your TV stolen last year, didn't you?" Bob was taken by surprise. For once he was at a loss for words and just kind of stammered an affirmative reply.

"I know," the boy confessed. "I was the one who stole it. I'm real sorry now, and I haven't stolen anything since. Do you think God can ever forgive me?"

Bob smiled kindly at the young man, his blonde hair tousled over the collar of his windbreaker, his eyes staring at him earnestly. "Yes,

God can forgive you. Have you ever asked Him to? Have you ever asked Him to come into your life and live in your heart?''

''No, but I sure would like to. How do you do it?''

Right there in that arcade, its lights flashing frantically, its bells clanging, its rock music blaring, Bob and the former thief bowed their heads and prayed. Bob led to Christ that very moment the young man who had robbed his home. Later, he sent him books and study material to help him to mature spiritually. Suddenly, the day wasn't so dismal after all.

Another place where the Schullers love to go to relax is Hawaii. In fact, I guess it's just about their most favorite place on the face of the earth, and I'm sure they'll probably retire there someday. In February, 1976, just before Donna and I had our fourth child, Bob invited us to accompany the Schuller clan to Honolulu for a few days. We were investigating the possibility of doing some taping for TV over there, and I jumped at the chance. Neither Donna nor I had ever been, and we were quite excited about it, even though Donna was nearly eight months pregnant.

We met the Schullers at the airport. All of them were going—Bob and Arvella, Sheila who was well into her twenties, Jeanne who was still a student at Wheaton College, Carol who was twelve, and Gretchen who celebrated her tenth birthday that trip. Only young Bob was absent. He was already married by then and he and his wife Linda, whose father owns a travel agency, had plenty of opportunities to travel on their own.

All four of the older Schullers were six feet tall or more, and the family together was a commanding sight as we approached them at Los Angeles International Airport. Carol was just beginning to shoot up in height; only Gretchen was still small. It was one of the children's first trips to Hawaii, and they were really excited, chattering and giggling as we boarded and made our way to our seats in the very back of the plane. We were traveling by the very cheapest fare; even our lunch wasn't included and we had to order one and pay extra for it.

We were all seated together across the sides and middle of a big L-1011, so it was easy to talk with each other. When the stewardess brought Donna's and my lunches, I paid her the three or four dollars for them and we settled down to business. That's when I glanced over at the Schullers to see which of the entrées they had chosen. To my chagrin, Arvella had brought out a large brown shopping bag, the kind they pack your groceries in at the market. She was passing out homemade sandwiches to all the kids, wrapped in cellophane. There were potato chips and fruit for them all in the sack lunch she had prepared, and everyone, including Bob, was eating with gusto as they passed bananas up and down the aisle of the plane. Donna and I just wanted to slink down into oblivion with embarrassment, feeling that we had been overly extravagant in ordering and paying for our lunch. But it was too late now.

When we landed in Hawaii, we were surprised at the city of Honolulu, even though we had been warned of its size. It was like any other large city in America, full of freeways and skyscrapers and traffic jams, but with its own unique flavor. The ocean was beautiful and blue and the early evening was full of exotic scents and flowers. The street names on the freeway overpasses were fascinating and unpronounceable.

All eight of us were crammed into a large blue station wagon Bob had rented; and we were in high spirits as we drove into the pinks and blues of a fading Hawaiian sunset, the liquid air of paradise dampening our hair and making beads of sweat stand up on our foreheads. To our delight, we drove through all the bustle of the city and headed out into what I thought Hawaii should have looked like to begin with. In the enclosing darkness, we could make out hills covered with palm trees and cascading flowers as we drove into the parking lot of one of the most lovely hotels I have ever seen.

We were escorted way up to the top of the Kahala Hilton, and the beauty of our room and its commanding view took our breath away. Bougainvillaea trailed scarlet blossoms from our balcony; and below, the lights of Kahala were just beginning to emerge from the darkened hillsides, twinkling and giving us teasing glimpses of what would await us on the morrow.

The next day, we met Bob and Arvella for breakfast. They were seated in their special table down in the front of the open air restaurant, the shimmering emerald and aquamarine of the Pacific Ocean stretched out before them, its sugary sands embracing the tiled floor of the coffee shop. Little birds flew in and out, every now and then pausing long enough to light on a chair back and cock their little heads, ruffling their feathers and staring quizzically at the diners. The Schullers were in swimsuits and coverups, totally relaxed, as they scooped up bites of pancakes smothered in coconut syrup. Younger members of the family popped in and out during the meal, but they didn't stay to eat. Sheila and Jeanne were watching their weight, and Carol and Gretchen were much too excited.

A stunning black-haired young waitress approached our table, her dark eyes glowing like coals in the midst of her smooth olive complexion, a radiant smile lighting up her whole face. Around her neck she wore a beautiful gold cross which I recognized immediately as one of ours, only more lovely. It was filigreed with the words "God loves you and so do I."

She beamed at Bob as he introduced us and shared with us their first meeting. She had recognized him right away, but couldn't place him. Even in his flowered shirt she had a vision of him in a flowing black robe, and guessed at first that he might be Bishop Fulton Sheen. But no, that wasn't quite right. "Robert Schuller!" she had finally gushed. She told him of her Christian commitment, and Bob had loved her excitement, her enthusiasm for her Lord and her life. "He promised me he would bring me a gold cross, and he did," the lovely Polynesian Christian told us. "I never take it off, and it gives me lots of opportunities to witness to others," and she flashed us another of her brilliant smiles as she rushed off.

Toward the end of our meal, I realized a group at another table was eyeing Bob. One of the men wore a gold medallion around his neck and on closer inspection I knew it was the same Good Shepherd that Bob and I also wore. I remember thinking, "Boy, that's dedication, to even wear it with a swimsuit." As we got up to leave, he and his wife came over to shake Bob's hand.

"We're Jewish," the gentlemen said. "In fact, our son is a rabbi, but we love to watch you, Dr. Schuller, and we're understanding more about the Christian religion. I always wear my Good Shepherd medallion; it's really special to me."

Later, out on the beach, we tried to relax in what seemed to be a full-fledged windstorm. I couldn't believe that these were what the natives called "moderate trades." The sky was full of billowing white clouds that raced around trying to catch the wind. Now and again they dropped a few drops of light rain on the sunbathers, but nobody bothered to get up and move. It was warm and humid. It seemed odd that the air could be so heavy and yet so windy at the same time.

Poor Donna was quite a sight. Once she lay down on her back in the sand, she was unable to get up and just collapsed there, her pregnant stomach towering over the rest of her and casting long shadows across the sand. Before long, Bob came over, his silver hair contrasting with his golden skin. He stood a moment looking at Donna. I knew he was searching for something positive to say. Finally he launched in, "You're just like these beau-tee-ful Hawaiian Islands," he smiled. "They are laden with wonderful fruit and so are you. You are the symbol of a fruitful marriage."

That entire trip was an experience for Donna. She was surprised to discover a different side of Bob Schuller, the father and family man. Like most people, she held him in high esteem, considering him mainly as a minister, imposing in his robes. But to see him joke with his family, to see the give and take with the children. Why, they really were like any family on vacation would be.

Bob was rank with puns and other forms of corny humor, making a joke out of everything. But the silly gags that would elicit howls of laughter from a church congregation brought different reactions from the Schuller girls. "Oh, Daddy," coupled with a look that said "I don't believe anyone could really be that simple," and a certain upward roll of the eyes.

"My gosh," Donna whispered to me, "his family will certainly keep him humble." But it was obvious that they adored their dad and that the feeling was mutual.

It was only three weeks later when our baby Shannon Michael was born. There were complications. He was a large infant, though born three weeks premature, and his shoulders were larger than his head. Donna was able to deliver the head easily enough, but the rest of him just wouldn't come out. Finally, after what seemed hours of Donna's pushing, and pulling and tugging on the little head by the doctor and the nurses, the little body slipped out into the doctor's hands.

It was black and blue from bruises and a lack of oxygen, and already air had escaped from the lungs making the head appear huge and misshapen. An hour or so later, Shannon suffered a complete respiratory arrest. No one had known that his collarbone had broken during the birth process and that it had punctured one of his lungs. When our pediatrician finally arrived at the hospital, Shannon had been without oxygen to his brain for some twenty minutes. He was cyanotic, and our doctor almost didn't try to revive him. It was a hard decision, because we already had one profoundly brain-injured child; he didn't want to give us another.

Shannon was placed on a respirator and rushed to the neonatal intensive care unit at Orange County Medical Center, with what the doctors told us would be certain brain damage. It was a devastating blow. When Bob found out, he was crushed. It's funny, but for a pastor he is sometimes so hurt himself by tragedy that he has difficulty dealing with it. I asked him if he would come to the hospital and baptize Shannon, as at that time it was doubtful that he would live. Donna and I are not great believers in infant baptism. Our little girl Christa, who was born three years earlier, we had had dedicated instead. But for some reason, we really wanted Shannon baptized. It comforted us.

I'll never forget the day Bob and I arrived at the intensive care ward. They almost wouldn't let him in, since only the parents were supposed to visit the babies, but he had his little bowl of baptismal water and the nurses finally relented. It was a big room full of incubators, quite elaborate ones with built-in life support and monitoring systems. Inside each one was an incredibly tiny bit of humanity. Some of their little legs were no longer nor bigger around than a woman's pinky finger, their heads the size of golf balls. It was inconceivable that they could live. There was a nurse on duty for each two infants, and she stood guard at the threshold of life for them, talking to them, stroking them. Buzzers would go off periodically, and we soon learned that one of the little ones had stopped breathing. The nurse would rush to its side and begin tapping briskly on its back. "Breathe, little mouse."

We located Shannon's incubator with tears streaming down our faces. He looked huge compared with the others, but nine pounds is still awfully small. His skin was all yellow as he was severely jaundiced in addition to his other problems, and he lay completely naked under a large, bright light which was supposed to treat the overabundance of bilirubins he had in his bloodstream. His eyes were covered with a black mask to prevent their being damaged by the intensity of the light, and he had an intravenous needle inserted in his ankle as he could take nothing by mouth. His head was still swollen way out of proportion, and he was black and blue and purple in splotches from the tip of his blond fuzzy head to about mid-chest.

Bob looked from Shannon to me, and the hurt in his eyes was almost unbearable. I was kind of numb, and I think Bob was feeling enough pain for both of us that day. The incubator couldn't be opened as it was a totally contained environment, but there was a little porthole on the side where a person could slip his hand in to touch and care for the baby. Bob carefully dipped his big fingers into his little bowl of water and inched his mammoth hand inside the opening and over to the downy head, caressing it ever so softly as he made the sign of the cross on Shannon's forehead. "I baptize you in the name of the Father and the Son and the Holy Spirit," he whispered. Then he prayed for Shannon's complete healing.

It was nearly a week later before Bob got up his courage to speak to Donna. He called her on the phone and tried to say the most positive things he could think of. He described the baptism for her and said, "My, what nice big hands and feet Shannon has, and so perfectly formed. He's got all his fingers and toes and everything." Then he excused himself as quickly as he could.

To make a long story short, Shannon was completely healed. I'm not saying whether it was the baptism, or Bob's laying on of hands and praying, or a combination of all the other prayers that were going up for him at the time. I only know that he is six years old now and every whit perfect. And I give the glory to God, who I believe performed a miracle.

Bob does not have a healing ministry, although he certainly believes in the healing power of God. One day many years ago a woman brought her young son to him. The boy had been born deaf and she asked Bob to pray for his complete healing. "You preach that all things are possible with God," she said. Bob hasn't been called to a healing ministry, and I think he feels a bit uneasy about requests of this kind. He went into what he calls "two-way" prayer. "God, what shall I do? Do you want me to pray for the boy's healing?" He felt that God answered him in the affirmative.

He put his hands over the child's ears and prayed, "Dear God, help this little boy to hear." Bob took his hands away from the boy's ears and opened his eyes. He clapped his hands. But the little boy heard nothing. Bob looked sorrowfully over at the child's mother. At least he had tried.

A couple of days later, the boy's mother had a friend come to visit. As she was preparing to leave, they walked together out to her car which was parked at the curb. The little boy was standing behind the car, holding on to the rear bumper and didn't hear the engine start. When the car pulled away and his mom saw what was going to happen, she ran toward him, but couldn't reach him in time. She stood by watching in helpless horror as her son was dragged behind the car, his little legs struggling frantically to keep pace. Finally the car reached a speed where the child couldn't continue to hold on, and he was thrown violently away from it, rolling over and over across the street until he landed in a heap at the curb.

His poor mother rushed to him hysterically, imagining the worst from the lifeless figure crumpled in the gutter. She picked him up, her hot tears washing over his blood streaked little face. In a moment, his eyes flickered and eventually opened, taking in his distraught mother. Other than bruises and lacerations, the child escaped the ordeal unscathed but for one thing. He could hear. And his hearing has been perfect since that day.

It is an accepted fact by those who know Bob well that he is not a particularly good driver. It's not that he doesn't want to be, but just that he is so consumed by other matters that it is hard for him to concentrate on the road and traffic conditions. I guess this predilection has given him a soft spot for others in the same predicament, and he is not therefore overly fond of traffic cops. Down the street from the church there is a Holiday Inn which has a large billboard positioned in its parking lot. One day on his way into work, Bob spotted a policeman hiding behind the sign, just waiting to give some poor guy a ticket. As he would say, it pushed one of his red buttons, and really made him mad. Some people would have driven by, swearing under their breath, but not Bob. He pulled his car into the lot and right up to the police car and got out. That poor policeman had to endure a scathing Schuller style lecture on the evils of entrapment.

One Christmas Eve, Bob was running late for the first of his five candlelight services. He and Arvella and Carol and Gretchen raced out of the house and hopped into the car, revving it down the driveway at full speed. More than likely, he was mentally rehearsing his sermon and neglected to move over into the left-hand turn lane when he approached Lewis Street. He didn't have time to go up and turn around, so he took a token glance in his rearview mirror and gunned the car, swerving jerkily into the left lane. He hadn't noticed the car that had been behind him, and he ended up cutting him off, nearly clipping his front bumper. He reached the intersection just as the light turned red, and was forced to stop.

From nowhere a large man appeared outside the car, motioning him to roll down his window. Bob was afraid to because it was obvious even in the darkness that the man was absolutely livid with rage. The blood vessels in his neck were bulging and he was swearing a blue streak so hot that it nearly melted the glass. Timidly, Bob put the window down and tried to apologize, but the string of obscenities was too stiff to cut. He tried smiling at the man, but it only seemed to antagonize him more. When at last he had to pause for a deep breath, Bob made his move. "Wait! This is Christmas Eve!" The man plunged into yet another line of vulgarities, shaking his fist in Bob's face. The next time he gasped for breath, Bob tried again. He looked him straight in the eye and spoke as quickly as possible so as not to be interrupted. "God loves you and I'm trying." The man's mouth went slack and a flash of recognition crossed his face, softening his features. Without another word, he turned heel and went back to his car and drove away into the night.

Yet another Christmas, after the gifts had been opened on Christmas day and the turkey eaten, Bob had to run up to his office in the Tower of Hope for a few minutes. Something made him ask Sheila, who was minister to girls at the time, to come with him. As they drove onto that expanse of concrete, it was totally empty but for two cars. One was that of the New Hope counselor on duty. The other car was parked way out away from the buildings. They walked up to the door of the deserted tower and were surprised to see a young woman huddled there on the ground. She looked to be about twenty-one, but she had lost the sparkle of youth. She just sat there, hugging a pillow that had no pillowcase on it. Her thin hands clutched that pillow so tightly, as if it were her only friend. It probably was.

Her eyes were puffy, her face tear-stained. She had spent Christmas Eve trying to sleep in the backseat of her car, and even in

Southern California that's cold and hard. She looked so pitiful and alone that Bob turned to Sheila. "Why don't we take her home with us?" So while Bob worked, Sheila took her home and Arvella fed her turkey and dressing and put her to bed between nice, clean sheets. She stayed with them a few days, sharing her past few unfortunate years with people she knew understood.

She and her mother hadn't spoken in eight years. She didn't give any details, but she had been placed in a foster home and her foster parents had run up three thousand dollars worth of bills on her credit. She had been a loner all her life, had even tried to commit suicide, and had spent one entire year in a psychiatric hospital with little improvement. Now she had no money, no home, no friends, and a host of bill collectors just waiting to pounce. The Schullers showed her Christ's love, free and full of acceptance.

A year later, Bob received a package of homemade fudge and a letter from the Christmas waif. It read in part:

> Dear Dr. Schuller,
>
> It's been a year since you found me in the alcove in front of the church. I just thought this would be a good time to share with you what God has been doing with my life. He used that miserable day as a beginning of something beautiful.
>
> I nearly went into bankruptcy this year, but then I started tithing. One miracle after another happened so that within one month from today I will be almost completely free from these extra debts. All my life I've been unable to relate to any peer group and I've never wanted to, but in the church I've found some beautiful people and I'm not alone anymore. But the biggest miracle is my mother. Through your ministry, I began to believe that it was possible to be reconciled to her. We've set things straight, and are now spending our first joyous Christmas together. The turning point came when I brought her to the Mother-Daughter Dinner that Sheila put on at church.
>
> It's a beautiful Christmas for me. Thank you.

Bob truly believes in the beauty and potential of each person. His creed of self-confidence goes something like this, "I am made in the image of God. Christ died for me. I am God's redeemed child, born again through the Holy Spirit, and that means I am somebody great. I am filled with the gifts of the Spirit. I am a wonderful, unique, beautiful person." Bob doesn't like to say anything that might give anyone a negative self-image. Of course, he can get mad just as easily as the next guy and say things he's sorry for later, but he never purposely sets out to hurt anyone.

He carries these values over to his managerial position at the church and the Hour of Power. From a human standpoint, management and organization automatically bring with them a certain amount of frustrations and a lot of those are people generated. Bob decided years ago that he would try always to look at frustration in a positive way and that in so doing he would never fire anyone. It's a fact he hates to fire people and will bend over backwards to avoid it. If he is frustrated and at a loss as to how to handle someone, he takes the attitude that they must be there for a reason. Maybe God is using them to help him grow or to teach him humility or patience. He leaves it up to God to remove the person from the position of irritation if and when He wants to.

This sounds great in theory, but it isn't always the best in actual practice. Some employees have left very hurt because they were never really told what they were doing that was not pleasing to Bob. Telling people their bad points just isn't Bob's style though. He has so set his life on being positive and building up self-esteem in others that he has difficulty voicing criticism unless he is really angry, even though he advocates venting rather than suppressing frustrations.

He and I have certainly had our share of disagreements, some of them quite vocal on Bob's part. I wouldn't call them arguments, but both of us can be quite strong in our positions. I think the maddest he has ever been with me was one Sunday after he returned from speaking to a large group of American businessmen on ethics in business. Apparently, some of these key people complained to Bob that he should address himself more to the controversial issues of the day, something which he has purposely never done.

It was fresh in his mind, and that Sunday he added comments about nuclear energy and genetic engineering to his nine-thirty sermon. It just wasn't Bob. Arvella and I, sitting in the television room, gasped audibly as he began; and as the cameras panned the congregation, it was easy to see that there were some people who agreed with him and others who did not. It was totally against Bob's whole philosophy; he just doesn't get into these subjects from the pulpit where his audience can't dialogue. It turned his role on Sunday morning from that of a therapist to that of making a one-way pronouncement on an issue. He had tried to deal with it in positive terms, but he hadn't pulled it off, and Arvella and I felt it hadn't gone over very well.

So in between services, we went into his office and tried to tell him as positively and as tactfully as we could, that he should consider leaving those remarks out of his message at the next service. We didn't pull it off very well either, I guess, because it made Bob furious. His face reddened and he even pounded his fists on his desk in frustration. "You aren't the ones who have to prepare the messages every week!" he exploded. "I'm the one who has to do that, and I get tired of being criticized all the time for not dealing with the critical issues! People say I'm just full of pie in the sky, and I just felt the need to speak out!"

"Bob," I began, trying to placate him, "I don't criticize you for speaking out. If you believe deeply in them, you should talk about them. But do you really want to use the "Hour of Power" as a forum for that?"

I think he knew I was right, and that only made him madder. He shook his fist at me. "Don't you ever forget, Mike Nason. You work for me!" And he stormed out of the room and disappeared into the sanctuary for the beginning of the next service. I sort of slunk, red-faced, into a back pew, and my head was pounding from the tongue lashing I'd received. But Bob got up beaming into the pulpit and delivered the same message, minus the controversial comments. Later, he apologized, as he always does.

He's a human being, just like the rest of us, and subject to human frailties. He loses his temper just like I do, and he gets hurt and he cries. And just like the rest of us, he picks himself up and starts over again.

But unlike most people I know, Bob seems to be on a one-man crusade to see to it that everyone else is happy, regardless. When he meets an employee in the elevator or crossing the parking lot, he will flash them that famous Schuller smile. "Isn't this a glorious day? How are you today?" If the person is smart, he will return Bob's smile with one of his own that is nearly as broad and say something to the effect of "Oh, I'm just great, just wonderful." If he isn't quite that positive, he's liable to be in for a lecture on the evils of negative thinking.

One day, we were having breakfast at one of Bob's favorite morning places, the Cookbook Restaurant. The waitress came up to take our order, and it was obvious that she had a bad cold. "Good morning!" Bob enthused. "And how are you this beautiful day?" She shot him a rather pitiful look.

"Oh," she replied, searching really hard for a smile which never quite made it, "I'm pretty good, I guess."

"Only pretty good?" Bob's voice boomed his disappointment. "We can't have that!" She was more than a little annoyed.

"Well, I'm sorry," she snapped. "I have a cold and I don't feel good and I wish I was home in bed."

Bob couldn't stand that. He is so sure that anyone can feel terrific, regardless of his circumstances, if he will only make up his mind to be. He wants people to concentrate on the good things about their situation and he just won't take no for an answer. He pestered that poor waitress through the entire breakfast, trying to get her to look on the bright side. He doesn't like to admit that there are some people who don't want to be happy all the time. To him, it's always an achieveable goal, there's always the possibility of happiness. He believes that if you make up your mind to be happy, you will be, even if you have to lie to yourself at first. Pretty soon the lie will become the truth and you will realize that you really are genuinely happy.

11

God's People— One-on-One

In this chapter I would like to share with you Bob Schuller as I've seen him ministering to people from all walks of life, the famous as well as the ordinary, church leaders, movie stars, cab drivers, stewardesses, political leaders, ball players, business men.

One such incident took place in a little fishing boat in the Sea of Cortez. We were out in the open sea, so far from the rugged coast of Baja California that I could barely make out its outline in the distance.

Along with the captain of the craft, and his crew of one, there were three of us aboard: Bob Schuller, Bob Pierce (the founder of World Vision International), and me. We were clad in shorts and shirts, and each of us had a hat pulled way down over our eyes, trying to escape the cruel, burning rays of the sun overhead. It blistered and taunted us as it danced on the water, lighting up each wave as it curled. Every now and then the thirty-foot vessel would lurch forward, sending a cooling spray of water our way. It tasted like salt and coated our skin, making it sticky. The wind that wanted our hats was salty too, and clean and wild and free and smelled of fish.

The two Bobs were reminiscing. They had a lot of years between the two of them. Bob Pierce was dying of leukemia. I think that's why Bob Schuller was treating us to these few days of marlin fishing. He wanted to share in some of the last days of this great man of faith, wanted to experience again his power and vision. And he hoped to impart some of his own strength to him, to let the clean sea air invigorate him and maybe do his part in helping to prolong his life, if only by a few days.

They had been working closely together these last few months. Bob Pierce had left World Vision. He was now directing another one of his own creations, The Samaritan's Purse. It was a small organization; I'm not sure if he even had a staff other than himself. We had pulled our troops out of Vietnam and most of the other organizations were through bringing out refugees. Bob Pierce was one of the last Americans in that strife-torn country, still trying to bring those he could to freedom.

His first love was, as always, the children, and Bob Schuller and the congregation of the Garden Grove Community Church had made his efforts their own. Together, we had brought some of the last Vietnamese to safety in the United States. Bob Pierce provided the know-how and the personal courage. Bob Schuller provided the money.

They were both relaxed. In fact, I don't think I've ever seen Robert Schuller so completely at rest as on the deck of that boat, his skin tanned a dark brown, his lips chapped from the sun and wind. Our poles were set in stands so we were free to move about, and there were two rigging lines over the sides of the boat. When that rigging line snaps, you know you've got a fish on the line. When a marlin hits, he hits hard, grabbing the bait and yanking, setting the hook. That first shiver of excitement comes as you take hold of your pole and feel the raw power unleashed at the other end.

And then it's a grim fight. The silver crescent leaps out of the water, pulling and straining the line, dancing for a second on the tips of the waves. Then it plunges, diving down deep under the shimmering surface and dragging the line farther and farther as it cuts valiantly through the water. It's man pitted against beast, muscle for muscle, strength for strength, courage for courage in a struggle that lasts for hours. The great fish lunges, you reel in your line; he darts to and fro, skipping, tossing his head; you fight to keep the line taut. You lose and he's off again, plowing across the billows in a headlong pursuit of freedom. You tighten up your slack, he jerks violently until finally one of you outlasts the other.

Each of us caught a marlin that day, each experienced the thrill of victory, the pride of accomplishment while every muscle in our bodies quivered and shook uncontrollably in protest. Bob Schuller had landed marlins before, and didn't like to kill the courageous creatures, so he had his tagged and let it go, taking great pleasure as it gracefully parted the waters and found liberty once more. Bob Pierce and I brought ours back to shore that evening at sunset. The beach was full of native women and children in bright-colored clothing, all waiting and hoping for fish. When ours had been cleaned and carved, they smiled, their teeth white against their dark faces. They would have fish for supper.

Bob Pierce bought me a tiny gold marlin charm. To remember. A few months later, he was gone.

Another occasion I'll never forget was the time I went to the Los Angeles Airport to pick up Bob and found him accompanied by the new manager of the LA Dodgers, Tommy Lasorda, and the Dodger's vice president, Al Campanis. They had all been waiting for the same flight from Chicago to Los Angeles in the Chicago Admiral's Club. Tommy and Al had been in Chicago for the annual National Baseball League dinner, which had been hosted by the Chicago Cubs that year. Once inside the airport, Tommy had spotted Bob and came over and introduced himself. It turned out that he was a regular viewer of the "Hour of Power."

They didn't have a car at the airport when they arrived in Los Angeles, so Bob offered to drive them home. I played chauffeur that day, and it was great. Later, Bob asked Tommy to be a guest on the "Hour of Power." He was such a down-to-earth sort of person, we all grew very fond of him right away. He and Bob really hit it off, and he issued Bob a standing invitation to come down to Dodger Stadium and see the Dodgers play and meet the players. Needless to say, Bob became a big Dodger fan. He loved Tommy's jokes about the Big Dodger in the sky.

On one occasion, Tommy invited Bob to conduct chapel for the Dodgers before a game. Bob thought right away of me and my son Mark, who is an undying Dodger fan, and called to ask us to accompany him. We were staying down at the beach at the time on vacation, and my mother was house-sitting. Dr. Schuller is her boss, as she works for the Hour of Power, but she wasn't about to let him have our phone number. "Please," Bob found himself pleading with her, "I promise not to bother Mike about work. I have a surprise for him. Really." Bob comes off sounding very quiet and meek on the phone, very much like a small child with a deep voice, and my mother was not going to let him get around her. "I'll call Mike and give him a message for you," she was firm, "but you can't call him yourself."

Of course, Mark and I were thrilled to be included, and were most appreciative of Bob's thoughtfulness. We accompanied him right into the Dodger locker room and the dugout and into one of their small training rooms for chapel. Nearly all the players were assembled there; chapel means a lot to them. Tommy John came in a little after the others, and as he reached to steady himself with a table as he sat on the floor, he accidentally knocked over a soft drink. It spilled out and ran off the side of the table, all over his hair and face and splashed all over his crisp white uniform. The Dodgers burst into gales of laughter. It was an embarrassing moment. But Tommy John was extremely gracious and very much in control. He sat there on the floor, his hair dripping with the sticky brown liquid, all the way through Bob's short message and prayer.

The next year, Tommy Lasorda invited Bob to give the invocation at the National League dinner, which was being held in Los Angeles. I went with him, knowing it would be a baseball fan's dream evening. We were in a large anteroom, all decked out in black tie and tuxedo, at a reception just before the dinner. Neither Bob nor I knew hardly anyone, and we were feeling a little uncomfortable.

All of a sudden there was a great commotion as a back door opened and Frank Sinatra and his wife Barbara entered. It seemed that every person in the room was dying to meet them, and soon a huge crowd had gathered about them, buzzing with excitement. We sure didn't know the Sinatras, so we didn't even bother to join the throng, but just stood back at the other end of the room. As they made their way through the crowd, Frank spied Bob. Immediately there was a spark of recognition in his eyes. He put his arms out in front of him and literally parted the mob, with people scattering to the right and the left as he made a beeline for Bob.

"Robert Schuller!" He beamed. "I watch you on television nearly every week before I go to Mass." He pumped Bob's hand warmly. I think Bob was in shock. You know, when you stand on one side of the television tube, you have no idea who is watching you at the other end. Frank shared with Bob how much his ministry had meant to him, and Bob was just thrilled to death. They've had an interesting friendship ever since, and Frank has been very supportive of Bob's work.

It pleases Bob to have been chosen of God to have a ministry to those who are rich and famous, but no more than it does to have a ministry to people from all walks of life. God loves us all, no matter who we are, and He plays no favorites. Bob Schuller tries to do the same.

He has lots of opportunities to meet people on a one-to-one level on his many travels around the country and the world. Most of his trips are in conjunction with speaking engagements. He gives motivational lectures with a positive Christian thrust to many large businesses, and also speaks to churches and pastors' groups. It has been my privilege to accompany him on many of his trips, and they are nearly always interesting in one way or another.

One time when Bob and I were flying together, a pretty blonde stewardess came over and literally poured her heart out to Bob. Her husband had left her for another woman some months earlier, and she had been left shattered from the experience. She had started watching the "Hour of Power" and had become a Christian and was beginning to let Christ help her put her life back together again. As Bob counseled her and prayed with her, her big blue eyes puddled up and spilled tears down her cheeks. Then when she went into the galley of the plane and the other stewardesses saw she had been crying, they were sure that the silver-haired gentleman had been unkind to her in some way. They stalked down the aisle, casting furtive glances at Bob, and if looks could kill, he'd have been a goner. When she realized the misunderstanding, she brought them over and introduced them to Bob, telling them of the transformation he had helped to bring into her life.

On another long flight across the country, Bob sat next to a successful-looking man in his forties. Right away, the man asked Bob what he did for a living. "I write books, and I'm a minister."

The man shot him a skeptical look, "What kind of minister?"

Bob smiled. "A Christian minister."

The man kind of raised himself up and put on a dignified air, "Oh," he said. "I know the Bible. But I don't believe in God. The Bible is a nice book and all that, but. . . ."

Bob Schuller loves a challenge, and he was challenged by his seat partner that day. "You are an intelligent man. You know the Scriptures. You must have a good reason why you don't believe them. Why don't you tell me about it?" Bob talked to that man all the way from one coast to another, and he introduced him to the personal Christ. As the plane landed, they had their heads bowed as Bob led his friend in a tearful prayer while the power of the living God washed over him.

On yet another occasion we were boarding a plane in St. Louis. It was nearly empty, and the stewardess who checked our tickets took time to look them over carefully. Mine said Mr. Michael Nason, Bob's said Dr. Robert Schuller. Later, after take-off, she looked us up. I think she was bored, since the plane was so quiet. She sidled up to Bob, who was sitting on the aisle. "So you're a doctor, huh?" she began. "What kind of a doctor are you? No, no, don't tell me, let me guess."

Bob shot me a look that said, "She'll never figure out this one." He just smiled at her. He loves a good joke, especially if he can play it on someone else.

She started out innocently enough. "Are you a pediatrician?"

"No."

"Are you an internist?"

"No."

"Don't tell me you're a leg man."

Bob smothered a choke. "No."

"I know," she said in her sexiest voice. "You must be a breast man." Bob turned about ten shades of red. He couldn't look her in the eye, but turned and looked pleadingly at me.

It was all I could do to keep from laughing. There had been a joke all right, but I wasn't sure whom it was on. I fished in my briefcase and pulled out Bob's press kit. It has pictures of him and the church and tells all about his ministry. I handed it to the stewardess, who was beginning to look awkward by this time. When she got a look at the pictures, I thought she was going to cry. She let out a gasp and her hand flew instinctively to cover her face. "Oh, my God," she muttered as she made a rapid retreat down the aisle. Both Bob and I felt so sorry for her, because she couldn't pass him without blushing. But we let her keep the press kit. And, who knows?

Recently, on a trip to Canada, Bob and I were taking a taxi through the city of Montreal. The driver was a surly fellow, and when someone cut in front of him on the road, he let out a string of blue language that would have made a sailor blush. Bob reached forward and tapped the man on the shoulder. "Sir," his voice carried authority. "That language is offensive to me. It insults my dignity as a human being." The cabby was shocked. I don't think anyone had ever talked to him like that before, and possibly he had never thought of foul language in quite that light. He actually apologized to Bob, and his entire manner took on a different quality.

In Washington, D.C., one time we rode with another singularly angry cab driver. He was a real cynic, cold and hard as tacks. He seemed to be bitter about everything, from the weather to the traffic to the unsatisfactory relationships he had had with three different women. He was a sixty-year-old man whose entire life revolved around an attitude of resentment. No matter what happened to him, he responded to it by getting mad.

It was a long drive across the city, and Bob had finally had enough. He steered the conversation around to religion. "Are you a Christian?" he asked.

"Sure," the driver snarled.

"What kind?" Bob countered. "A real one or a hypocrite?"

He was insulted. "A real one, I guess."

Bob took the plunge. "If you think you are a Christian, then answer me one question. If you died tonight, where would you go? To heaven or to hell?"

The driver sounded puzzled. "I'm not sure." His tone said, "What's it to you, buddy?"

Bob put on his best preaching voice. "I can tell you how to be sure."

The cabby looked into his rearview mirror suspiciously. "Hey, what are you anyway?"

Bob smiled. "I'm a minister and I write books and I can tell you how you can be sure." He didn't pause long enough to let the man open his mouth. "What you need to do my friend, is to ask Jesus Christ into your heart. Jesus promised, 'Him that cometh to me I will in no wise cast out.' What you have to do is come to Jesus and admit that you've sinned. Your bitterness and resentful negative attitude are your worst sins."

The cab driver shot Bob an incredulous look in that mirror and Bob met it with a steady gaze.

About that time, we pulled into the parking lot at the airport. "I'm not getting out.'' Bob was emphatic. ''You can keep your meter running if you want, but I'm going to let you have the opportunity right now to become an authentic Christian. An authentic Christian doesn't go griping through his life. He accepts Jesus as his Savior and lets Him change his attitude.'' Bob led the cabdriver in a prayer for forgiveness and new life. I watched his countenance change. It was a beautiful, moving sight.

''Now listen to me.'' It was Bob's voice of authority again. ''If by some quirk of circumstances you arrive tonight in the very presence of God Almighty, whatever you do, don't start rattling off a list of all the good things you've done. He won't be impressed. You just call Jesus and remind him of His promise. He's a man of His word, and He promised you He wouldn't cast you out. You can depend on Him. You know, you're not the same man you were ten minutes ago.''

I took a good look at him, and Bob was right. The anger was gone, the bitterness, the tight, nervous set of the jaw. All gone. The man was radiant.

One day Bob answered the phone in his office. There was that crackly, hollow long-distance sound. A pleasant voice on the other end said, ''Robert Schuller? I need to talk to you. I'm in Belfast, Northern Ireland, and I've just got to hear something positive.'' Bob laughed and regaled the stranger with a few of his one-liners. Then the caller continued in his wonderful Irish brogue, ''I've just read your book, *Move Ahead with Possibility Thinking*, and I think its fabulous. My name's Leslie Hale, and I'm a possibility thinker myself. I was beginning to think I was the only one.''

Leslie pastored a small church in the war-torn city of Belfast, and he had a dream, a dream so big and so impossible it had to have come from God. ''I want my church to expand. I want it to be a place where true Christians can come together and worship God, no matter whether they are Catholics or Protestants.'' Bob was captivated. He saw to it that Leslie Hale had his way paid from Belfast to Orange County and that he was able to attend the next Institutes for Successful Church Leadership. Bob was touched by the first-hand account of bombings and guerrilla warfare, the terrorism of civil war and the havoc it wreaked on everyone, especially children. He was especially saddened by religious prejudice.

Bob issued an invitation to the dynamic Irishman to come back the next summer for a month and bring his wife and children for a respite from the struggle. He could preach in Bob's place, get paid for it, and have the chance to relax and regroup his thoughts. Leslie loved the idea, and churchmembers and visitors that year had a unique treat in the preaching of the Irishman with all the unusual stories of God's provision in an explosive and exploding city.

Leslie Hale went on to make his dream a reality. He pastors a large congregation of Christians from every denomination, striving for unity in a divided land. Later, Bob had made up and sent over to Ireland some two hundred thousand bumper stickers that say "God loves you and so do I." Through the auspices of Leslie's church they began to distribute them, and when they were all gone, more were printed. Soon cars could be seen all over Belfast sporting "God loves you and so do I" stickers. The Catholics had them, the Protestants too, even the police cars. Those who posted the stickers smiled and waved at each other, regardless of religious persuasion. And it started with a book.

That same book, *Move Ahead with Possibility Thinking*, has recently been translated and published in Mao's script on mainland China. It became an instant bestseller. Last summer, Bob traveled with his son Robert Anthony, now a minister in his own right, into the cities and villages of that ancient land. Together they walked the Great Wall of China and bargained with the people for down comforters and other fine native handcrafts.

The Chinese people are very small in stature. The Schullers loomed above them, standing several heads taller. This fascinated the Chinese, who would stare and point at the tall Americans. Bob found them to be very friendly and anxious to practice their English. Later in their visit, they discovered another reason why the people in Shanghai had been so friendly and interested in them. The American Embassy there has a large billboard that looks out onto the street. On it are pictures of different typically American scenes, from fashion to food to cities to people. Included in the collage was a picture of the Garden Grove Community Church and another one of its senior pastor, Robert Schuller.

One evening, just as the sun was going down, father and son were walking across one of the many bridges in Shanghai. They were stopped by two young Chinese students from the University of

Shanghai. In their halting English, they said, "We know you. Your picture is at the American Embassy. You are ministers, aren't you?" The younger Bob answered "Yes." A crowd of curious onlookers gathered as the three young men spoke together. "We would like to know more about your God."

The twenty-eight-year-old, second generation Robert Schuller shared with them a loving, living God who wanted to be their friend. They were hungry for more. Young Bob reached into his pocket and brought out a copy of Campus Crusade's Four Spiritual Laws. It's just a small tract, outlining the steps a person must take to receive Christ into his heart. They nodded their heads in acceptance as he went over the booklet point by point.

When he was finished, they asked him eagerly, "Can we pray the prayer right now?"

Bob was astounded, looking around uneasily for the police. There were none. "Well, sure, if you want to." And there, on that bridge surrounded by the pagodas of Shanghai, as darkness overtook the day, they bowed their heads unashamed before the crowd and asked Jesus to forgive them and come and live within their hearts. Young Bob gave them a copy of the Bible, a small translation that he had carried in his pocket, and they hugged it to their breasts.

Their parting words as they turned to go were, "We're not going to keep this miracle, this Jesus, to ourselves. We're going to tell everyone about him."

Bob looked at his son in the light of a lamp that shone in the darkness. The crowd was dispersing, and a sliver of moonlight could barely be seen through the clouds. Night had come to China. Bob thought back to the years of raising his only son. He had hoped for more boys, and goodness knows he and Arvella had tried, but the Lord had given them four beautiful daughters instead. That his son had grown up to follow in his father's footsteps as a minister was one of his greatest joys. When his son had first started reading the Scriptures and giving the prayers on the "Hour of Power," it had been all Bob could do to keep from bursting into tears. Now here in the Orient his son was carrying on a work that had always held a special place in Bob's heart.

It hadn't been too many years earlier when Garden Grove Church had given three hundred thousand dollars to build the Keochang High

School in Korea, a Christian high school where hundreds of young Koreans could learn a positive faith. Later the church had given nearly as much to finance the printing of the Bible into Mao's script and had also helped to distribute copies of it in the very land where they now stood. He reached over and put his arm around young Bob's broad shoulders, and the two of them walked over the bridge into the night.

Bob Schuller's positive faith and personal charisma have made him appealing to people from all walks of life, many different countries, and the entire political spectrum. He steers clear of politics as much as possible, and most people don't know where he stands politically, which is how he wants it. That way he is free to minister to a broad field of persons who will not be hung up on his politics. If they're not worrying about his politics, then they can concentrate on his theology.

After Senator Humphrey died and his wife Muriel resumed his office, she wanted to introduce Bob to more of the lawmakers on Capitol Hill. He had been extremely well received at Hubert's funeral, and many in Washington watched the "Hour of Power" regularly. Senator Robert Dole and his wife Elizabeth were also staunch supporters of Bob personally and of the "Hour of Power," and they too wanted to give him credence on the Washington scene. The three of them hosted a luncheon for Bob in one of the Senate dining rooms.

About fifteen senators were in attendance; Republicans, Democrats, liberals, conservatives were all represented. I accompanied Bob that day and saw firsthand, as I have so many times, the amazing draw the man has for all types of people. Jacob Javits from New York was there, and Jesse Helms of North Carolina. Strom Thurmond from South Carolina was also present.

Ted Kennedy had been invited and had wanted to attend, but had a conflict that day. He asked if Bob couldn't meet with him on another occasion, as he was anxious to spend some time with him. So on another trip to D.C. Bob made a point of arranging an appointment with the Senator. We found ourselves back in the elegant Senate reception area, the same place where Bob had met Hubert Humphrey years earlier. Ted Kennedy bounded off the floor of the Senate and greeted Bob cordially. He was as tall as Bob, a big man, and the two of them stood, framed by the tall French windows, as they talked for a full fifteen minutes. Kennedy found something in Bob that generated hope within him, something that touched off a positive chord in his own life of challenges, bitter defeats, and sorrows. They spoke of the Kennedy family and the unique pressures of membership and the unique possibilities, too. Bob is always very close-mouthed about his meetings with people, the famous as well as the ordinary. He takes his position as a minister very seriously and never betrays a confidence. I was over to the side as they spoke, taking pictures. Senator Kennedy had tears well up in his eyes many times during the conversation.

Another interesting incident occurred one day when someone in the letter-opening division of the Hour of Power opened a letter which contained a handwritten check for $100,000. The woman who opened the envelope was so stunned, she just sat there for a moment, speechless. Was it real? Although the Hour of Power gets lots of mail, less than half the letters contain donations, and most all of them are small, the average being around five dollars. Any time a sizeable gift is received, it has usually been solicited in some way other than the television program. Perhaps Bob has visited with the person, or maybe a special direct-mail piece has gone out like our current Eagle's Club which asks for a membership fee of $500.

The check and letter were sent over to the church to Bob. It was from Ray Kroc. The letter openers didn't know who he was, but Bob did. Ray Kroc was the owner and founder of McDonald's Hamburgers.

He and his wife had never heard of Bob Schuller or the "Hour of Power." They were just turning the channels on their television set one day and somehow he caught their attention. They watched the whole program and loved it. Mr. Kroc was so impressed that he sat right down and prepared to write out a check for $200,000. "Oh, don't do that," his wife advised. "They won't believe it's real. It's too much." So she talked him into cutting the check in half. Bob was ecstatic. But this was the beginning of a friendship between the Krocs and Bob, three creative possibility thinkers.

Bob is very ecumenical. He hates majoring in minors, but prefers to concentrate on the points that all Christians share. He tries to cultivate friendships with everyone and likes to cement bonds and build bridges. I guess that's why he had a burning desire to meet the Pope. He was given an audience with Pope John Paul II, whom he admires very much. He attended a mass there in the Vatican first, and was impressed by the love and concern the pontiff showed for each of the communicants. He treated each one as if they were special to him, and just radiated love, from his eyes, from his smile, from his touch. It meant a lot to Bob to be there, even though he was not allowed to partake of the sacraments. The brief visit he shared with the leader of much of the Christian world only served to strengthen his love of Christians everywhere.

Bishop Fulton J. Sheen had long been a favorite of Bob's. Back in the fifties he never missed one of Bishop Sheen's television programs. Bob loved his syncretization of theology and psychology and the way he often spoke in short stories and parables, just as Jesus had done. Bob says that Bishop Sheen has been one of the major influences on his own theology, and lost no time having him as a guest on the "Hour of Power." Bishop Sheen came to the church twice, and taped three different programs. He is one of the few men to whom Bob has relinquished the pulpit for an entire message.

The first time he came, they had to set up chairs in the parking lot to handle the overflow. Bob was delighted to see the great number of Catholic nuns and priests who came to hear their bishop. It was a great day. Bishop Sheen's next visit was disappointing to Bob in that very few of the Catholic clergy came to see him. He knew they had enjoyed him and admired him on his previous visit, and was saddened to learn that the upper echelons of the church had put out the notice for them not to attend the service.

When Sheen passed away, it was my privilege, under Bob's direction, to prepare a special memorial service for TV using clips from his visits to the church. We dedicated an entire hour to this great Christian churchman and gave him the accolades he so richly deserved.

Another of the men who have influenced Bob's theology and ministry the most is the great evangelist, Billy Graham. Bob has spoken at many of Graham's Schools of Evangelism throughout the world, and has always held him in the highest esteem. Both Billy and Ruth Graham are fairly regular viewers of the "Hour of Power," especially Ruth.

When Billy held his last Las Vegas Crusade, he invited Bob to have a part in the program one night and speak to the crowd. Bob doesn't like to travel to Las Vegas by himself, and Arvella dislikes the place immensely. Usually I, or another aide, will accompany him to the city known as the sin capital of the country.

This time I was able to go with Bob, and I was really excited to think of meeting Billy Graham for the first time. I had always enjoyed his crusades on television, but had never been to one in person. Bob and I normally stay at the MGM Grand Hotel when we go to Las Vegas. The hotels there are so huge that it's just easier to always stay at the same one; that way we know where to find the restaurants and even how to find our way in and out. But the Graham Crusade was held in the convention center, which is right next to the Hilton, so his staff made our reservations there.

That night we met Billy and Ruth Graham in a small side room of the convention center before the Crusade began. They were both tall, beautiful people, who could light up a room just by being there. Each possessed a quiet dignity and enormous personal charisma. They spent about twenty minutes with Bob, sharing their ministries and visions, talking about the current crusade. They let Bob know by their comments that they had been watching the "Hour of Power" recently, and that pleased him very much.

That night at the crusade, Bob shared what the living Christ had meant in his life and told about the time Billy had touched his life during Bob's days in seminary.

The next morning my phone rang as I was getting dressed. It was Bob. "Go look out your window," he said. "Do you see any smoke?" There was a thin black column rising from the backside of the MGM Grand. "Looks like maybe a truck or something caught fire outside in the parking lot of the Grand," I reported. "Let's hurry up and meet for breakfast. Maybe we'll see more on our way down to breakfast." Bob never wants to miss anything, and I'm afraid I'm just as bad. I turned on the TV, hoping for a news report, but quite a while went by before they interrupted the program with the news that the MGM Grand was on fire.

When we went by taxi to the airport, we could see the helicopters trying to rescue people from the burning building. The balconies were full of screaming persons, many trying to jump. It was terrible, like a battle zone. The air was pierced constantly by sirens, all sorts of emergency vehicles snaked through the streets. There was a lot of commotion. Back home, Donna, who thought we were at the Grand, was going through torture. It wasn't until we were on the plane that we realized what a narrow escape we had just had. What if we'd been at the Grand as usual?

On another trip, I accompanied Bob to Oral Roberts University where he was to give a motivational address for a rally on positive speaking. We also had an appointment to meet Oral Roberts in his office at the chapel building. Bob and I were really impressed with the University. It jutted up out of the prairie in modernistic simplicity, and the students' faith and warmth were obvious. When we met the founder of ORU, we found him to be a man of boundless energy, exuding enthusiasm and vitality. He greeted Bob with a warm embrace like an old friend, and the two of them went into Oral's private office for a time of close fellowship. A supportive relationship emerged.

They both have a great deal of respect for each other, and they reach a lot of the same people, or the same kinds of people, with their TV ministries.

Bob invited Oral to come be a guest on the "Hour of Power" sometime. We really hoped he would, but knowing the busy schedule of a man in his position, we doubted he could work it in. It was an exciting day when Bob got the call that Oral was in California and would come by for a visit. It was one of those stormy winter weekends, where the sky just opens up and lets loose with everything it's got. Nevertheless, they met, the Roberts and the Schullers, for dinner Saturday night. It was a highly spiritual time, one which Bob will never forget.

Oral had had a vision. He saw the "Hour of Power" and the Robert Schuller ministries as a team of wild horses out of control. "You've got to get the reins, take control," he told Bob and Arvella. They were visibly shaken. They knew of certain situations within the ministry, different personnel and people problems, that were very much out of control at that time. A lot of it was the result of the rapid growth, and Bob, who hates to fire people and make changes in staff, was grappling for a solution. But no one outside the Hour of Power could possibly have known. The message was obviously from God.

Oral went on further to warn Bob not to get too much hay on the fork, to weigh his priorities carefully. He had quite an impact on Bob and gave him the impetus to make some decisions that had needed to be made for some time.

Another prophecy that Oral made which had a profound effect on Bob was regarding the growth of Bob's ministry. "I see it growing like a great banyan tree in the years to come," Oral prophesied, "it's roots spreading, its trunk growing, its branches reaching out to a massive size and strength."

The next morning, when Oral stepped up to the pulpit in the sanctuary, the choir burst into a rousing rendition of "Something Good Is Going to Happen to You." He loved hearing his theme song, and the congregation of several thousand gave him a standing ovation. After the service, Oral gave Bob a lot of prayer support. It was at the time when we were first starting construction on the Crystal Cathedral, which he called the Crystal Palace, and he had a feel for the pressures that were about to begin.

I was struck by the care and concern that Bob and other Christian leaders have for each other. They realize, more than the general public, I think, that their efforts are combined ones. They are not in competition with one another, but serve the same God for the same purpose. The next few years Bob would need their support as at no other time in his life.

12

The Crystal Cathedral—Monument or Instrument?

When I came to work for Bob in 1973, he was already complaining that the existing sanctuary was too small. It was a fact he lived with daily, and it chafed him and gnawed at his very soul, even then. It was unthinkable to abandon that building, to just cast it off like an old shoe. One of Bob's favorite analogies when it comes to church growth is in likening the church to a foot and the church buildings and property to a shoe. He says, "The shoe must never tell the foot how large to grow! If the shoe is growth-restricting, it's got to be removed."

He lived it. He believed it as he believed the very gospel of Christ. But in his own case, he just wasn't ready to pay the price. The scars he had received during the two years of deliberation that resulted in the Lewis Street property were still there. He would swear that God had turned them into stars, and He probably had, but that still didn't make him over eager to jump into the fray again. So, for a period of years he just stewed over it. It stuck in his craw. I think it bothered him because he saw himself as being hypocritical. He really believed that God wanted his church to grow, and he knew it was at capacity and couldn't continue to expand as it should. He understood the problem and knew the solution rested in the construction of a new sanctuary. Not to move ahead with it was selfish on his part and went against his concept of himself as a servant first.

The "Hour of Power" television ministry was threatening the Garden Grove Community Church. Each week, some three to five hundred visitors arrived from all over the country, persons who watched the "Hour of Power" on TV and wanted to worship in the church while in Southern California on vacation. The regular members of the church couldn't find a place to sit. It was a huge growth-restricting problem, the result of success. Depending on his mood, Bob will chuckle or frown when he says, "Success doesn't eliminate problems, you only exchange those you've got for bigger ones."

He figured he was looking at a four- or five-million-dollar project, and it frightened him. He rather halfheartedly had different architects draw some schematics for a new sanctuary, but none of them suited him and only served to help him procrastinate more. Richard Neutra was dead, or perhaps the two of them could have come up with another design as exciting as the glass-sided, international-style sanctuary. But as it was, Bob just couldn't get enthused about building something ordinary. Not for that kind of money. "If I'm going to take the criticism to raise the money to build the building," he said, "I want a design people won't forget." He never liked to be involved with anything that didn't excel. Excellence, to Bob's way of thinking, produces excitement. Excitement produces energy. Energy creates momentum. And momentum makes things happen. To raise that much money for a building, it had to be unique, outstanding. Nothing else would do. God waits to pour out His abundance, but He doesn't give it to small-thinking people. He only gives it to those who think big.

Bob's indecision lasted for years. He just couldn't make up his mind. Then one week a funeral was held at the church for a small boy who had drowned in the backyard pool of his parents. They were a young couple, with no church affiliation, no personal faith that could help them cope with their loss. Bob knew that. And they were hurting. Bob wanted to reach out and touch them, to pass on to them the faith it took to get through the crisis. He invited them to church on Sunday.

Sunday came, and it was cold, one of those rare Southern California days when the sky was slate, unfeeling and uncaring. From atop the Tower, Bob could see the people pouring into the sanctuary, the wind whipping at their coats and hair. He could see the several hundred chairs which had been set up out in the Garden of the Twenty-Third Psalm. The sanctuary was full. Again. People began filling up the outdoor seating, their hands jammed inside their pockets for warmth, huddled together under blankets the church provided.

When Bob entered the pulpit area high above the congregation, he scanned the crowds. There, in the last rows of garden seats, sat the young couple he had hoped to see. Their faces were tense, and the woman's long hair blew in the wind. Every now and then she would reach a hand from under the blanket and try to smooth it down.

As the service began, it started to drizzle thin, dreary sheets of water. Inside, the choir was singing, the television lights were bright, reflecting off the golden brass of the trumpets. Outside it was dismal. Depressing. As the minutes wore on, some of the women's hair matted in clumps about their damp faces. A few had umbrellas. Many did not. By the second anthem, people were beginning to abandon the garden sanctuary. In groups of twos and threes they rose, leaving their blankets to soak there in the rain, which was increasing in intensity. Bob watched them from the corner of his eye, frustration mounting within him. Then it happened. He sat helplessly and watched the bereaved couple get up from their chairs. They had brought no umbrella, and the husband put his arm around his wife protectively as they walked away. Bob saw them walk through the rain out into the parking lot toward their car. They looked so small and so alone. "Wait! Come back!" he wanted to scream at them, but he spoke the words only in his heart.

At that moment he knew he couldn't let his selfishness, his fear, control his decision making any longer. He let his mind wander over his lectures at the Institutes. "Leadership looks for growth-restricting obstacles and sets goals accordingly. Your goals must be in accordance with your own deepest value system." He squared his jaw and moved up to the pulpit for his morning message.

Both Bob and Arvella started really concentrating on finding a suitable architect. It was top priority. They searched for no less than the greatest living American architect to build the new sanctuary. They wanted a building so beautiful that it would bring glory to God and to the human family. As Bob says, "God wants us to be shining stars in a dark world." Nothing but the best would do. One summer day in 1975, on a transcontinental plane flight, Arvella drowsily leafed through a *Vogue* magazine as Bob slept in the seat beside her. All of a sudden she clutched at his arm. "Bob, wake up. Look at this."

His eyelids fluttered open, and he fumbled for his glasses, perching them on top of his nose as he focused on the magazine Arvella held in front of him. There was a photograph of a maze, of angular concrete walls and trees and plants and cascading water. He read, "The Water Gardens in Forth Worth," and repeated the words over to himself. "This is fantastic, Beau-tee-ful." Even the tone of his words embraced the design. "Who did it?"

"Philip Johnson, honey. See, it says so right here." Arvella pointed her long, angular finger at the print. "I think he must be a landscape architect."

When they landed in New York, Bob lost no time in looking up the famed architect. He arrived at the impressive offices of Johnson/Burgee without even an appointment, so great had been his rush to see them. He approached the receptionist confidently. "I'm Robert Schuller from California. I'm here to talk with Mr. Johnson about a job." She looked unimpressed. He tried a different tack. "I've worked on some projects with Richard Neutra." She got up and disappeared into another office for a few minutes, then returned. "I'm sorry. Mr. Johnson is out of town and Mr. Burgee is in conference right now. Perhaps if you'd care to leave a resume . . ."

Bob laughs about it now. "They thought I was a draftsman looking for a job."

Communication was finally established. The firm of Johnson/Burgee was much more interested in talking with a potential client. Bob spoke with John Burgee and arrangements were made for Philip Johnson to fly out to California to meet him and look over the property. In the meantime, he would watch the "Hour of Power," which he had never seen, and get a feel for the man and the ministry of Robert Schuller.

I drove Bob to the airport to pick up Philip Johnson on his first visit to the church, witnessed the first meeting of these two men who were destined to make architectural history together. Mr. Johnson was an impressive figure as he strode confidently through the concourse and out into the terminal. He's the sort of man who stands out in a crowd, partly because he's so tall and thin and possesses such an air of dignity, almost of aristocracy. He's an older man, well into his seventies now, with a shock of white hair and dark-rimmed round glasses. He was very New York proper, dressed in an immaculately cut black suit with a white shirt, black tie, and white handkerchief positioned just so in his coat pocket. When he caught sight of Bob, he broke out in a wide smile, greeting him with a handshake that was warm and friendly. I don't think the two of them ever stopped talking from that moment until way after I let them off at the base of the Tower.

Mr. Johnson's reputation in the field of modern architecture has been that of undisputed excellence for decades, some of his buildings considered to be the finest in the world. He was an early follower of the pioneer of modern architecture, Mies van der Rohe, and he expounded the theories of the international style that Bob Schuller also believed in, "less is more" and "form follows function." Long before the Crystal Cathedral, he was famous for designs like the Pennzoil Place, a pair of trapezoidal skyscrapers in Houston, Texas, and the American Telephone and Telegraph building in New York with its classical arches and cabinet-like granite cap.

He listened enthusiastically as Bob described the mammoth project he had in mind, a huge edifice that would open from the inside out and bring the outside in, a church large enough to seat four thousand people with ease. And a building that would harmonize with the Neutra structures. They spent time walking over the grounds, looking at the existing architecture, and just getting to know each other before Philip Johnson had to leave for New York.

In a few weeks time, he was back with his first sketches of the new church. He had borrowed concepts which he had used in the design of the art gallery on the grounds of his own home in Connecticut, a design with opaque walls and a transparent roof. Bob hated it. It was far too visually confining, too conventional. "I want something striking. So striking that it will cry out to be built. We don't have any money, so it doesn't matter how much it costs. If the building is striking enough, it will raise its own financing."

In speaking of that day, Bob asserts that he was politely nonaffirmative. Philip Johnson says he nearly threw him out of the room. "Please," Bob finally asked, "can't you make it all glass?"

A short time later, Mr. Johnson was back, this time with not a drawing, but a model. It was six inches high and secured to a piece of masonite, shaped like an elongated four-pointed star, and shimmering with ten thousand pieces of mirrored glass. Bob thundered his approval. It was perfect. He never changed even one pane of glass.

To Bob, it was the answer to his desires for a building that didn't inhibit views of the outside world. As before, he wanted people to be able to look out and see cars and sky, and he wanted them to be able to see the gardens that would eventually surround the church, he wanted to re-create for them the peace and tranquillity of the Garden of Eden within a modern structure.

Johnson had been inspired by Victorian England's Crystal Palace and the amphitheater at Epidaurus, Greece, as well as by Mies van der Rohe's angular, multifaceted office project built in 1919. The design also bears some resemblance to the University of Oklahoma's Crystal Chapel in its exclusive use of glass for walls and roof as well as its complicated nonrectilinear geometry and extensive interior and exterior fountains and pools. He was delighted with his own creation. "I've always wanted to build a church."

Philip Johnson, as a modern architect, starts with structure and function. First he determines the purpose of the building, then the best way of building it, and then integrates the two. "Religious buildings are really what architecture is all about," the austere Johnson maintains. "A church has no purpose other than backing up the ritual of the liturgy. You don't have to worry about where to put the kitchen or the toilets. You just have to make the space as moving as you can. To me, architecture is the design of interior space. And, oh my God, this is the most exciting space I've ever done. I'm overwhelmed by it."

The dimensions were breathtaking, even though at that time they were still hard to imagine. The distorted four-pointed star measures 207 feet along its two axes, its ground coverage equivalent to that of a 186-foot square rectilinear building. Its ceiling soars to an unimpeded height equal to that of a ten-story building, and it's been said its length is longer than that of two football fields. Bob asserts that it is larger than the Cathedral of Notre Dame in Paris, but its usable interior space is actually a little more than half that size.

Almost immediately it was dubbed the Crystal Cathedral. In the strictest sense, a cathedral must contain a bishop's throne—"cathedra" in Latin—and serve as the bishop's official or principal church.

Nevertheless, the dimensions and ambitions of the Crystal Cathedral certainly approach those of a cathedral. Some have said that its surging lines have put Robert Schuller in the same architectural camp as Counter-Reformation popes and cardinals who often used pomp and drama in their buildings as well as in their services.

As Bob told *Newsweek* magazine in an early article about the Cathedral, "I wanted a building that would be a lasting work of art. I happen to believe that a work of art is good for a man's spirit. It's a cathedral of ten thousand windows—an all-aglow structure without a single gloomy corner."

There may not be any gloomy corners in the all-glass church, but it certainly took five gloomy years to bring it from its inception to its glorious completion. These years represented joys and tragedies heretofore unknown by the Schuller family. The Crystal Cathedral represented the culmination of all Bob's work, it stretched back through the years to a small boy with bare feet and a dirty face who wanted to be a preacher some day. Those five years should have been fulfilling, exciting times, like experiencing the birth of a much-wanted baby. But they weren't.

They were so full of misery and pain at times that Bob didn't get to enjoy them. They were sad for him all the way around, personally and professionally. He went through hell trying to build that building, and his ups and downs permeated the entire ministry, from the top echelon right on down to the bottom rung.

There were great mountain-peak experiences that helped sustain all of us through the rest of the time when we were deep down in the pits of despair, and I think that's a sign that God wanted the building built. When things got so low that we thought we couldn't stand it a minute longer, God always stepped in with an assurance of His love and support. Without that, I doubt the Cathedral would have been completed.

It got off to a good start, with no real hints of the difficulties to come. November 1975 was the twentieth anniversary of the church, and seven thousand members attended the celebration at the Anaheim Convention Center. Bob held up the model of the Crystal Cathedral, turning it around so that the lights would catch its prisms and make it shimmer and glow. The congregation caught the fire, the excitement of the challenge and pledged their support overwhelmingly.

Even so, we knew the membership couldn't build the church alone. To this day they are a basically middle-class group, many lower on the economic scale and some higher, but certainly not in possession of great wealth. Bob challenged them to double tithe, give twenty percent of their incomes to the church and they responded. But it still wasn't enough even for the original seven million dollar budget. He went to the banks and tried to enlist their support, hoping they would loan us the money to build. They wouldn't. We were encouraged to raise the money and pay for it as we went along so that when completed it would be a debt-free building, and Bob decided that would be the best way to go.

I was the one who finally convinced Bob that we would have to go to the greater community for financial support. After all, the "Hour of Power" was broadcast all over the world, and everyone who watched the program would benefit from the Cathedral. Not only that, but our congregation on any given Sunday contained hundreds of visitors from all over. They would like to have a part in the construction of the new sanctuary. We were sure of it.

Bob selected Victor Andrews, a prominent Orange County resident, but not a Christian nor a member of the church, to spearhead the building committee. It was a good choice, not only for us, but for him. Bob and Victor would meet each other for breakfast at Cocos Coffeeshop in Newport Beach near Victor's home to discuss plans, and they soon became friends. One morning, toward the middle of construction, Victor told Bob how much he admired his faith. "I wish I had your faith, Bob," he said over ham and eggs. "You have an immaculate faith." Bob smiled. "You can, Vic. All you have to do is ask for it." And there in that busy cafe, they bowed their heads and Bob led Victor in a prayer, asking God to forgive him in Jesus' name and for Jesus to take up residence in his heart by the power of the Holy Spirit.

At the twentieth-anniversary celebration, Bob had surprised everybody by saying he believed someone would give a million dollars for the construction of the Cathedral. The convention center had rocked with laughter as the people pondered the impossibility of such a thing. Certainly none of them had such a capacity.

As he had done many times before, Bob hired a professional fund raiser, but a different kind than he had used earlier. Doug

Lawson's expertise is in knowing the very wealthy people in the country who have large sums of money to give away. I realize that it is hard for most of us regular people to comprehend, but there really are such people who have plenty of money and plenty of compassion and who also can benefit from the tax advantages of donating part of their resources.

Bob doesn't like fund raising. He enjoys meeting people and talking with them, but he doesn't like asking them for money. It makes him feel presumptuous. It was only his belief in the project that gave him the courage to ask. He knew it had to have support or it wouldn't happen. Bob believes that the dreams that come from God always seem impossible, in fact they really are impossible apart from God's intervention. He also believes that the bigger the problem the bigger the miracle. For Robert Schuller faith in action is to dream, then have the nerve and daring to make that decision, before the problems are resolved. It is to announce to the whole world what is going to happen. And that's just what he did with the Crystal Cathedral.

He views frustrations as mosquito bites; if you scratch them, you make them worse, so he tried not to scratch. Only to forge ahead and start trying to raise that money. On Maundy Thursday of 1976, he screwed up his courage and went with Doug Lawson to visit John Crean. He was a local rancher down in San Juan Capistrano, with a beautiful Spanish-style home that sat up on a hill overlooking the San Diego Freeway and the fertile Saddleback Valley. Mr. Crean had made a fortune in recreational vehicles and was well known locally for his philanthropy.

Bob shared with him his dreams of an all-glass cathedral and told him it needed a lead-off gift of a million dollars to get the momentum going. Would he make that gift? Mr. Crean looked thoughtful, rubbing his chin between his thumb and index finger. "I'm sorry." He would like to, but just couldn't at that time. Bob was disappointed—it had been his first attempt to secure the million-dollar gift, and he had really hoped to be successful. But, before he left, Bob asked John if they could pray together about the situation. John agreed and Bob prayed these words: "O God, I'm so thankful he wants to give a million. Is it possible for You to figure out a way for him to do what he'd like to do, but can't?"

The next day was Good Friday, surely one of the holiest days of the year. Bob was busy preparing for services to commemorate the sacrifice of Christ on the cross for the sins of the world, having temporarily forgotten yesterday's failure. The phone rang. It was John Crean. He had thought about it, prayed about it. God wanted him to give that million dollars. He would do it. It was not a matter of if, it was a matter of when and how.

When Bob announced it to the congregation that day, I thought his heart would burst with gratitude and thanksgiving. We all felt God had given His blessing to the project, and with the gift coming through on Good Friday, it seemed especially symbolic.

But already there were other signs that portended more bad than good; previews of rising construction costs frightened us. Even there, though, God brought His people to the rescue. We received a letter with a check for five hundred dollars. "Dear Dr. Schuller, why don't you sell the windows in the Cathedral for five hundred dollars apiece? I'll buy the first one." It was a great idea, not Bob's nor anybody's on our staff, but from someone we didn't even know, someone who had caught the excitement of what we were trying to accomplish.

There were 10,661 windows going in the cathedral, each one six-feet-tall by two-feet-wide, each one made of silver mirrored glass, and we began a mammoth campaign to sell each one. The purchaser could dedicate his window to whomever he chose, and they would be numbered and marked with that name. At that time it was purely promotional. People had to take us on faith that we would in fact build a cathedral and put up the window with their name on it.

By that next November, the window program was going full blast, and we were all getting really excited about the Crystal Cathedral, even though it was still no more than Bob Schuller's and Philip Johnson's dream. At the twenty-first-anniversary celebration (Bob always celebrates each year), he unveiled a large illuminated model of the proposed cathedral. It was encased in lucite for protection and, as Bob said, sparkled like a jewel. He installed it in a place of honor in the lobby of the Tower of Hope, a brilliant symbol of his goal.

Of all the five years, I guess 1977 was the best, even though we could see inflation soaring and the costs of our cathedral following right along behind it like the tails streaming behind a kite on a windy day. We were well into the project now, with much of the preliminary work being done and funds already pouring in.

That January we moved over into the new Hour of Power building across Chapman from the church. We had it all to ourselves until the Crystal Cathedral Academy opened that September and the voices of children at play echoed down the halls.

The congregation of the Garden Grove Community Church single-handedly raised enough money to buy a helicopter for the Missionary Aviation Fellowship and presented it to them that March. It has been used in the jungles of New Guinea ever since to bring missionaries and natives out of the brush and deliver them to modern hospital facilities when they are ill, also to take drugs and other supplies into the back country where cars cannot go. I have often wondered, in the ensuing years of criticism about our supposed lack of concern for missions and the poor, how many of the complaining churches had ever given an equivalent gift to mission work. I imagine many had never given that much if you added all their gifts over the years together much less one single gift at a time, and that during a building campaign.

That May marked the long-awaited opening of our Community Garden Towers with 210 units for senior citizens to live in Christian community just down from the church. Many had been waiting for years for the governmental paperwork and HUD delays to finally make this dream a reality, and it was a major achievement for us all.

Then, in August, the 116-rank, 108-stop Fratelli-Ruffatti organ, with its more than 6,000 pipes, was installed in the sanctuary. That was surely a great day for the Schullers, as much as they all love fine organ music.

But all these were only teasers for the main event coming December fourth. We were finally going to break ground for the Crystal Cathedral. It had been two full years since Bob had first shared the tiny model with the congregation. Now we had admired the large model for a year, and finally something concrete was happening.

Bob has always gone in for pageantry in a big way, and the groundbreaking for the Cathedral was certainly no exception. He had a large crew ready to man the shovels, trying to represent all the different facets of our local and Hour of Power congregations as well as those who were donating money for its construction. We all started in the Neutra sanctuary. Barbara and Toby Waldowski, who are regular singers on the "Hour of Power" and who also headed up the children's choirs, had composed a unique musical program, which made use of all the choirs, especially the children's choirs. The children told in music and song the story of the Garden Grove Community Church. They sang songs like "Inch by inch, anything's a cinch; I will build my church, says the Lord;" and "Whatever happened to Rosie Gray?" and "Come as you are in the family car." The successes of the past and the hopes for the future were reflected in their open faces, and it was especially touching for me to see Carol and Gretchen Schuller singing in their robes with the others. Jeanne had been singing with the choirs when I started with Bob, but now she was a sophomore at Wheaton College. It seemed I was watching three of the Schuller children grow up along with my own.

At the close of the program, the organ swelled to Widor's powerful Toccata (Opus 42, #5) and the entire congregation marched en masse out of the sanctuary and onto the cleared ground where the Cathedral would one day stand. A long line of dignitaries stretched in front, with the Schuller family leading the way. Among those breaking ground that day were the rich and famous like Glenn Ford and John Crean and Athalie Clarke, whose father, Mr. Irvine, owned half of Orange County. And there were also those who nobody would recognize by either name or face, but they were important to the church, to God, to Dr. Schuller. One of those was my own daughter Tara, who Bob chose to represent the handicapped that day. She was dressed in her Sunday best, and even though she had a great deal of trouble maintaining her sitting balance in her wheelchair, she was prouder than I'd ever seen her, her special little shovel laying across her lap as she listened to Bob's message.

When it came time to turn that first shovelful of dirt, all were poised and ready. In the center of the group were Bob and Arvella; Sheila, then in her late twenties; young Bob and his wife Linda; Jeanne Ann, home from college for the occasion; Carol, celebrating her thirteenth birthday that day; and Gretchen, eleven. In the usual thriftiness of the Schullers, Carol and Gretchen were wearing the junior bridesmaids' dresses they had worn at their big brother's wedding several months earlier. It was a proud day for them all, and they each one looked like the Cheshire cat from *Alice in Wonderland* As they ceremoniously dug their shovels into the ground, a large earthmover dug its giant shovel into the parched ground behind them, its engines whirring solemnly over the organ music.

At last we had really begun, and as 1978 began, the earthmovers were busy at work digging the foundation and the basement of the Crystal Cathedral. They prepared a giant hole in the ground, and then it started to rain. California's rainy season comes in the winter, but none of us had seen a winter like that one. It turned out to be the rainiest winter in over a hundred years. The gaping orifice was soon nicknamed the Crystal Lake as day after dreary day poured rain from the stormy skies.

It was a fitting beginning for what was to become the worst year in the history of the Schuller family and the Garden Grove Community Church. The only bright spot in that black year concerned Sheila. For years she had wanted nothing more than to fall in love with a wonderful young man and get married and have children, and for years it seemed that God had other things in mind for her, no matter how much she implored Him. She was lovely, in a tall, striking, fashion-model sort of way, as are all the Schuller girls, and possessed a keen mind and good personality. But the men in her life were few and far between, probably due to a combination of her high moral standards and the awesome authority of her Dad. There were days when Bob would tell me with tears in his eyes of how lonely Sheila was. And it hurt him so to see her suffer.

A few years earlier, I had hired a young artist by the name of Jim Coleman to work for me over in Mascom—Hour of Power's in-house advertising agency. He was talented and bright; that's why I hired him. But he was not a Christian; far from it, and he had a long ponytail that hung halfway down his back. There were many at the Hour of Power who were quite surprised when they saw our new "hippie" artist, and it wasn't long before Bob started hearing rumblings from the troops. I'll never forget what he said. "This is the very best place for him to be. How else is he going to learn about Jesus unless we show him Christ's love?"

Over a period of time, I had seen Jim soften. It's interesting that during the sixties and early seventies there was a lot of talk about the length of a person's hair and the cut of his clothes being unimportant. I don't think those people had given a lot of thought to the underlying rebellion that the hair and the clothes symbolized. And in the next couple of years I watched the transformation of Jim Coleman and saw that it quite often manifested itself outwardly in a new haircut or a change of clothing style. It was very gradual, both outwardly and inwardly. The hair went from waistlength to midback to shoulder to just over the ear. And Jim went from a practical nonbeliever to a committed Christian as he was constantly exposed to the love of Christ by our people.

He was very nice looking and had a good sense of humor. I knew that quite a few of the single girls there at the Hour of Power had their eyes on him, Sheila Schuller included. But he didn't seem to take much notice. Then suddenly, in early 1978, when God's timing was just right, it seemed as if cupid aimed two of his arrows straight for the hearts of Jim and Sheila. Overnight a casual friendship blossomed into a real romance that was the talk and the delight of the Hour of Power and Bob and Arvella Schuller as well.

It is so beautiful that along with the severe tests, God always sends a way of escape, a silver lining for the stormclouds, and in 1978 Jim and Sheila were everyone's ray of sunshine.

The costs of the Cathedral were escalating almost daily, not by the thousands, but by the millions. What had started out as a seven million dollar project had mushroomed into the teens. We didn't know it yet, but it wouldn't level out until it hit twenty million dollars—a staggering sum. I don't think Bob Schuller would have ever begun the task of building it had he known in advance what the bottom line was going to be.

He thought for sure that he had bitten off more than he could chew. He was going to fail. This time he had done it. He felt his entire career was on the line, everything he stood for, all his work, possibility thinking, and the theology of self-esteem—all teetered in the balance. A great big unfinished building would make him the laughing stock of the whole country, maybe even the world. He really had only two choices: either he left a rotting skeleton on his church grounds or he saw the project through to completion. Either alternative scared him to death.

To make matters worse, a real storm had been brewing in the church consistory and matters were coming to a head. When Philip Johnson had delivered his original model of the Crystal Cathedral, its acceptance by the church board had been instantaneous and unanimous. However, in the ensuing months, great controversy had arisen over the financing of the building. One member in particular had been increasingly insistent that his personal broker be retained to aid in the raising of money through the sale of bonds.

Bob had employed that method successfully on other occasions, but felt that the Crystal Cathedral was different. He didn't want a long-term mortgage. The building must be dedicated debt free, and he fought tooth and nail for it.

Inevitably, there was a showdown one night. Feelings were high, but Bob won. They would raise the cash. The board member who had led the opposition was livid with righteous indignation. At last he jumped to his feet, his face purple with rage, and strode angrily toward the door. He jerked it open and started to walk through, but stopped, whirled around, and looked Bob squarely in the eye. "Okay, Bob Schuller," he shouted, shaking his fist, "*you* go out and raise the money!" And he slammed the door and was gone, never to return.

It was as if Bob had been physically assaulted, and he felt that the man had been correct in his parting attack. It was up to Bob Schuller, and he alone, to raise the money for the Cathedral. Nothing else happened to relieve Bob from this solitary pressure. The weight of it rested on his shoulders.

Toward late spring of the year, a million-dollar payment was due for the construction to continue. Bob didn't have it. The church didn't have it. The Hour of Power didn't have it. Bob pushed and shoved all he could, and then he was out. Out of ideas, out of energy, out of enthusiasm. He actually sat down and wrote the bulletin for that Sunday, announcing total failure and inability to complete the Cathedral. For a goal-oriented sort of person like Bob Schuller, it was the most unthinkable humiliation. I doubt he would have been able to live with himself afterwards.

That day, a letter arrived from Belfast, Northern Ireland. It was from Leslie Hale. A continent and an ocean away, he hadn't been in contact with Bob or anyone from the church for some time. All he knew was that in his spirit he felt a heaviness that wouldn't go away. It pushed and weighed on him constantly and had done so for several weeks. He didn't know why, but God kept speaking to him about his friend Robert Schuller. God had a message for Bob Schuller, and

Leslie Hale was supposed to deliver it. Try as he might, he couldn't shake the feeling. Finally he sat down and took his pen in his hand, writing the words God gave him—words of encouragement and love.

Bob read the letter, and the words might as well have been emblazoned in fire. They sent shivers through his body and he kept shaking his head in amazement. These words meant so much to Bob that he had the letter framed, and to this day it hangs behind his desk. As he did throughout the entire three-year construction period, whenever Robert Schuller was at the end of his rope, God sent in the backup team. This time it took the form of a letter from halfway around the world and a suggestion from a friend.

Bob was in no shape at the time to think up something like the Million-Dollar Sunday. Howard Kelley, minister of Stewardship, came up with the idea of having one Sunday where the congregation would give whatever they could in an attempt to raise the needed million-dollar payment. It was put up to the people, like a vote of confidence. Many of them were already double tithing and had bought or were paying on the windows, but they dug down deeper and gave even more that day in June. Bob started it off by selling his apartment at the beach in Laguna. He had bought it many years earlier for $36,000, making the cash down payment with his total inheritance from his family of $9,000. Since then it had increased in value to a total of $175,000. After paying the mortgage, Bob collected a cashier's check for $150,000. He gave every penny to the church, feeling an immense satisfaction in knowing how his action would have pleased his father. Carol sold her beloved horse and gave the money for the Cathedral. Others did what they could. And on Sunday, June 18, 1978, the offering at the church was so large that it had to be carried away in wheelbarrows and cement buckets. When it was all counted, it totaled one million five hundred thousand dollars.

And the construction went on.

Bob and Arvella were relieved of the immediate danger of a construction stop and were able to leave for the Far East with relatively clear minds. The two youngest girls flew to spend the first part of the summer with their cousins in Iowa, as they have done for most of their lives, while their famous parents travel and speak and write. This time Bob was touring the East, visiting churches in Singapore, Hong Kong, Bali, and Seoul, lecturing and giving courses to pastors and laymen on church growth much as he does at the Institutes here.

While they were gone, it finally happened. Jim asked Sheila to marry him. I think half the Hour of Power staff felt like successful matchmakers. I know I sure did. She called her folks in Korea, and her joy was matched by theirs.

It was only a week later when I received a phone call toward bedtime on a Friday night. I was to call Henry Schuller in Iowa right away. Carol Schuller had been in an accident. I phoned the number they gave me, a payphone at a hospital in Sioux City, and I was shaking all over. Donna stood next to me there in our kitchen huddled at our wall phone. Henry, a shy, quiet man of few words, so like his father and so unlike his brother, answered. He was even quieter now as he stammered out details of a terrible motorcycle accident. I went white. "Where is Bob?" he wanted to know. "Can you reach him? Tell him?"

I raced through the house, searching for an itinerary. Where was it? It must be here. It must be. I tore into my briefcase, racking my brain for the name of a hotel. Donna and I went upstairs and sat together on the edge of our bed, going over the few details we knew. It wasn't until later that we learned all that had occurred that fateful night. I kept saying over and over, "How could she be riding on a motorcycle?" Bob hates motorcycles. All of the Schuller children are forbidden to ride one.

But Carol's cousins love motorcycles. I didn't know that then. Her cousin Mark, who was twenty, had taken her for a spin on what was to have been her last night with the family that summer. He had insisted that she wear a helmet as they took a leisurely drive down a country road. Suddenly, the car in front of them braked to a halt. Mark knew he couldn't stop in time, so he swerved to avoid it, only to end up being crushed in between the stopped car and one passing to the left going the other direction. The motorcycle was mangled into an unrecognizable mass of chrome and metal, and Mark broke his foot. But it was Carol's left leg that took the brunt of the collision. She was thrown eighty-nine feet through the air, landing in a ditch by the side of the dark road.

Her femur had been broken in four places, her entire left side from the pelvic area down mangled, and the femur had plunged through her thigh. She lay there alone in that ditch, speared by her own leg, bleeding to death. She was thirteen years old. And she was scared. "When I walk through the valley of the shadow of death, I will not fear for Thou art with me. Thou art with me, with me. I will not fear. Through the valley of death." She repeated the words over and over to herself for what seemed like an eternity. She was dying. She knew it. And the pain. It was unbearable.

She lost nearly seventeen pints of blood there in that ditch next to an Iowa slaughterhouse, where it mingled with the dirt and stench and bacteria. When at last she arrived at the hospital, she was in extreme shock. She had no blood pressure and no pulse. They just kept giving her blood transfusions until the vital signs returned. Amputation seemed the only way to save her life.

Donna and I just sat there—stunned and hurting for Carol. How swift an accident can happen. One split second in eternity marking the end of one life and the beginning of another. I cried. Donna cried. Remembering, eight years ago this very time of year when we had been the ones to get a phone call. Our daughter. Our Tara. Lying in a coma at Children's Hospital. We had left her perfect and well, and we never saw her that way again. Ever.

My hands were shaking as I dialed for the overseas operator. What time was it in Seoul, Korea, anyway? Would Bob be in his room at the hotel? What if he wasn't? I didn't even want to think about it. I could hear the phone ringing. Bob answered. I gulped and flinched involuntarily.

"Hi, Bob. This is Mike."

"Mike. How are you?" His voice was tired, but relaxed. He had lectured for two hours every morning and another two hours every night for a week to over ten thousand Korean ministers each time on church growth. I took a deep breath and swallowed. I could feel my Adam's apple bob up and down in my throat. "Well, Bob, I've got bad news. It's Carol. She's been in a motorcycle accident. Bob, they may have to amputate her left leg."

Silence.

"She's in the emergency room in Sioux City, Iowa. Here's their number." Bob's voice was weak. "Thanks, Mike. I'll try to get the first plane out of here. I don't know when it'll be. Northwest Airlines is on strike. But assuming that we can get on the KAL flight that leaves in about five hours, please see what you can do about arranging the fastest connections into Sioux City from LA. And Mike," he paused. "I'm glad you gave me the news. It makes it easier to take."

Bob hung up the phone, shaking. After calling the hospital and talking to the doctor, he began pacing back and forth. Where was Arvella? When was she going to return from her outing with the Korean women? "I need you," he cried out silently to the empty walls. At last there was a knock on the door. He sprang for it and reached for Arvella, holding her close for a second. She began to talk, but he interrupted her. "We've had bad news," he began. "But it could be worse. Carol's leg has been mangled in a motorcycle accident. I've already spoken with the doctor in Sioux City, and she's severed an artery. They don't think they can save her leg."

Arvella was surprisingly calm. She walked over and stared out the window. She saw nothing. Her mind was a million miles away. She's such a strong woman. "Carol mustn't lose her leg," she said to herself, remembering Bob's message from yesterday about visualizing healing through prayer. With tremendous concentration she forced her thoughts to center on that leg, "Now I must visualize, for Carol's sake," she told herself, picturing in her mind the leg being repaired in surgery right that minute, the severed artery being attached. "Jesus Christ," she prayed, "please surround Carol with Your loving presence and give her the strength to cope with the pain."

Bob left to make arrangements, and Arvella was alone, still visualizing and praying as she packed her suitcases. The phone rang. It was Sheila. "Mom," she blurted through her tears, "they can't save the leg. They're amputating it right now." Arvella was stunned speechless for a moment. Her prayers . . . her faith. She began to cry, and then through her tears she forced the words to come, "All things work together for good to them that love God."

Minutes later, when Bob returned, her voice broke as she struggled for composure. "It's gone. Carol's leg is gone."

Pastor Cho, minister to one of the largest churches in the world, has hosted the Schullers on many visits to Korea. He personally went to the airport and arranged the Schuller's flight, fixing it so they could be spared the pain of customs, at least in Korea. He and his wife were waiting for them at the airport and stayed to pray with them until they boarded. "We don't know how," he said in his beautiful Korean accent, "but God will work this out for many blessings."

Bob recognized the words as his own, remembered the many times he had offered them to grieving families. For the first time they were now directed at him. For the first time, he found them unconvincing. His own sermons haunted him. "It's not what happens to you that matters; it's how you react to what happens to you that matters." "Trouble never leaves you where it finds you—choose by an act of your will to accept positively what you cannot change and you will find the strength and peace you need."

Once on the plane, Bob and Arvella were each lost in their own web of pain. It would be a ten-hour flight to Honolulu, followed by probably two hours of customs and another five hours on to Los Angeles. God only knew how they were going to get to Sioux City, Iowa. Bob glanced at the stewardess. She had two pretty, shapely legs and a pair of feet that fit nicely into her high-heeled shoes. The tears began to flow. "Carol only has one."

Bob jumped from his chair and raced back to the lavatory, as urgently as anyone about to be airsick. He made it just in time, closing and locking the door as sobs began to rack his body. A hideous volume of grief poured from his throat, nearly choking him in its intensity. His mental tape recorder played before him the sounds of the ten thousand Korean pastors at prayertime. "Alleluia. Alleluia. Praise the Lord." He contrasted it with the ugly sounds that were gushing from his own mouth. How typical. "Schuller," he lectured himself, "if you have to bawl, turn it into a ball. Praise God while you cry."

By an act of sheer will, he forced his mouth to shape the words, turning each heartwrenching sob into "Alleluia. Alleluia." Gradually serenity replaced the sobs, and he was able to return to his seat, only to be greeted by the slender crossed ankles of the young woman across the aisle. He choked up. "God, help me." A thought entered his mind. "She only lost a leg. You're exaggerating it all out of proportion. She will still be able to do all the things she really wants; be a veterinarian, play the violin and piano, the guitar. Play it down and pray it up."

Bob and Arvella did little talking all those long, frantic hours. They couldn't sleep. They cried a lot, and Arvella read her Bible.

God gave her the last part of Psalm 57. "Oh God, my heart is quiet and confident. No wonder I can sing your praises! Rouse yourself, my soul. Arise, O harp and lyre! Let us greet the dawn with a song!" (vv. 7, 8, TLB). As she read these beautiful words, Arvella glanced out the window and saw the tapestry of a Pacific sunrise from thirty-five thousand feet. "Your kindness and love are as vast as the heavens. Your faithfulness is higher than the skies" (v. 10, TLB).

They landed in Hawaii, but it held no charm for them now. It was Saturday noon there, six hours earlier than in Sioux City, Iowa. What had happened to Carol during that ten-hour flight? They phoned the hospital, their mouths as dry as cotton. Jeanne was there, and Sheila and Jim, too. Thank God. "Carol's vital signs are stable. Her spirit is great."

Then they were airborne again, another long flight over the Pacific. All the time they were traveling, our home had been like Grand Central Station. The phones were ringing off the hook, both of them, and I was making call after call. Somehow, there must be a way to get Bob and Arvella to Sioux City that night. They just couldn't be made to wait overnight in Los Angeles for a Sunday-morning flight and then make the transfers to get them into the small Iowa town. I had been through it all before; I understood the burning anguish of a mad dash to reach an injured child. Mine had only been from San Francisco, and I thought I would surely die before I reached her.

I knew the best way was to rent a Lear jet to fly them nonstop from the airport as soon as they arrived and right into Sioux City. But they were expensive. I didn't have the money and neither did Bob. Finally, in desperation, I called Athalie Clarke, and she agreed to pay for the flight. I met the Schullers at the airport and helped them transfer their bags and saw them off once more into the night sky. They looked tired and drawn.

The jet cut through the blackness like a knife, and soon they were cruising at fifty thousand feet. Over the Rocky Mountains, at that altitude, they emerged from the earth's shadow and the sky exploded into a riot of color. Their second sunrise. "Let us greet the dawn with a song."

But as the sleek aircraft descended for the approach to Sioux City, darkness once again engulfed them. And the lights on the landing strip greeted them, a perfect lighted cross shining from the darkness.

It was four o'clock Sunday morning, and Sheila drove them from the airport to the hospital. She was as high as Bob has ever seen her, almost elated as she described the courage of her sister.

They paused for a moment outside the intensive care unit, gathering their composure, their courage. It was the Lord's day. Thoughts flickered across Bob's mind, fleeting images. Was this the day that God had made? Could he possibly rejoice in it? As they entered the room, the sky outside was lit with delicate pinks and blues. Their third sunrise in one long, incredible day. Again the Psalm spoke to them, "Let us greet the dawn with a song."

And there was Carol. She lay in a bed surrounded by equipment, tubes, bottles, monitors, and bandages. Her dirty blonde hair lay in a mass of tangles, matted against cheeks that were scraped, bruised and so puffy that you had to search for her nearly buried blue eyes. It seemed that a tube had been placed in almost every orifice, and her whole body was black and blue and swollen out of shape. She lay naked save for a thin sheet that covered her, and suspended in midair was a short, round, well-bandaged stump of a leg. Bob and Arvella each stiffled a cry as their eyes traveled down to the end of the bed, where five manicured toes dangled out from under the sheet.

Carol opened her mouth to speak, closed it quickly to keep back a sob, then forced it to curl up at the corners. "Hi, Mom." "Hi, Dad," she croaked through the oxygen mask that sustained her. Arvella rushed to embrace her, to love her pain away, but the moment she made contact with the bed, Carol shrieked with pain. Soon they found that if they very carefully stroked the foot and toes of her one leg or her forehead, they could at least impart a little of their love to her without hurting her more.

From out of their swollen sockets, her eyes focused on Bob. "Dad, I think I know why this accident happened." She had to pause a moment, knitting her eyebrows from the pain. "God was testing me. God has a special ministry for me to people who have been hurt like I am hurt."

Later the doctor spoke with Bob about the night Carol had been brought in. "She was in terrible pain when she arrived and asked for medication to relieve it. I couldn't give her any; it would have depressed her condition further. She accepted the pain patiently and quietly, even though it was very intense. I cannot recall any patient ever so strong. You can be very proud of your daughter."

Bob was proud of her. He was overwhelmed by her. She was living proof of everything he had believed and taught all his life. She illustrated that a positive faith made the difference between life and death, heaven and hell. He prayed for her healing, visualizing it in his mind, using all the techniques he had ever taught or even studied. He heard God's voice. "No miracle can be carbon copied; then it would be the result of human manipulation. Seek Me; trust Me. I can and will perform miracles of healing in Carol's mind and body and soul. But let Me do it—My way."

Throughout all that painful period, he could feel the prayer support of people around the world. His friends in Korea, the members of Garden Grove Community Church, and churches all over America were praying for her. Billy Graham and Oral Roberts had both called and were praying. There was a tremendous outpouring of God's spirit.

Mostly, Bob and Arvella were praying that Carol would be able to keep her knee. Her leg had been amputated just below it, and the chances of saving the rest of the leg were slim at best. The knee and thigh were badly mangled, and infection had set in, too. But if she could only have her knee, maybe she would be able to maintain a normal walking gait someday.

Cory SerVaas, a medical doctor and editor of the *Saturday Evening Post,* called to urge that they get Carol to a replantation center, where she would have the greatest chance for saving the remainder of her limb. Arrangements were made to transfer her by ambulance jet to Children's Hospital in Orange County on Monday night. Bob, Arvella, Sheila, Jim, and Gretchen stood by as the special intensive care nurse eased the stretcher carrying Carol's bruised and broken body into the little plane.

As it streaked its way through the blackness, the family, cramped as they were in the small space, tired and hungry, sat numbly staring first out the windows and then at Carol as she grimaced from the pain. Bob started singing quietly at first, then with more volume, and the others soon joined in.

Praise God from whom all blessings flow.
Praise Him, all creatures here below.
Praise Him above, ye heavenly hosts.
Praise Father, Son, and Holy Ghost.

It was a difficult flight, especially for Arvella. Carol insisted that she hold her hand, and Gretchen slept with her head on Arvella's free shoulder. Her feet were bunched up on top of Carol's two large canisters of oxygen. But that wasn't the worst part. An incredible stench came from Carol's stump, strong and nauseating, and Arvella practically hypnotized herself to keep from vomiting from its intensity. What was causing this odor? The fear inside threatened to consume her.

It was a relief to find their son Bob and his wife Linda waiting for them on the ground at Orange County Airport. Linda took Gretchen home with her and their four-month-old baby Angie. Bob's eyes held a million questions, and top on the list was "Why?" Why the family athlete? Why anyone in their family at all?

They were ushered into the special care floor at CHOC, and Carol's aching body was eased gently into bed. "I'm glad to be home," she sighed. Once more, she was wheeled into surgery, knowing that there was a good possibility she might wake up minus more of her leg. As she gazed at her mom and dad, she spoke with determination. "I know one thing for sure. If I need more amputation, it won't change God's plan for my life."

For the time being, their prayers were answered. The knee remained. Through a haze of antibiotics and pain relievers, she issued the victory cry. "We did it!"

But it was not the end, it was only the beginning. There would be years of highs and lows, intense pain and blessed relief, soul-shattering doubts and mind-boggling faith. The days faded into each other, turning into months as one infection after another raged within Carol's battleworn body. The filth of that slaughterhouse ditch by an Iowa roadside was stubborn, containing bacteria that was resistant to any known antibiotics. Phantom pains assailed her day and night, wrenching her with the suffering of a leg and foot that weren't even there.

Bob spent every moment he could possibly spare by her bedside, and a lot that he couldn't spare. At first he was tempted to exaggerate the tragic element of the situation. But he remembered the words God had given him on his trip from Korea that first night. Play it down and pray it up. He was inspired by the courage of Carol herself, and amazed at the strength she found in his own corny little sayings. "There is no gain without pain." "When the going gets tough, the tough get going." "Look at what you have left, not at what you have lost." In times of the most excruciating pain, she would just repeat the name of Jesus over and over again. "Jesus is my reliever," she said. Even though she often bordered on hysteria from the pain, she rarely felt sorry for herself, rarely said, "I wish this never happened." Only once did she cry out, "I wish I had died in the ditch."

Bob gently rebuked her. "Those thoughts do not come from Jesus. Don't ever say or think you wish it hadn't happened. Futile regret is a negative spirit. Claim Jesus as the author of only inspiring and positive thoughts."

One day she asked her mom to reach her Bible for her. "Open it up to first Corinthians chapter thirteen. That's my favorite, and I have a letter there." Arvella carefully unfolded the piece of notebook paper. It was dated Winter Camp, February 26, 1978.

> Dear Jesus, I know that a lot of this is going to be . . . I want this or I want that. But it's also to be thank yous. Well, I guess I'll start out with—thank you for being my friend and coming into my life—thank you for dying on the cross for me. I love you and—Please never leave me. I'll write again soon.
>
> Carol

She endured yet another surgery, and the pain was so excruciating, Bob wondered how she could stand it. Even morphine didn't bring much relief. Her face was as white as the sheets, partially hidden by an oxygen mask. The ever-present tubes were sticking out of everywhere, it seemed. Plastic bags of antibiotics hung above her, and a bag full of dark blood, her twenty-fourth pint so far. She was put into isolation due to the serious infections that had invaded her knee and thigh, and her temperature soared daily—103°, 104°. Bob sat beside her bedside, praying and visualizing healing, praying and reading his Bible.

He cried aloud as he read the last chapter of Job. "So the Lord blessed Job at the end of his life more than at the beginning" (Job 42:12, TLB). And Job's beautiful confession of faith, "I know that you can do anything and that no one can stop you" (v. 2, TLB).

Bob drove home to check on Arvella. She was asleep. She'd spent an especially trying night with Carol. He went into the big country kitchen and found a piece of paper. In big, bold letters he wrote:

GOOD NEWS
CAROL MUCH BETTER
SHE WILL BE O.K.
DR. VERY POSITIVE

Then he taped his little poster to the doorframe where Arvella would be sure to find it.

The hot, dry summer turned into an even hotter, drier fall. It was a blessing that Carol's accident had happened in the three-month vacation Bob and Arvella take from the ministry of the church each year. That way at least they had breathing room and the time to adjust somewhat to the trauma and the change in lifestyle. But now Bob was back in the pulpit again. Production of the season's "Hour of Power" had begun. He must have dug down deep inside himself to find the faith and courage to get up there and preach each Sunday that year, beaming from ear to ear as he raised his arms and proclaimed, "This is the day that the Lord has made."

The Cathedral was taking shape, the balconies stretching their arms skyward were already changing the landscape of Orange County. With this increased visibility came increased support and also bitter criticism. Bob had to deal with it all—fund raising, criticism, preaching, the running of the church and the Hour of Power. In addition there was Sheila and Jim's February wedding to plan and Carol's suffering to cope with. It was a crushing load, even for the likes of Robert Schuller, and we all staggered under it.

Bob was moody and withdrawn. Several old-time church members left. It hurt him deeply. Those of us who worked closely with Bob during those times lived constantly under the same cloud of gloom that rained on him all day. He was so down lots of times that he dragged us down with him, and we in turn spread the despair to the lower ranks at the church and the Hour of Power. There was a turnover in staff. Those of us who stayed were constantly upholding Bob and Arvella and Carol and the Cathedral in prayer. It was prayer support that helped keep us going against all odds.

There was a brief respite in late October when Carol was allowed to come home in between surgeries. Arvella was exhausted from her care, passing a lot of her duties at the church over to Sheila. Bob had cut out most of his outside speaking engagements in order to spend more time with Carol and Arvella. But Wheaton College in Illinois was asking again. He had always turned them down, sensing trouble with their fundamentalist student body. He knew from bitter experience that fundamentalist Christians had a hard time understanding Robert Schuller and were often quite blunt about it, sometimes even brutal.

But there was Jeanne Ann to consider. Wheaton was her college, the one she had dreamed of attending since childhood. And she wanted him to come. It meant a lot to her. And he hadn't really seen her since those first few days following Carol's accident. Almost against his better judgment, he consented to come speak at one of their morning chapels. He could fly in the night before and see Jeannie, speak the next morning, and then come straight back home to Carol.

About that same time, there was a vicious attack against Bob and the Crystal Cathedral in the *Wittenberg Door,* a satirical fundamentalist Christian magazine. They took a full page of the magazine and drew a line down the center. At the top was printed something to the effect of "What to do with fifteen million dollars." On one side of the midline they wrote, "Build a Crystal Cathedral," on the other side were listed a long line of philanthropic endeavors. It was a popular magazine with the students at Wheaton, and they became inflamed over what they saw as an outrage just before Bob arrived.

Jeanne was so proud of her dad. She loved him so much and believed so in his work. She had grown up at the Garden Grove Community Church. It was her home. Most of her friends were there. She understood all the good her dad had accomplished all through his life, and she was excited that he was coming to her school to share with her classmates some of his vision and his inspiration.

The morning he was to address the chapel, there were posters in the college library protesting his appearance—signs that read, "Schuller doesn't preach the gospel," "Schuller is building a monument to himself," "Give the fifteen million to the poor." Bob glanced over at Jeanne. Her large brown eyes were as big as saucers, and tears had welled up and begun to spill over her lower lids, smearing her mascara as they trickled down her cheeks. She looked confused. "How could they?" she wondered to herself. There was nothing Bob could do but make his way into the chapel, give his message, and get out of there as soon as he could. Maybe with him gone, the students would calm down.

The next morning I was in his office. He looked so tired, so defeated. The phone rang, and it was Jeanne. Bob's face turned red and then white and then red again. Tears flowed freely down his cheeks. Jeanne's classmates were making cruel remarks to her about her father. She wanted to come home. Bob tried to talk her out of it, and eventually succeeded in convincing her to at least stay long enough to finish out the quarter. She could come home for Christmas, and if she still felt the same, she could stay.

Bob hung up the phone and started to pound his fists on his desk. He choked out great sobs. "It's not fair!" he cried, gulping for his breath. "They can attack me, they can hurt me and criticize me—but not my family. Not my children. Oh please," he blubbered, "please don't hurt my children. Please God. Please don't make them suffer on my account."

A few weeks later, Carol was back in the hospital for more surgery. They were going to release the muscles in her knee so that hopefully her leg would become more functional. The doctor was pleased when he found no pockets of pus in her knee and thigh when he opened them. But three days later, the bacteria that had lain dormant for some time erupted with a new and unprecedented fury. Carol's temperature shot back up in the range of 104°. And stayed there. Her stump of a leg continued to swell. The infection was a wildfire out of control. Bob and Arvella were frantic.

Sheila was having a wedding shower. There were bridesmaids' dresses to be found. Money needed to be raised for the Cathedral. Christmas was coming. Presents must be bought, the five candlelight services planned. And hour after hour Bob and Arvella sat paralyzed by Carol's bedside, holding her hand as she cried. Even the sounds of sirens or the sight of an ambulance on TV would send her into hysterics. They would come home and find Gretchen in Carol's room, stroking one of her stuffed animals, just looking at her things. And they'd think "Oh, God. Is it ever going to end?"

About that time, the Federal Drug Administration released a new antibiotic, one that was needed in the treatment of the particular strain of bacteria that Carol had picked up in that ditch. She was the first person in Children's Hospital to receive it. Within hours her temperature began to drop. Her leg had been left open so that it could bleed and so that they could take cultures to check the progress of the disease that raged within it. The cultures began to show improvement, until one day shortly before Christmas one came back with no bacteria growth at all.

One Saturday night, Arvella told Bob she had a surprise for him. He was to stay home and wait. He paced the length of the living room for some time, and finally saw the lights of Arvella's car. He ran to the front door and threw it open. "Now Bob," Arvella said, "you have to go back in and wait. Wait by the Christmas tree."

The door opened, and he heard rubber scrape against the wooden floor—the rubber tips of Carol's crutches. She stepped in through the open door and just stood there. Arvella had taken her straight from the hospital to the beauty salon. She'd had a permanent. And there she was, a lovely fourteen-year-old girl, her golden curls framing her face. As his eyes traveled down, he smiled as he saw two legs, two ankles and two shoes. She was wearing her new prosthesis. Bob says that was the happiest Christmas of his whole life.

Jeanne soon came home for Christmas. She didn't go back to Wheaton College that year. Her own wounds were still too fresh.

Early in January, Bob drove Sheila into Los Angeles to pick up her wedding gown. It was one of the most exciting days of her life, and she was happy to have her dad share it with her. "I know it was expensive, Dad," she found herself saying. "And with Carol and the new cathedral and all—well, I guess I just want to thank you for buying it for me."

"Sheila," Bob began, "it gives me great joy to buy you this dress. I'm so happy to see your dreams come true. We waited a long time, but you have been greatly blessed, and I want you to have the most beautiful wedding dress in the whole world." He looked thoughtful, "Some people think a wedding dress is worn only once, but I think it is worn more than any other dress a woman ever has."

Sheila looked at him expectantly. Her dad had such a way with words. "You wore your wedding dress the day you received your first bride doll. And everytime you have dreamed of getting married, you put it on. You will be radiant in it on your wedding day, and you will wear it every time you look at your wedding pictures."

That long-awaited wedding day finally arrived one crisp February day. Bob was so excited and so happy, as was the whole family and a lot of the rest of us, too. He was not only going to walk the bride down the aisle and give her away. He was going to perform the ceremony too, as he had for Bob and Linda when they got married. It had been such a tumultuous year, so full of highs and lows, so much emotion had washed over the bridge, and he hadn't recuperated from it yet. He was worried that he would start to really cry during the service and spoil everything. He knew he had to think of something to help him keep his emotions under control. At last, he came up with the perfect solution. When he felt he was losing control, he would just tell himself, "Remember Dad, you're paying the bill!"

It was a family affair, with Jeanne, Gretchen, and Carol as the attendants. Ever since the accident last July, Carol's one burning goal was to walk down the aisle at her sister's wedding. There were those of us, and I must admit I was one of them, who thought it was an unreachable goal. When I would hear the Schullers, that familiar glint of determination in their eyes, promise people, including Carol, that she would do it, I felt maybe they were being a little unrealistic. They were expecting too much. But they firmly refused to ever utter a negative word on the subject. That glorious day, when Carol walked down that long aisle on her crutches, I don't think there was a dry eye in the house.

I wish I could say that all our troubles were over at that point, that 1979 ushered in a new year of health and prosperity and happiness for everybody. It didn't. Prices on the Cathedral had hit the sky, and the criticism went up right along with them. Between fending off insults and trying to raise money, there wasn't a lot of Bob left to go around. Everyone was clutching at him, pulling at him, and he had no reserves left from which to draw. He was downright cantankerous a lot of the time, not that I blamed him. He cried easily over his own problems and everybody else's, and when a crisis came up, we knew what to expect. He would just throw his arms up in the air. "I can't take any more! I can't handle it!" And he would bury his face in his hands and start to cry. We were all praying for him. After all, everyone has his breaking point.

Just where Robert Schuller's was, we didn't know. And we didn't want to find out.

Now, when he is criticized about the Cathedral, I think it makes him more angry than anything else. But during the construction, it nearly broke his heart. It's so difficult to be misunderstood, and to have so little ability to answer your attackers. Most of the more caustic attacks came from either the fundamentalist Christian community or the extreme secularist community. It was one of those rare times when they have been in agreement with each other.

It was like the old adage, "When did you stop beating your wife?" There just isn't any graceful way to answer a question like that. There was little Bob could do to defend himself during that time. The expense of the Cathedral was a real problem for everybody, Bob included, but he had gotten himself into it, and he was bound and determined to get himself out of it with dignity and honor. It wasn't his fault that inflation was rampant in the building industry. He was just trying to finish the project as best he could.

Sure, he would have liked to give twenty million dollars to the poor, or to mission projects, or to build hospitals, or lots of other things. But he knew from experience that it is next to impossible to raise that kind of money for those purposes. Not only that, but if you could raise huge sums of money to give to the poor, they would still be poor. "If I just collected money and gave it to the poor," Bob said on the "Phil Donahue Show" one day, "the poor would still be poor and I would be poor too. The poor can't help the poor."

Bob saw the Crystal Cathedral as a power base. He felt he could use that base to generate income or other spiritual, psychological, or emotional resources to help the people who are really down. He has basically a missionary outlook, a missionary heart. He wants first to be a missionary to his own community, and then to reach out to the world. His goal was to dedicate the Cathedral debt free so that he could then take the offerings and use them to establish a chain of Good Samaritan Inns around the world. They might be hospitals or day-care centers or schools or whatever the people needed the most. But the Cathedral had to come first.

A lot of people couldn't grasp that concept. If Bob were a materialist and not a Christian, he admits that spending the twenty million to build the Cathedral would have bothered him a lot more. But, as he says, "I don't worship money. Money only means helping people who are hurting. If it costs twenty or thirty million dollars annually, I could care less. If I wanted power based on money, I would be a materialist. But I don't. I am basically a servant; the money is used to serve God.''

When the Crystal Cathedral was complete, every dollar of the twenty million dollars spent to construct it had been used to help people—to reduce unemployment, to pay salaries to all the hundreds of people who worked on it, to increase the nation's productivity.

In the beginning, Bob had made a covenant with God. ''If you want it built, Lord, I'll take the criticism if You'll provide the cash.'' He expected criticism about the money, but I don't think he had anticipated the comments about the monument aspect of the building, at least not to the extent that they developed over the five years.

It was the snide comments about Schuller's monument to himself that cut at Bob most deeply. I don't think he ever had considered the Crystal Cathedral in that light. All you have to do is look at the other buildings he has built to know that as a person he is committed to excellence. He has never done anything in his life that wasn't the very best he could do. That's just not his style. There are some people who naturally are interested in the practicality of things. They don't particularly care what they look like, just so long as they are functional.

Bob is just the opposite. He loves beauty. Beauty comes from God. Just look at a snow-covered mountainside or a stormy ocean or even a bright blue sky. God never did anything halfway. He didn't stint when it came to beauty. And when it came time for Bob to build a new sanctuary, he just naturally wanted it to be the most beautiful building, the best building, he could possibly build. Not to build a monument to himself, but just to build a monument of beauty. He wanted to build something beautiful for God, a soaring landmark that would lift man's spirits and cause them to think of higher, purer, better things.

There were many who caught the vision, and as the steel framework pierced the cloudless Southern California sky, we all knew that the new Cathedral was going to be beautiful indeed. There was still all the fund raising to be done. We had sold the windows. To that we added ten thousand crystal stars, which would hang from the ceiling of the completed structure, and the sixteen thousand steel pillars that actually helped provide the support of the building. Of these three projects, it was the windows that sold the best, even though by the time we got around to the stars and pillars the building was no longer in a purely promotional state. I think people really liked the idea of having a visible symbol of their involvement, like a legacy, to leave behind, something that could bear their name.

Bob had been able to secure five gifts of a million dollars each. One was the original one from John Crean, and one came from W. Clement Stone in Chicago. Hazel Wright donated a million dollars for the construction of the organ, and a couple of elderly Chicagoans gave two million dollars anonymously. It's interesting, but the largest gift, the two million dollars, was not solicited at all. One day a letter came to Bob from a man he didn't know, a man he hadn't even heard of before. It told of how he and his wife were devoted viewers of the "Hour of Power" and of how excited they were about the construction of the Crystal Cathedral. He closed his letter rather nonchalantly, asking if a million dollars would come in handy about that time.

Needless to say, Bob lost no time in locating the kindly gentleman and his sweet wife. He found them to be a delightful couple, well into their retirement years, with no children with whom to share their wealth. And yes, the million dollars was greatly needed and much appreciated. Sometime later, on a trip through the midwest, Bob decided to call on the couple. They invited him to lunch and were most gracious in their hospitality. All the while they teased him, saying they had a little something for him but weren't sure whether to give it to him or not. Their bright eyes twinkled merrily as they played out their charade all through the meal. At last the wife said, "Oh, do give it to him, dear," at which point the husband pulled out a plain white envelope and handed it to Bob. Inside was a cashier's check for a million dollars. He was so overwhelmed by their great generosity that for once he was stunned speechless.

The year wore on, and each day measurable progress was being made on the Cathedral. Soon the panes of glass arrived. They were stacked one on top of the other in the parking lot, in groups of seven. Bob had known from the start that a new landmark was being created. He sensed its importance, and always hoped to have the press turn out each time a major milestone was reached in construction. It was my job to get them there, and sometimes it was no easy task.

One of the first big breaks we had was when Frank Berkholtzer, the

Los Angeles correspondent for NBC evening news, came to do a story on the Cathedral. I really can't take the credit for the piece, though, because it was actually Frank's mother who convinced him to come. She's been a fan of Bob's for a long time, and he brought her with him. She opened up her purse to show us its contents. It looked like she had just about every medallion and cross we had ever offered on the "Hour of Power" stored in there. She was a dear soul, and Bob gave her a big hug there in the open cathedral and had his picture taken with her. At the close of the interview, he shared a prayer with her. Frank had tears in his eyes.

It didn't seem possible, but the glass was going up so fast, rippling and waving across the angles of steel, covering up the lacy framework of white that we had all come to love. The ninety-foot-high doors that would open for the drive-in worked, and so did the fountains. Underground, the offices were taking shape in the basement. Despite the hardships, Bob was like a kid with a new toy. Few days went by when he wasn't there, hard hat on, to see what had been added.

Arvella was found to have cancer of the breast that summer, and a total mastectomy was necessary. Carol was still having bouts of recurrent infection in her stump. Despite the fact that they had managed to keep her knee, it didn't work properly and she had great difficulty walking with it. The normal gait they had so prayed for proved an elusive thing. Young Bob had graduated from Fuller Seminary, and Sheila and Jim were expecting their first child.

Time was drawing to a close on the construction of the Cathedral, and with the ever-spiraling costs, Bob was still four and a half million short. It was finally decided to sell the seats. There weren't nearly as many as Bob had originally wanted. I guess that's one of those times when perhaps the problems should have been solved before the final decisions were made. As it turned out, they were only able to fit 2,866 seats inside the great cathedral, 1,134 short of their goal. At that, they were small and extremely close together, hardly affording space for a grown man's knees in between the next row.

Beverly Sills, thought by many to be the greatest coloratura soprano that ever lived, was in her retirement year and agreed to give her last solo performance in the nearly completed Crystal Cathedral on May 13, 1980. It would be the very first event to be held there, and the tickets were priced at fifteen hundred dollars apiece. That included the price of the seat, which would bear the name of the donor or someone of his choice. They went like hotcakes. I guess everyone likes to be a member of the winning team. Most were bought by those who hadn't given to the project before. Seeing it standing there, majestically captivating the skyline, drawing visitors like a magnet, was exciting to nearly everyone.

Workers were really busy trying to get the interior completed and cleaned up in time for the gala event. Bob was there nearly every day showing dignitaries around and consulting with the foremen. One day a workman raced down a flight of steep steps from the balcony and approached Bob a bit timorously, holding his hat in his hand. "Dr. Schuller," he asked breathlessly, "can you tell me the significance of the three crosses?"

Bob looked surprised. "What crosses?"

The workman pointed with his hand, "There," he said, "the three crosses in the marble, just under the pulpit." The exquisite salmon colored marble had just been cemented in place all along the altar. It had been quarried in Spain and cut in Italy, then numbered so that our workers could put it up in the correct order.

Bob stepped back for a better look. He caught his breath sharply, stopping short. There, in the creamy veins of the marble, were the unmistakable outlines of three crosses. Each one was perfectly spaced in distance from the other, all were in perfect proportion and perfectly centered under the pulpit and across the broad expanse of altar wall. How could it be? They looked for all the world like a piece of fine art, but they were only randomly selected cuts of marble. No one had planned them, they hadn't been designed. Not by human hands, that is.

Bob has often said that God is in the details. I don't think He wanted us to ever forget who really built that Cathedral or for whom it was really constructed. In the smooth, shiny surface of salmon marble, right at the focal point of the entire structure, He had signed His name.

May thirteenth was quite a night. We've not seen the likes of it before or since. It glittered with beautiful people in furs and diamonds. But by far the most beautiful was the Crystal Cathedral itself. It was one of the first times I had seen it with the lights on at night, and from the outside I could look in and see its white lace superstructure. It glowed eerily, like some living thing from another planet, its soft lights bouncing and dancing from one mirror-clad geometrical plane to another.

The press was out in full force. All the local papers and TV stations were represented. The three major networks. The wire services. It was a PR man's dream come true. Bob wore a tuxedo, Arvella a formal gown, and the cameras whirred and clicked and flashed. As the lights dimmed, Bubbles swept majestically onto the stage, her long satin gown floating across the salmon marble, like a princess in a palace. She paused. The orchestra began to play, and she burst into song.

I'm not much of an opera buff, but as a television producer-director, I do know acoustics. It was the moment of truth. Her rich soprano leaped along the walls, bouncing from one plane to another. I was horrified. Of course, I rationalized, it's only a temporary sound system. The permanent one will be ever so much better, I'm sure. But I wasn't sure. And I had to produce a television program from this beautiful twenty-million-dollar echo chamber in September.

The next day the *Los Angeles Times* ran a scathing review. Martin Bernheimer said the world famous opera star sounded like the fat lady singing the "Star Spangled Banner" at a baseball game. Well, gee, I hadn't thought it was that bad. She had remained gracious throughout the entire evening, bravely seeing it through to the very end. A night or so later, she was a guest on the Johnny Carson show.

"Say," the ever ebullient Johnny asked, "I hear you sang over at the Reverend Schuller's Crystal Cathedral the other night."

She smiled sweetly. "Yes," she quipped. "My voice is still there now, ricocheting from one glass wall to another, trying to find a way out."

Even so, the evening was a stunning success. All us possibility thinkers always try to think on the bright side of any given situation. We're experts at finding it, wherever it is. It was only four months until the formal dedication of the Cathedral, and that meant we all had a lot of work to do. That's all.

Both Bob and Philip Johnson became quite adept at dodging embarrassing questions about what one reporter called their reverberating airplane hangar. "The church was not planned as a concert hall,'' Mr. Johnson commented dryly on many occasions. ''It was not designed for acoustics, but for electro-acoustics [using amplification to override the building's natural sonic structure].'' He had a way of making a reporter feel sorry he had asked. My job was the lighting and the sound, and I intended to leave no stone unturned.

Bob hates television equipment. He doesn't like anything that distracts from the beauty of the building and the moment. I knew it must be made to be as unobtrusive as humanly possible, and then it would have to go the extra mile. With all the light streaming in from the glass walls, I was worried about glare for my cameras. We decided to install a forest of ficus trees and ferns behind Bob to cut down on the sunshine. Individual pewback speakers were installed behind every other seat in the Cathedral in an effort to cut down the echo. Some of the beautiful terrazzo-like floors were carpeted to help absorb the noise.

We were all gearing up for the big day—September 14, 1980. It had taken five long, hard years from beginning to end, but the end was really here at last. We had all grown through the experience of building the Crystal Cathedral, Bob Schuller most of all. He had been forced to lean even more heavily on the strong shoulder of his Lord as he fought and clawed his way up that mountain. But he hadn't quit. It had been a uniquely humbling experience for him.

So many people all over the world had given and given again to make the Crystal Cathedral possible. We wanted to help them share in the excitement and the enthusiasm we all felt at the opening of the church. Sunday, September seventh, Bob planned to transfer all the articles of worship from the old sanctuary into the new. They could have just been carried over during the week, but it seemed too hallowed a moment not to share with everybody.

We started the service in the old sanctuary for the last time. The hymns were sung, the sermon given. Toward the close, the organ boomed triumphantly and was answered back by part of the new organ that was still being installed in the Cathedral. The congregation rose and began to file out. It was a solemn, beautiful procession, led by Dr. Schuller and the other ministers, followed by the church consistory. Held lovingly in Bob's arms was the big old black pulpit Bible. Each minister and board member carried some article of worship, from the baptismal bowls to the communion cups.

I had eleven TV cameras there and one above in the Goodyear blimp in an effort to capture the joy and the dignity of the moment. As I watched my monitors in the new television room underneath the Cathedral, I realized tears were streaming down my face as the long line of people snaked across the grass and into the shimmering edifice. The seats filled, and Bob ascended the marble steps into the pulpit area, carefully placing the Bible in the place of honor. Other ministers positioned the articles of worship. A hymn was sung, a joyous hymn of thanks to God who gave the dream and made the miracles happen. Bob rose to give the benediction. "May the Lord bless you and keep you. May the Lord cause His face to shine upon you and be gracious unto you. In your going out and in your coming in, in your labor and in your leisure, in your laughter and in your tears, until at last you come to stand before Jesus, in that day in which there is no sunset and no dawning. Amen."

The organ roared its applause.

When the service was over, and I had wrapped up production, after the customary coffee and rolls in Bob's new small office beneath the Cathedral, I walked up into that sparkling building and just sat there, thinking. It had been a long, hard five years. Everyone had suffered for the construction of that building, Robert Schuller most of all, but there wasn't a one of us who hadn't been touched. I know there were times when I had asked myself if it was really worth it.

I looked up ten stories straight into the white space-frames of welded steel tubing that comprise the walls and roof of the Cathedral. Three dimensional, modular, and continuous, they repeated their pattern over and over again so many times that they became a delicate, lacy filagree, a latticework over which the sun skipped and jumped. Above was the glass, thousands and thousands of panes, each letting in an equal amount of sunlight. Philip Johnson was right, it did feel like swimming with open eyes in a sunlit pool. Subaqueous.

And yet the enormous dimension of the Cathedral didn't make me feel uncomfortable. Light, space, and structure were wedded into one awesome entity that somehow excited me and made me feel tranquil and relaxed at the same time. It was magnificent to just sit there, bathed in that soft, pearly, luminous light.

The giant balconies soared into the air, three points of the star, and the fourth point stretched before me, rich in marble. The altar with God's gift of those three incredible crosses (or were they faces), etched in stone by the skillful hand of time. To the left, the tall, slender, gold-leafed cross rose majestically into the air. Behind were the organ enclosures, still under construction. It would be more than a year and a half before its 12,688 pipes were installed and the true volume and purity of the instrument would be incorporated into the throbbing vitality of the Crystal Cathedral.

I'm not sure how long I sat there, mesmerized by the very reality of a dream come true. Finally I rose to go, walking backwards, then turning around, trying to take in the entire structure at one time. Yes, it was worth it, it was worth all of it, to build something so beautiful, something so soaring that it made you think of the vastness of God, dwelling in perfect purity and holiness in the quality of life that is eternal, above time and space.

As I walked out that day, I could almost hear the laughing voice of Bob Schuller echoing from one glass-skinned wall to another. "Of course, it was worth it. The gain is always worth the pain. The tassel is always worth the hassle. There can be no goal-reaching without sacrifice. The cross always sanctifies the ego trip."

Sunday, September 14, 1980. Probably one of the greatest days of my life, really euphoric. Like Carol Schuller had said, I wanted to shout to the world, "We did it!" God, our Father; Jesus Christ, our Lord and Savior; the Holy Spirit, working through Robert Schuller and Philip Johnson and all the engineers and carpenters and welders and glass workers and stonemasons and people great and small all over the world.

People were streaming into that great, shimmering, star of a building by the thousands. The nation's and even some of the world's press were there in astounding numbers. Outside the sun beat down that hot fall day, and inside it filtered through glass and steel, gently filling the Crystal Cathedral with a spectacular diffusion of light and space.

I had eleven cameras again that day, and overhead the Goodyear blimp cruised leisurely by, affording our viewers a bird's-eye look at a glistening star surrounded by gardens and reflecting ponds and giant fountains spraying into the air. The organ swelled and the trumpets sent their sweet high notes spiraling into the white trusswork of the ceiling. The choir and the congregation began to sing. "The church's one foundation is Jesus Christ her Lord."

Up in the pulpit area, right above the three marble crosses, Robert Schuller held out his arms, the black of his robes in stark contrast with the salmon and beige earthtones below him. As our cameras caught a close-up, I could see he was blinking to keep back the tears. His whole life played before him at that moment, and he raised his voice and sang out loud and clear the call to worship that had become synonymous with his name.

It was not one of Bob's better sermons. I think he had been too excited to prepare adequately, and he was so choked up anyway that he had difficulty keeping control. I don't think it mattered much that day. Everyone was gaping at the cathedral, paying more attention to the wonders of its architecture than to anything else. The service concluded with a color guard of local Boy Scouts, each one carrying a flag representing one of the countries where the "Hour of Power" is broadcast. The pageantry, the symbolism of the dedication service were beautiful, but they were dwarfed by the dramatic pageantry of the Crystal Cathedral itself.

Not everyone agreed with the building of the Cathedral, but the day it opened, it immediately increased Bob Schuller's credibility. He had accomplished what he had set out to do. He wasn't just a music man who came to town for a week; he was solid. He had invested half of his life in one place, caring for his community and giving it something beautiful to keep, a landmark that would stir the good in us all. Everyone involved felt a sense of personal accomplishment and fulfillment. I guess little Tara summed it up for everybody when she said, her dark eyes flashing proudly, "Hurrah! Hurrah! The Crystal Cathedral is finished! That's the church that I built!"

13

Peak to Peek—Ever-Expanding Goals

THE CATHEDRAL WAS finished. A major goal of a lifetime reached. Robert Schuller had changed an entire landscape; because of him tons of steel and glass now pierced the skyline of Orange County. But was he satisfied? He was fulfilled for the moment, but a great climber doesn't stop at the mountain peak, no matter how hard it has been to get there. Bob always says that the process of becoming is more exciting than the experience of arriving. The *is* must never catch up with the *ought*. If you set a goal and reach it and can't expand, you start to die.

Fortunately for the driven Dutchman, there were certain problems that had been inherent in the construction of the Crystal Cathedral that still needed his attention. For one thing, his relations with his congregation had slowly deteriorated over the three years of construction. The pressures of fund raising and the criticism he had received, coupled with the trauma of Carol's accident, had taken their toll on him. He had gradually withdrawn from the mainstream of church life. Of course, for several years, ever since the Neutra sanctuary had been completed, he had let his staff of ministerial specialists take over much of the close, one-to-one fellowship with church members. His job was to stand in the pulpit Sunday mornings and uplift and inspire. He was the main attraction that brought the people in; the other ministers were to take it from there.

But the Cathedral had caused rifts, there was no doubt about it. Bob had known it would. Some people just don't adjust well to change. Now was the time to begin patching broken relationships, to start building those bridges and to make them stronger than ever. Bob knew how to do it, and the church mattered so much to him that he was willing to pay the price. He was past the ringing doorbells stage, but there were other ways—subtle, but effective.

First of all, the acoustics in the Cathedral still needed a lot of work. People don't want to come to church if they can't understand the pastor when he speaks. He set out to find a permanent, acceptable solution. It took him over a year, but at least a compromise was reached. I don't know if he'll ever really be happy with the sonic temperament of the building, although I doubt he would admit it.

Now that he is no longer under such intense stress, Bob has been able to increase his visibility somewhat at the church. And when he is there, especially Sunday mornings, he is able to be really quite jovial. All during the construction and the great sorrow he had to bear with Carol, Bob promised himself that he wouldn't be gloomy from the pulpit. Sometimes he got up there with a weight on his heart that was so heavy and hurt so badly that he longed to share it with everyone, to just pour out his soul and let it stand naked before them.

But he said to himself, "Schuller, give them a lift or give them a load." He didn't want to give a load to his listeners. After all, they had enough problems of their own without hearing about his. So he never did. He talked a lot about Carol and the construction, but always tried to couch his feelings in positive terms. The trouble is, it's nearly impossible to pull that off; maybe on television, but not in person. There is that sixth sense people have, that ability to read in between the lines, to pick up vibrations. They may not know how to interpret the signals, but they know they are there. I think this was one of the factors at work within the church. The congregation sometimes read those unspoken words as a lack of interest or concern when actually they were neither.

Bob has really applied himself since the Cathedral opened to the cementing of the congregation, to meeting them at their level, where they are, and opening up to them on a more intimate plane. Often he will go outside and shake hands with the people in cars in the drive-in, or just be there and available on Sunday mornings after services. He's really searching for ways to say "I care," because he does.

With the Cathedral completed, he turned the old sanctuary into what is probably the world's largest fellowship hall. *Fellowship hall* is far too mundane a term for Bob Schuller, though. He installed green carpeting on the floor and put mirrors on one wall and hung plants from the ceiling and calls it the Arboretum.

Next has been his concern for the Good Samaritan Inns project he had hoped to inaugurate with the opening of the Cathedral. He had promised everyone that since the Cathedral was to be dedicated debt-free that he would be able to use the offerings collected there to build Good Samaritan hospitals and schools around the world as a mission outreach. But soaring inflation has hit hard. Not only does it cost so much more to maintain the church and pay the salaries of the employees, but the congregation itself has been hard hit and revenues are down, both in the Cathedral proper and from the "Hour of Power." The surplus of money he had planned on just hasn't been there. I think, too, people look at the beautiful completed Cathedral and heave a sigh of relief, saying "Well, thank goodness Schuller doesn't need my money anymore. He's got that fabulous church built and doesn't owe a dime on it. His congregation must be rich, and I'll either keep my money or give it to someone who needs it more than he does."

Bob's first project was to have been a thirty-five-bed hospital down in the impassable jungles of Chiapas, Mexico. There, descendants of the noble Mayas, most of whom don't even speak Spanish, live without any medical care. He has spent a year and a half trying to raise the money to build that hospital, and it has only served to prove the validity of his own words. People won't give to the poor and needy like they will to an exciting building project that excels. He once said it was easier to raise a million dollars for a Tower of Hope than it was to raise eighteen hundred dollars for a new dishwasher. Now he could say with equal accuracy that it was easier to raise twenty million dollars for the Crystal Cathedral than it is to garnish one million for a jungle hospital.

In his own words, "Excellence succeeds because excellence attracts attention. The average American is so busy that if you want to get his attention, you must first impress him. Whatever your idea is, it's got to have a superlative in it." So far, he hasn't found the right way to sufficiently impress enough people to build his hospital. But he hasn't given up by any means. Somehow it will be built. All it takes is a better idea. As Bob says, "The problem is never a lack of money, it is a lack of ideas. Money gravitates to good ideas."

Actually, the first Good Samaritan Inn was built a few years back. It's a child-care center on 146th Street, South Bronx, New York City. There the children can come for care and good nutrition while their parents work. Bob believes that charity begins at home. That's why he picked Mexico, California's closest neighbor, for the second project.

Some years back, Bob saw Bob Jany's living nativity at the New York City Music Hall in Rockefeller Center. He loved it. The live camels and sheep, the fabulous costumes, the music. He tucked it away in his fertile mind, and when the Crystal Cathedral was completed, he began to envision a spectacular, beautiful Christmas present that he could give to Southern California. This was the birth of what was to become known as the "Glory of Christmas."

He contacted Bob Jany, who does a lot of work for nearby Disneyland as well as New York's Radio City Music Hall, and who he has known for some time. Could he produce a living nativity at the Cathedral? Of course. The two of them worked out the details for the better part of the year. Bob wanted a longer, more elaborate nativity than the New York counterpart. It had the Rockettes to take up time and add excitement, but Bob wanted pure Christmas story, in its beauty and its simplicity. He wanted the most gorgeous of Christmas music, the familiar carols, the drama of drums and trumpets, the glory of strings. He knew instinctively that the Cathedral would be the perfect setting, and he was right.

They needed volunteers, hundreds of them, for the two alternating casts. No one would speak during the presentation, the story would all be told by the soaring, swelling music. The vocals would all be performed by the Hour of Power choir. I remember Arvella telling a group of us at breakfast one morning about the animals. "They're professionally trained, acting animals. They won't make a mess." She was a farm girl. She knew about animals. I hoped she was right.

One day during the summer, Bob was good enough to let Donna and me use his office on the twelfth floor to work on this book. With our four children home from school, peace and quiet were at a premium. He has added a spectacular library onto his home, and usually works from there, so we weren't expecting to see him at the church. We were embarrassed when we arrived at his office to find he was conducting a meeting there. Nothing would do but that he and his guests gather up their papers and adjourn to the small secretarial area just outside his office door to conclude their meeting so Donna and I could spread out in his office. As we were setting up inside, we realized that they were discussing publicity for the "Glory of Christmas." Bob was talking about the overhead bridge that spans Chapman Avenue from the church to the Hour of Power building. "I know the city said we couldn't advertise with signs from the bridge," he speculated, his dark eyes shining. "But they didn't say a word about putting live camels on the bridge."

The tickets were to be sold through the church, at a reasonable price. The original production cost somewhere in the neighborhood of five hundred thousand dollars, but with the revenue from ticket sales for twelve performances it would probably be recouped in the first or second year. It was merely capital outlay, as it is anytime someone puts on a play.

The night they held the press preview, the coverage exceeded anyone's fondest dreams. All the big guns from the media were there. The next evening Dan Rather of CBS News concluded his evening broadcast with a report on the "Glory of Christmas." And the news articles were excellent. How could they be otherwise? Bob Schuller and his Crystal Cathedral were creating a new Christmas tradition for Southern Californians, something people would come to see year after year. They were making available to their community a beautiful way to experience something of the wonder, the love, the perfection of that first Christmas night when Mary brought forth her firstborn son and wrapped him in swaddling clothes and laid him in a manger. What a way to celebrate the Nativity! What a way to put Christ back into Christmas! With all the cheap commercialism, with all the secularism of schools and public places, here was a place to come and recapture the true meaning of Christmas.

There was only one sour note sounded in all the press coverage. It was unfortunate that it came from so prestigious a publication as the *Los Angeles Times*. It was an error on their part, and was certainly not done intentionally or maliciously, but they misquoted the cost of the production. They printed it at a million dollars, quite a tidy sum indeed. It's funny the things people pick up on. We have Christian neighbors who I know would have loved the "Glory of Christmas." It is truly the most beautiful, awe-inspiring, faith-producing Christmas program I have ever seen. But all they could do was criticize Robert Schuller for spending a million dollars on its production. They missed the point entirely. I'm afraid others probably did, too, and that makes me very sad.

Why are we so quick to jump to conclusions without really knowing facts or thinking through the motives and the outcome? I guess it's just part of human nature. Here a man tries to do something beautiful for God, to provide something beautiful and uniquely special for his community. And even there, he is misunderstood. How tragic.

Fortunately, others were not so judgmental. The phones started ringing off the hook the next morning and didn't stop until the ten-day production was over. The "Glory of Christmas" was a rousing success. Bob has already begun work on next year's program, which he promises will be even more spectacular. Why can't the angels fly out over the audience like Sandy Duncan did in *Peter Pan*? Well, why not?

The night we went to see the "Glory of Christmas," we had to admit that it was as though the Cathedral had been built especially with it in mind. It was a perfect set, glowing as though it had been bathed in the very light that must have shown around the Holy Family that Holy Night. The entire altar and organ bay area of the Cathedral had been turned into a giant stained-glass window that kaleidoscoped with the most beautiful paintings of Madonna and Child, and there in the center was an exquisite portrayal of Christ on the cross, a reminder of His mission on earth. Christmas would have no meaning without Easter; Easter couldn't have happened without the incarnation of God that took place that night in a stable in Bethlehem.

Everything, from the artwork to the lighting to the music to the live camels and little lambs and the costumes, was designed to take the audience back in time nearly two thousand years. When the ninety-foot glass doors parted and a great light entered, seemingly from way out in space, and shone on the baby Jesus in the manger, it was as though we were actually experiencing the Star of Bethlehem's blinding purity. Grown men reached for their handkerchiefs.

One Sunday shortly after Christmas, early in 1982, Bob was

explaining salvation in terms of being invited into the presence of the perfect ideal One and being accepted and loved by Him. He began by telling his audience and guest—former president, Gerald Ford—that he had never been invited into the Oval Office in the White House, but that it must surely be a great honor. Then he talked of the honor of being sought after by the God and Creator of the Universe.

President Reagan's daughter Maureen and her husband Dennis Revell just happened to be watching the program the day that message ran. She knew her dad watched the "Hour of Power" sometimes, too, and the next time she spoke with him, she asked, "Did you know that Dr. Schuller has never been in the Oval Office? You should invite him sometime." To make a long story short, he did. Bob and I pulled up to the east gate of the White House, and military guards checked our identification. Then we were escorted across the acres of grass and into the west wing lobby. The president's wing. It was a cold, gray day outside. And it felt good to step in out of the cold.

We waited there about fifteen minutes, two men who felt very excited and very out of place. There is such an aura about the presidency. Power just seemed to exude from the walls of the reception area. Bob and I made small talk, but we were each lost in our own private thoughts. His hands were folded nervously in his lap. He felt the dignity, the honor of the moment.

Then Elizabeth Dole, Assistant to the President for Public Liason, came to take us on a personal tour of the west wing. She's the highest level woman in the White House, wife of Senator Bob Dole, and a long-time friend of Bob's. I'd been on the regular tours, but they don't include this private sector. Once, when an old high-school friend was working at the White House, he took me through the west wing, around midnight, even gave me a peek inside the deserted, darkened Oval Office. It had been one of the biggest thrills of my life, but it couldn't compare to this. Bob had been to the White House some years back when the "Hour of Power" was one of the first television programs to institute captioning for the deaf onto its videotapes. He had met Mrs. Carter and even sat in on a press conference. But this was different.

The White House is a work of art; everywhere we looked, there was craftsmanship, beauty. Even the walls and the ceilings were richly inlaid and contained fine oil paintings and intricately carved thick wooden moldings. It was like stepping back in time to a day when gracious living and elegance and perfection in detail were wrapped up in the pride a craftsman took in his work. Mrs. Dole completed our tour with a visit to the cabinet room. It took my breath away to think of the decisions that had been made in there.

And then we were there, standing at the door to the president's private office. The Oval Office. The lustrous mahogany door opened revealing a large oval-shaped room.

A cheery fire crackled in the fireplace, but I had chills down my spine when President Reagan rose from his chair behind the desk and walked over to greet us. I had met him before, on many occasions, when he was governor of California and before and after. But he had not been the president then. Both Bob and I had expected to feel awe-struck with the sheer power of the presidency. I know I had been when I had first met Richard Nixon. But Reagan was different.

He was so friendly, so unaffected, as he grasped Bob's hand in a firm shake. "Bob! . . . welcome, good afternoon."

Bob was truly delighted. "Mister President, I haven't seen you since your election." (Reagan had been to church in Garden Grove a couple of times prior to the campaign.) The President beamed. "I've seen you—on television."

There were staff photographers there snapping pictures. Keepsakes we would never forget. I sat down. Bob and the President stood for the twelve minutes we were there. They spoke of the mail and volunteerism, which is a subject dear to both their hearts. Bob shared with him a little of the church's Christmas cookie project to prisons and invited him to come to services in the Cathedral some Memorial Day when we unfurl the world's largest American flag.

All too soon the audience was over. Bob put his hand on Reagan's left shoulder and the two prayed, eyes open. Bob quoted a scripture from Isaiah 40. "They that wait upon the Lord shall renew their strength. They shall mount up with wings like eagles. They shall run, and not be weary; and they shall walk, and not faint" (v. 31, TLB).

He thanked God for the President's recovery from gunshot wounds and for his good health.

Then President Reagan escorted us to the door, and we said good-bye.

The winter of 1982 had been an eventful one. Not only was Robert Schuller invited into the Oval Office to see the President, but his ministry was also the recipient of a fabulous gift. John Crean, the man who had given the lead-off gift for the Crystal Cathedral, was ready to leave the green hills and orange groves of his home, Rancho Capistrano. He and his wife Donna had raised their children there on that fertile hillside. They were grown now, and the huge ninety-acre ranch was a lot to run and maintain. So they gave the ten-million dollar ranch to Robert Schuller Ministeries.

Just off the freeway in the fastest growing, southern part of Orange County, the ranch has long been a landmark to passing motorists. The Creans always kept its name, Rancho Capistrano, emblazoned in flowers on the lower portion of the hill. They had generously donated its acres of rich green grass to local service organizations, who have used it free of charge for years for camp-outs and the like. Both my daughters have enjoyed its open vistas and shady trees and swimming pool during day-camp in the summer.

The Ranch is an exciting project. Bob plans to turn it into what some would call a retreat center. He dislikes the word retreat though; it's so negative to his way of thinking. He is calling it a Renewal Center. Plans are under way to construct bungalows for the conferees to stay in and to turn the six-thousand-square-foot ranch house into a conference center and dining room. It's still in the thinking and dreaming stages, and the fund raising remains to be done. But it will happen. You can be sure of that.

Robert Schuller is only fifty-six years old. He's got a lot of years left. He is inspired by Bishop Sheen and Norman Peale who both have preached well into their eighties. As he said when the Crystal Cathedral opened, his ministry had only just reached the halfway mark. Only God knows what Bob will accomplish in the second half. He is a man of fast moving, ever-changing priorities, a man of vision, a dreamer. Even he has only vague glimpses of the future at this point, but it is for sure that he is going to waste no time in getting down to the business of what he feels God has for him. He has a strong sense of urgency about everything he does. There are so many things he wants to accomplish that he knows he's got to rush to cram them all into his life span. His mother used to drill him with the idea that lost time is never found again. He's never forgotten.

Ever since the "Hour of Power" gained national prominence, his life has never been the same. He wanted to do something great for God, but I don't think he had really thought seriously about the notoriety that would come with exposure. He is a famous personality, but not because he set out to acquire wealth and fame. They have been by-products that have surprised him and not always pleased him.

He is recognizable all over the country. I travel with him. I know. He can't go anywhere without being recognized, and he grows more protective of his time and his anonymity with each passing year. He has to. Once, when he took Arvella back to the hospital for her cancer check-up, he noticed a man following him down the hall. He was kind of down at the time. He didn't feel particularly inspirational. He kept walking, hoping the man would go away. He didn't. In desperation, Bob ducked into the first open door he could find. It was a broom closet.

He and Arvella love to eat out in restaurants, and having their meal interrupted time after time got old in a hurry. Once they were having breakfast in one of their favorite coffee shops. They had a family situation they needed to discuss and were deep in conversation when Arvella noticed that some people across the room were staring at them. Bob was intense, concentrating on the problem at hand, when she broke into his train of thought. "Smile, Bob. Those people recognize you." He answered her through clenched teeth. "I-don't-feel-like-smiling."

He just wants to be himself. Yes, he is an unusually positive person, but that doesn't mean he's perfect. He gets angry and hurt and unhappy just like everybody else. That's part of what makes him a real, honest human being.

Arvella washes dishes and polishes silverware to get out negative emotions. Bob likes to work in the yard for the same reason. They both love to run, sometimes covering as many as seven miles a day. They still have children in the house, and probably will have for a few more years. Gretchen is sixteen. Carol is eighteen. She has undergone more surgeries, eventually amputating the mid-knee she fought so hard to save. She's had a rough time of it, times of great depression, but she's always come through. She loves sports. When she wanted to go out for baseball, Bob tried to discourage her. "How are you going to run around the bases?" Her answer was pure Schuller,

"Dad, when you hit homeruns, you don't have to run!" She spent the better part of the winter of 1982 in Winterpark, Colorado, with a ski coach, hoping to make the U.S. handicapped Olympic team for the 1984 Winter Olympics.

As far as the Crystal Cathedral and the Hour of Power are concerned, Bob is totally committed to both. They are very closely related at this time and will remain so as long as Bob is present in them, but they are not tied together. Each is its own separate entity; they are two financially separate corporations. The church is not dependent on television for its survival. It's a member of the Reformed Church in America, and it's a church of the laity. Bob expects it to continue to flourish until Jesus comes again.

But the Hour of Power is different. It's a personality-centered operation. There are some who wonder whether Bob is grooming his son, Robert Anthony Schuller, in hopes that someday he will be able to take the reins and be the driving force behind the Hour of Power. Bob is quick to admit that this assumption is correct. It is the desire of his heart that his son carry on his work, including the Hour of Power, but he knows that the final decision is up to God alone.

Bob sees his son making excellent progress as a communicator, showing increasing promise. Young Bob's own church, Capistrano Community Church, located in the south of Orange County in the historic city of San Juan Capistrano, is thriving and reaching out to its community. Bob is extremely proud of his son and his accomplishments and credits him with a deep spiritual emphasis in the power of prayer.

Once Bob was asked in an interview, "Dr. Schuller, you've built the Crystal Cathedral, written sixteen books, your church has over ten thousand members, the 'Hour of Power' is seen all over the world. Isn't it possible that your entire ministry is turning out to be one big number?"

Bob looked thoughtful and cleared his throat, but he didn't really have to search for the answer. "If I were a doctor in charge of innoculating children in the community, I wouldn't cut notches in my syringe and add up how many kids had been vaccinated. I would only look at those who haven't yet been immunized. The unfinished task is what sets the goals. I'm not going to quit until I have helped everybody who can conceivably be helped by my ministry."

I spoke with Bob shortly before this book went to press. He has received many honors. I wondered which ones mean the most to him. First, he told me that he sees his honors as more illustrative than definitive. High on his list are several honorary doctorates he has received. Most prized are those from his own alma mater, Hope College in Holland, Michigan. He is proud to have been one of the first four persons to receive the Distinguished Alumnus Award from that venerable institution. A few years later, they bestowed upon him an honorary doctorate. Bob is also especially pleased about a recent honorary doctorate which he received from a prominent university in Seoul, Korea. It is unusual for colleges to give such degrees to people from other countries. This one was given in appreciation for his work as a television missionary to the people of Korea as well as for his efforts on behalf of church growth in that country.

"I have more than enough honors," Bob told me, "but my greatest honor is my family. The love and faith of my first and only wife, Arvella, and the positive family we have built together, these are the most important. The lives of our children are great honors to us both. They are all committed to Judeo-Christian values. Each knows Christ as his personal Savior. Each is deeply involved in an active Christian ministry. My children are my greatest joy and pride.

"There is no way anyone will ever know the real Robert Schuller better than my own children. They know the real inside story—the story of the life I live behind the closed curtains of my home. And I can say to you in all honesty, if you want to know me, look at my children—all five of them.

"They aren't carbon copies; each is strong-willed in his own right. I give you permission to ask any one of them about their father. And they will answer you truthfully. I am nothing but a sinner saved by the immeasurable grace of God."

Bob sincerely believes that there must be meaningful struggles all through life or a person will die before his time. And he's certainly not ready to even think about stopping. His life will go on the same as it always has, going from peak to peek to peak. And he says:

"My goal is to come to the end of my life with pride behind me, love around me, and hope ahead of me."